Sensible Self-Help

The First Road Map for the Healing Journey

*How to Measure
Your Healing,
Make the Most of
Your Efforts,
and Get the Results
You're After*

Sensible
Self-Help

The First Road Map
for the Healing Journey

DAVID GRUDERMEYER, PH.D.

REBECCA GRUDERMEYER, PSY.D.

LERISSA NANCY PATRICK

Willingness
Works
Press

The Twelve Steps of Alcoholics Anonymous (page 406) used by permission of Alcoholics Anonymous World Services, Inc.

Permission to use Ann Landers column (page 139) granted by Ann Landers/Creators Syndicate.

The Val Kilmer quote (page 25) appeared in the July 9, 1995 *Parade* magazine article by Elinor Klein.

The Michael Murphy quote (page 180) and the Chogyam Trungpa Rinpoche quote (page 326) appeared in *What Really Matters: Searching for Wisdom in America* by Tony Schwartz (Bantam, 1995).

The Richard Friedenberg quote (page xxviii) is from his screenplay for *A River Runs Through It*, adapted from the novella by Norman Maclean.

Publisher's Note: The case histories in this book are derived from actual interviews and research. The relevant facts are real, but all of the names and other identifying details have been changed to protect the privacy of the individuals. While the book discusses certain issues, situations and choices regarding therapy and other emotional healing work, it is not intended as a substitute for professional mental health advice.

Willingness Works Press
1155 Camino Del Mar #516
Del Mar, CA 92014

ISBN 0-9648648-0-0
Cover and interior design by Troy Scott Parker, Cimarron Design.
Cover photo near Lost Lake, Mt. Hood National Forest, Oregon, © 1995 Troy Scott Parker.

Printed in the United States of America by Publishers Press.
10 9 8 7 6 5 4 3 2 1

Acknowledgments

SINCE THIS BOOK IS GENUINELY THE CULMINATION of all that we have been through in our lives—both personally and professionally—it is impossible for us to acknowledge everyone individually. If you do not see your name here, we hope you know that, nonetheless, you have our gratitude.

We are grateful:

To our therapy clients, workshop participants and those who attended our *TGIFs for Healing People*, for their support of our work, their wonderful questions and requests—and their tolerance and forbearance as we put this book together.

To our colleagues and mentors—Robert Firestone, Ph.D.; Roger Daldrup, Ph.D.; Martin Rossman, M.D.; David Bresler, Ph.D.; Francine Shapiro, Ph.D.; Margaret Paul, Ph.D.; and Jordan Paul, Ph.D.;—who, even if they didn't realize it, showed us how to fill in missing pieces in this book's road map.

To our parents, Bill and Mary Meyer and Steffi Gruder, whose interest and support in this project, and of us as a couple, have been there from the start. And to the memory of David's father, Alex Gruder, who we feel certain knows and approves of this book from the other side.

To David's Mom's partner, Charlie Aquilina, for providing enthusiasm and support for this project that reflected the commitment of a "real" parent. Thanks, Charlie!

To our sister and brother, Carol and Stevan Wittenbrock, for rooting for us and allowing us to love their son, our nephew, William George, to whom we leave a different legacy.

To our community of friends, including Wayne and Patti Germain, Nancy Ragon, Kim and Russ Gutner-Davis, Lyn Dahm, Diana Hoppe, Jan North, Patsy McIntyre, Sherryl Parks, Colleen and Larry O'Harra, and our Tuesday night *A Course in Miracles* study group, for their emotional and spiritual nourishment and their unrelenting reminders to keep taking care of ourselves throughout the book-birthing process.

To our administrator, Laura Thoren, for increasingly taking the day-to-day administration of Willingness Works off our hands so we could complete this book.

To Samantha Morgenstern, for keeping our household together, and feeding our souls as well as our stomachs. Thank you for being the world's best *chatelaine*!

To our cat, Ketzelah, for always knowing when we were in need of cuddles.

To Jean Seifert, who kept bugging us—until we finally gave in—to record our presentations for those who couldn't attend.

To our presentation support staff—Lyn Dahm, Samantha Morgenstern, Jean Seifert, Wayne and Patti Germain, and Dee Morse, Ph.D.—for all their hard work.

To our prior therapists, support group members, workshop leaders and book authors: you so profoundly touched our minds, souls and hearts that somewhere in our book you will find the mark you left.

To *A Course In Miracles*, which gives us our grounding and underlying framework.

To our book designer, Troy Scott Parker of Cimarron Design, for your patience, diligence and timeliness. It is your talent that brought this book its beauty and elegance.

And, finally, to Lerissa, our co-author, without whom this book would not have been written anywhere near as superbly and rapidly as it was, for patiently interviewing us, for sifting through, editing and organizing thousands of pages of our material, and for sculpting and massaging it to accurately voice our message and our hearts.

– D.G., R.G.

BOOKS COME INTO BEING through the efforts of many, many people. Sometimes it seems that everyone who touched my life—everyone who traveled with me for a while—deserves credit for part of this book. But space limitations being what they are, I must limit my thank-yous.

Thanks to Brian Woolsey—whose commitment to this book was as deep as my own—for functioning as volunteer editor, human guinea pig, consultant, friend, godfather and cheerleader. His almost-daily encouragement kept me going on the days I thought I would never finish.

To Steffi Gruder, for her eagle copyeditor eyes; Laura Goodman, for ruthless and yet constructive editing; Pam Novotny, for sharing her wisdom and for cheerleading; Karen Woolsey, for feedback, putting up with all the phone calls and being secure enough to support her husband in being one of my best friends.

I am especially grateful to all those who offered emotional support and love at various points along my journey—love and support that may seem to have had nothing to do with this book but were very much a part of the reason it came into being.

They include: David Chambers, who, I am beginning to think, may never give up on our friendship; Mom and Dad, for giving me their best, always; Phoebe Carroll, for a supremely sane attitude about work and for raising my consciousness about active voice; Halimah Butte, for insightful questions and opinions and precious conceptual material, as well as sisterly enthusiasm and support; Toes, Jake, and Dancer, for keeping me company during the long hours at the computer; Fran Cutright, midwife to my own rebirth, and Walt Rutherford, co-midwife; Bus Lankford, without whom I might have marched self-righteously down another, bleaker road; L.J. Barbee and Laurel Pennybaker, who model artistic vision, loving self-care and the art of womanhood; Jackie Leeba and Sandy Peterson, whose growth, honesty, courage and tenacity always amaze and inspire me; and all the other staunch friends, helpers and co-travelers, seen and unseen, on this healing journey.

I am grateful to Barbara Wohlander for raising my consciousness to the possibility that my life was, very literally, my own creation.

Thanks to Fred K. Berger and Donald Martindill for helping me discover and correct my physiological imbalances.

Thank you, Jill Fitzgerald, for getting the whole thing started.

I am deeply grateful for the influence of the *latihan kejiwan* of Subud and for the support, both silent and spoken, of my Subud sisters and brothers.

Thanks to my former employer for laying me off when I needed it most.

And of course, I am grateful to my co-authors, David and Rebecca, for their faith in me, their vision of the future of this book, their willingness and courage to be vulnerable, and their love. You have opened my eyes.

– L.P.

Dedicated with love and gratitude to our parents
Alex and Gloria (Steffi) Gruder
and
William and Mary Meyer
who didn't know a better way, but who cheered us on,
each in their own particular style,
in finding one.

Dedicated as well to everyone who,
like us, struggled and fumbled their way
through their healing process
without a road map to smooth the way,
and to all our therapy clients and workshop participants,
who showed us that there
is
a road map.

To George and Veronica Patrick. Thanks.
Your parents can be your friends
when you learn to drop them as parents.
– Henry Rabin and Ben Weininger

Contents

Acknowledgments   v

Preface   xix

Prologue   xxv

☙

SECTION I

WOUNDING AND SURVIVAL

I

ONE

Connection: The Foundation of Your Emotional Well-Being   5

    Connection   6

    Broken Connections   9

    Four Ways to Disconnect   9

    A Note of Compassion to Parents   13

    Another Note of Compassion, to the Newly Aware   14

    Exercises: Discovering Your Broken Connections   16

TWO

The Genesis and the Power of Wounds   19

    Two Examples   20

    Anatomy of a Wound   21

The Power of an Unhealed Wound   24
We're All Wounded   27
Exercises: Identifying Your Wounds   28

THREE
The Survival Plan: An Overview   33
The Choice: Survival Plan or Death   36
Who Dies?   38
Who Survives?   39
Elements of the Survival Plan   40

FOUR
Leg One: The Happy-Ending Fantasy   41
How the Happy-Ending Fantasy is Born   41
False Hope and the Happy-Ending Fantasy   43
The Staying Power of False Hope   46
False *Hopelessness* and the Happy-Ending Fantasy   47
Your Happy-Ending Fantasy Today   49
Exercises: Identifying Your Happy-Ending Fantasy   54

FIVE
Leg Two: Rules   55
The Rule Book   56
The Inner Critic: Keeper of the Rules   56
The Inner Critic's Limitations   61
Exercises: Describing Your Inner Critic and Its Rules   62

SIX
Leg Three: Anesthesia   67
The Function of Your Anesthesia   67
Especially Dangerous: Addictive Substances   70
Exercises: Unmasking Your Anesthesias   71

SEVEN
The Survival Plan Takes Its Toll   73
How Your Survival Plan Uses Your Life Energy   74
What is the Price?   74
Exercises: Determining the Price of Your Survival Plan   78

EIGHT

The Survival Plan Falters   79

> Wake-Up Calls   81
> Custom-Designed for Your Needs   82
> The Volume Rises   83
> Exercises: Wake-Up Calls I: Survival Plan Failure   85

NINE

Avoiding Wake-Up Calls   87

> Fix the Survival Plan   87
> Enter a Window of Willingness   91
> Slide into Purgatory   97
> Exercises: Wake-Up Calls II: Past and Present   99

TEN

How to Answer a Wake-Up Call   101

> Surrender to Healing   102
> The Purgatory About-Face   105
> Exercises: Wake-Up Calls III: Lessons and Consequences   107

✿

SECTION II

THE SELF-RESPONSIBILITY SOLUTION

108

ELEVEN

Self-Responsibility as Growth Indicator and Growth Catalyst   113

> Dismantling Your Survival Plan   115
> Self-Responsibility and Healing vs. the Happy-Ending Fantasy
>   and Victimhood   117
> The Benefits of Self-Responsibility   118
> Pain Is Inevitable   119
> One Woman's Journey into Self-Responsibility   121
> The Nine Indicators of Self-Responsibility   126

TWELVE

The Feelings Indicators: How Do You Deal With Hurt?   129

    Ability to Feel, Grieve and Heal   131

    Response to Pain   131

    Exercises: How Do You Deal With Hurt?   135

THIRTEEN

The Personal Power Indicators: Who's In Charge?   137

    Boundary-Setting Skills   138

    Foundation of Self-Esteem   145

    Investment in Victimhood   148

    Exercises: Who's In Charge?   151

FOURTEEN

The Connection Indicators: How Do You Join?   153

    Attitude Toward Unfinished Business   153

    Mission in Life   157

    Quality of Relationships   159

    Quality of Relationship with Your Spiritual Resources   163

    Exercises: How Do You Join?   167

SECTION III

THE SEVEN STAGES OF PERSONAL HEALING

169

FIFTEEN

An Overview of the Seven Stages   171

    What Are the Seven Stages?   171

    Map, Business, Pyramid, House   174

SIXTEEN

Early Healing   177

    Stage One: Willingness   177

    Stage Two: Foundation   179

SEVENTEEN

Middle Healing   181

     Stage Three: Feelings   182
     Stage Four: Healing   184

EIGHTEEN

Advanced Healing   189

     Stage Five: Rebirth   190
     Stage Six: Clear-Hearted Relationships   194
     Stage Seven: Clear-Hearted Service   199
     Where Are You?   201

NINETEEN

Your Dominant Healing Stage   203

     Why a Healing Self-Assessment?   203
     Getting a Clear Picture of Your Healing   205
     Self-Assessment Instructions   206
     The Self-Assessment   207
     Scoring Your Assessment   217
     Dealing with Your Reaction to Your Score   219
     Interpreting Your Score   219

TWENTY

Your Secondary Stages   223

     Checklist Instructions   223
     Stage One Mastery Characteristics   225
     Stage Two Mastery Characteristics   226
     Stage Three Mastery Characteristics   228
     Stage Four Mastery Characteristics   230
     Stage Five Mastery Characteristics   232
     Stage Six Mastery Characteristics   235
     Stage Seven Mastery Characteristics   237
     Determining Your Secondary Stages   238

TWENTY-ONE

Healing Plans and the Nature of the Journey   239

     The Influences   240
     The Rubber Band Effect   243
     How a Healing Plan Helps   250

TWENTY-TWO

How to Create Your Own Healing Plan   255

The Long-Term Healing Plan   258

The Weekly Healing Plan   265

Re-Thinking Your Plan   274

Troubleshooting Your Plan   281

つ

SECTION IV

A STAGE-BY-STAGE LOOK AT HEALING REQUIREMENTS
283
It's Up to You   287

TWENTY-THREE

Stage One: Willingness   289

Goal: Get Honest   289

Emotional Work: Hit Bottom   290

Self-Responsibility Key: A New Response to Pain   292

Activities: Re-Orientation   292

Stage One Pitfalls: Diversions from the Pain   296

Stage One Healing Resources   297

Stage One Healing Exercises   298

TWENTY-FOUR

Stage Two: Foundation   301

Goal: Re-Organize Your Life   301

Emotional Work: Break Up with Your Anesthesias   302

Self-Responsibility Key: Hiring a New Manager   302

Activities: Enhance Your Healing   302

Stage Two Pitfalls: Too Much Talk, Too Little Action   314

Stage Two Healing Resources   316

Stage Two Healing Exercises   319

TWENTY-FIVE

Stage Three: Feelings   323

Goal: Make Friends with Your Feelings   323
Emotional Work: Meet the "Inners"   324
Self-Responsibility Key: Owning Your Feelings   324
Activities: Learn the Tools   324
Stage Three Pitfalls: Avoidance of Feeling Work   325
Stage Three Healing Resources   328
Stage Three Healing Exercises   332

TWENTY-SIX

Stage Four: Healing   335

Goal: Learn to Recognize, Expose and Heal Your Wounds   335
Emotional Work: Traverse Your Abyss   336
Self-Responsibility Key: A New Perception of Pain   341
Activities: Intense Therapy and Lots of Support   342
Stage Four Pitfalls: Avoidance of Feeling Work   346
Stage Four Healing Resources   357
Stage Four Healing Exercises   361

TWENTY-SEVEN

Stage Five: Rebirth   367

Goal: Welcome the New You   367
Emotional Work: Expand Your Comfort Zone, Forgive   368
Self-Responsibility Key: Full Acceptance   368
Activities: Apply Self-Responsibility   370
Stage Five Pitfalls: Resisting Full Self-Responsibility   371
Stage Five Healing Resources   374
Stage Five Healing Exercises   376

TWENTY-EIGHT

Stage Six: Clear-Hearted Relationships   381

Goal: Deep Joining   381
Emotional Work: Blending   382
Self-Responsibility Key: Vulnerability   382
Activities: Develop Relationship Skills   384
Stage Six Pitfalls: Insufficient Abyss Work   385
Stage Six Healing Resources   387
Stage Six Healing Exercises   388

TWENTY-NINE

Stage Seven: Clear-Hearted Service   389

>   Goal: Create a Service Role   389
>   Emotional Work: Vulnerability and Love   392
>   Self-Responsibility Key: Preparing for Union   392
>   Activities: Service   393
>   Stage Seven Pitfalls   394
>   Stage Seven Healing Resources   394
>   Stage Seven Healing Exercises   395

Epilogue: Stages Eight Through Infinity   397

APPENDIX

>   Long-Term Healing Plan Form   400
>   Weekly Healing Plan Form   402
>   A Stage-by-Stage Guide to Healing Activities   404
>   The Seven Stages of Personal Healing: Some Analogies   405
>   Love, Wounds and Self-Responsibility   406
>   The Twelve Steps and the Seven Stages   408
>   How Self-Responsibility Grows Through the Seven Stages   410

Glossary   413

Index   425

Preface

IT WAS THE EARLY 1980S. I didn't know how I made it through each day. I felt as though I were free-falling in a dark, bottomless pit. Somehow, my coping skills took care of my outer obligations—at work and in completing my doctoral program— while I secretly writhed in emotional pain in my inner darkness.

I stumbled through therapy with a Jungian therapist, doing inner imagery work and sand trays. I agonized over how I could be so successful professionally and academically, yet feel like a failure at love relationships and feel so bad about myself inwardly. I don't think I ever conveyed to my therapist the depth of my emotional agony during our year together. But I sweated out the time between our weekly sessions, and finally made it to the other side of what I later came to term my abyss.

This was a pivotal therapy in a series of therapies I have been through. Thank goodness my doctoral program at the California School of Professional Psychology required I be in one therapy or another for the entire four years of the program. No aspiring therapist should be spared this experience.

I didn't fully comprehend it at the time, but I was dealing with some of my deepest core wounds, sustained while growing up in a family that didn't look all that unusually dysfunctional to me—or to many others. With all my formal training and all the therapy and workshops I'd been through, I hadn't understood why I had gone through such profound pain during that therapy. But I did know that I shouldn't have had to go through that kind of hideous darkness without three things:

The tools necessary to navigate it

Clarity about the nature of this abyss experience and how to lean into it rather than resist and be terrified of it

Vision about what makes the journey through the dark night of the soul to the other side worth the pain and effort.

I knew there had to be a better way. I didn't yet know what it would look like, but I was determined to find it.

When Rebecca entered my life in 1985, I was finally healed enough to be able to build a vital, sustainable, loving, residue-free relationship with her. She, too, wanted to find a way to help the healing journey become clearer, less frustrating and more efficient for others than ours had been for us. Together we discovered, with the help of our therapy clients and workshop participants, what neither of us had been able to decipher on our own: how to go through the task of healing deliberately, with clarity and the necessary skills. We didn't want others to suffer the way we did—or take nearly as long as we took—to make it to the point where they felt good at their core about themselves, could enjoy durable, loving, residue-free relationships and were free enough of their own baggage to make a significant difference in the world.

I truly wish I had access to the information in this book from the beginning of my healing journey. I take profound comfort, however, in the fact that Rebecca and I have nevertheless been deeply helped by this material, both while helping to birth it and since. *Sensible Self-Help* is the child of Rebecca's and my deep joining and abiding love. We conceived it, birthed it and raised it to maturity, and now send it out into the world to have a life of its own.

This book marks the end of a long journey for me. It is a thrilling accomplishment to be able to offer you some hints about how to make your journey more productive and less torturous than mine has been and how to do it in less time than mine has taken.

It also marks the beginning of a new and exciting journey: Rebecca and I doing our parts to make sure that those who can benefit from this material are exposed to it. The more of us who heal to the point that our relationships can be loving and durable and where we can make truly remarkable contributions to the world, the more we'll help our planet out of the mess it's in.

I'm grateful to be at the point in my life where I can play some small part in this. I am even more grateful that my soul mate and I can be life partners in it.

I wish you, the reader, a clear path through a healing journey that allows you to be who you've wanted to become and give back beyond what you thought possible.

> — David Grudermeyer
> Del Mar, California
> July 1995

I'VE ALWAYS KNOWN I'd write a book combining psychological and spiritual principles. What I realize now is that, as we heal our wounds, understand ourselves psychologically and learn what makes us tick, we very naturally begin to open up to our spirituality. Sometimes it's our spirituality that awakens in us first, inspiring and leading us to our healing.

While I do not claim to know the secrets of the universe, it does seem to me that a path of growth and awareness ultimately, at some point, requires us to honestly search out all that interferes with our awareness of love. My own path has been at times difficult, at times painful and at all times, worth it. I believe that, had I not rigorously pursued every opportunity to heal and been deeply willing to do the necessary work, I would have missed out on my destiny.

Meeting David in 1985 was the single most life-changing event in my existence. His appearance was foretold to me one day when I was four, playing under a Japanese maple tree in my parents' yard. Suddenly, without fanfare, I *knew* that I would be called doctor and would help a lot of people. I *knew* I wouldn't be a doctor like Dr. Nash, my pediatrician. I also *knew* I would marry and work with a man named David and that he would be Jewish.

I have no explanation for how this information came to me or how, as a four-year-old, I could know things that were out of my realm of knowledge. Nevertheless, knowing about David was helpful more than once, as I came close to taking paths with other loves that would have led me away from my destiny. I am certain that all the therapy, workshops, twelve-step work and honest looking at myself gave me the necessary skills and stamina to be with my soul mate. I am glad I studied, so I was prepared for the final exam—otherwise known as living peacefully and happily with another human being.

This book is the expression of our work together. We have had many excellent teachers (disguised as clients, friends and family) along our way, and their influence is on each page. To everyone who has bravely shared their journey with us and allowed us to share as well, to those who supported, encouraged and humored us along, I thank you.

What David and I have done is to show people a map for healing the wounds that most of us have, and how removing these blocks opens the path to our spirituality. I wish I'd had this book to guide me through my journey. I gladly offer it to you, the reader, with my hope it will be helpful to you. Peace.

> – Rebecca Grudermeyer
> Del Mar, California
> July 1995

IT TOOK ME THREE YEARS to work up the nerve to attend a *TGIF for Healing People*, David and Rebecca's once-a-month, two-hour lecture and experiential workshop. I had heard about the Grudermeyers in 1989 from a woman I met at my new job as an instructional designer for a San Diego firm. I dithered about going for all the usual reasons, but I believe now it was pure instinct that kept me away. Going too soon might have scared me away for good.

When I finally did go, I was struck by the sense of loving acceptance I felt from David and Rebecca. But I found it nearly overwhelming. Being exposed without warning to people you realize you can't fool, but who clearly love you anyway, is like walking into bright noon sunlight from the dark of a movie theater; it almost hurt.

I went back, though, and a few months later, signed up for their one-day seminar, *The Seven Stages of Personal Healing*. I floated out at the end of the day on a deep sense of relief and hope about myself, my life and my healing process. If David and Rebecca were right, I was on track; I could trust myself, trust the process I instinctively followed, trust the nature of the healing journey. All I had to do was continue to be willing to do the work.

Now, this was by no means the first healing seminar I attended that had inspired my hope and insight. But this time, unlike most other times, the feelings didn't dissipate within a few weeks. This workshop transformed the way I thought about my healing. Through the Seven Stages, I began to understand that my struggles, far from being proof that I was damaged beyond hope, were appropriate and predictable for people in my stage. And as I applied this understanding to others—the understanding that they, also, were doing their work in their respective stages—I began to find the courage to give up burdens that I had dragged along my whole life.

For example, I began to give up trying to convert other people into beings who could meet my needs; to figure out who was right and who was wrong in conflicts with friends, family, and lovers; and to force people to see things my way. As I found a new respect for myself in my struggles, I began to respect others in theirs.

That day, I knew I had found something I wanted to bring into my life. Before I left, I told Rebecca that, should they ever need an instructional designer to polish an existing seminar or create a new one, I would love to work with them. To my complete surpise, they did, and thus began the adventure in collaboration that eventually produced this book.

Writing *Sensible Self-Help* changed me. As I described the journey through the Seven Stages, I found it impossible not to examine my own life and unhealed wounds. In fact, it became clear that if I were to truly understand the material and write about it in the same compassionate way that David and Rebecca spoke about it, I would *have* to heal the wounds this work exposed. Because my co-authors practice what they preach, they supported and encouraged me in my healing work, often leading the way with their own open hearts and willing vulnerability. I had never experienced a business relationship like this one. It stands as a model for me of the way people are meant to work together—and can work together, if their first commitment is to healing their wounds.

If I have one goal for this book, it is to convey the respect and care that Rebecca and David seem to bring to their interactions with everyone. If I have succeeded, *Sensible Self-Help* will leave you feeling the way I do after a visit with them: hopeful, joyful, grateful, recharged. It is my hope and prayer that, with the loving aid of all those who have witnessed and helped the birthing of this volume, I have achieved this goal.

> – Lerissa Patrick
> San Diego, California
> July 1995

Prologue

The Work of This Generation

Until the second half of this century, life for most of the planet's human inhabitants was a tentative proposal. A human infant who made it to his first birthday (and statistics show that nearly half of them did not) still faced daily challenges to his hold on life. Starvation, disease, predators, outlaws, accidents, domestic violence and a host of other threats often brought life to an early end. For most people, the overriding concern of each day was to secure enough food, shelter, adequate clothing and basic safety to stay alive until tomorrow.

Now, for the first time in history, civilization has produced a large population of human beings for whom mere physical survival is not life's overriding concern. For many people in the western world, food, shelter, clothing and basic safety are the givens of everyday life. Hard times still come, and can still be devastating. But for us blessed few, rarely do hard times mean a daily life-and-death struggle.

One of the most obvious results of this release from the struggle to stay alive, as psychology pioneer Abraham Maslow noted, is a search for meaning and purpose in life. The search has been carried out in ashrams, love-ins, college classrooms, drug-induced hallucinations, monasteries, bookstores, churches, personal growth seminars, sex clubs, twelve-step meetings—and in the offices of psychotherapists like us. The searchers have sometimes been called self-indulgent, self-involved and ungrateful. No doubt, some of them are; being human, we all are self-indulgent, self-involved and ungrateful from time to time.

However, we view this generation of searchers from a slightly different perspective. Just as staying alive from one day to the next was the job of generations past, we believe those who search for meaning and healing are doing the work of *this* generation. This work has never been done on such a scale. Some searchers have run up a number of blind alleys and have detoured into a variety of addictions; others have blazed new trails.

Today's searchers need a different set of skills than those cultivated by their ancestors. For example, if you are not certain how you were going to feed the family tomorrow, there is no time to take care of what we call emotional unfinished business. Survival depends on being able to ignore disruptive feelings and get on with the business at hand.

But when survival is a given, and the business at hand *is* the unfinished business of disruptive feelings, it is time to adjust priorities and learn new skills. It is impossible to go backward, to pretend that life is about what it was about for our parents and grandparents. It is possible only to move forward, to find a way though the underbrush and to lend a hand to others climbing the same trail.

Sensible Self-Help carries this message to the searchers: You are not flawed. You are not here to correct conditions that keep you from being like "everyone else." You are not working to return to a mythical ideal world where no one worried about self-esteem and personal fulfillment.

You are working to create a new world—first within your own spirit and soul, and then with your children and the people whose lives you touch. This new world isn't like any we've seen before. We don't know exactly what it will look like. All we know is that it will be different. And we know that its birthing is likely to be a difficult and lengthy process.

With *Sensible Self-Help*, we don't claim to have captured the corner on truth. We do have one path through the thickets, and a willing hand to lend to those who want it. We have an idea of what the new skills might be, and possibly, what it is we are all searching for.

How to Use This Book

Sensible Self-Help is not a one-size-fits-all proposition. While we have seen that people tend to heal in the same general sequence, we also know that your healing journey is as unique as your fingerprints. Therefore, what we provide here is a way to create a healing plan customized for your needs.

Planning complex work is nothing new. If you are building a home, for instance, you start with a blueprint. If you want to expand your business, you start with a strategic plan. If you decide to get a college degree, you start with a curriculum. If you want to build a successful retirement portfolio, you start with a sound financial plan. If you want to organize your life energy, time and activities, you start with a specific method of time planning. What *is* new is applying the tenets of sound planning to emotional healing.

In Sections I and II, we map out the territory that the healing journey must cover and describe the skills you must develop to blaze a trail through your wilderness. In Section III, we provide an emotional compass so you can figure out where you stand before you begin. Then we show you how to develop a healing plan that will meet your needs. Section IV provides the information you need about each stage so you can keep your healing plan current. (You'll find blank versions of the long-term and weekly healing plans in the Appendix; photocopy these forms so you'll have extras available to use when you need to update your plan.)

The Exercises

Many chapters conclude with a few exercises. We recommend completing them as you read, rather than coming back to them later. The exercises are intended to just whet your appetite for self-exploration. The suggestions you'll find in Section IV for activities and reading will lead you to additional exercises you can use to deepen your self-understanding.

Someday, when you're ready, you might tell our family story. Only then will you understand what happened, and why.

— Richard Friedenberg

You may find that the exercises bring up strong emotions. It furthers your healing process to have time to feel those feelings. For that reason, we recommend setting aside quiet time to do the exercises.

Many of our clients use a three-ring binder to help them track and update their progress. They divide it into three sections: one each for the exercises, their healing plans and photocopies of the self-assessments. Others do written exercises in their journals and keep their healing plans and self-assessments in a separate file. Whatever method you choose, be sure you *write* the exercises. Doing them in your head or just talking them through never seems to be as valuable as seeing your thoughts and memories in a tangible form.

The exercises can also provide a springboard for discussions with a support group.

Study/Support Groups

People often ask about setting up groups to study our material. We heartily recommend support groups; none of us heals in isolation. Support groups can be a wonderful, healing experience—or a repetition of painful, old family patterns. In groups, conflict inevitably arises, and without a facilitator, it can be almost impossible to keep the group from self-destructing. If you wish to study *Sensible Self-Help* with a group, we suggest you hire a therapist or counselor you trust to facilitate.

How do you find potential study partners? As always, willingness is the key. If you are willing to join others on the path, you'll find that opportunities will open up for you. Try mentioning your interest to people you meet at support-group meetings, seminars, lectures, retreats and bookstores.

Whether you read this book alone or with others, some kind of emotional support is essential for getting the most out of this material. When you choose healing, you choose a rewarding path. The journey, however, can be long and arduous. It's best to travel with friends.

The Glossary

We tried to keep special vocabulary to a minimum. Where we do use words in a special way, we provide clear, concise definitions as we introduce them. However, if you do encounter a word you haven't seen before, or forget a meaning, check the glossary at the back of the book.

One concluding suggestion: don't rush. Budget your time with *Sensible Self-Help*. Give it enough time, and it will tranform your life.

The Seven Stages
of Personal Healing

ONE

Willingness

TWO

Foundation

THREE

Feelings

FOUR

Healing

FIVE

Rebirth

SIX

Clear-Hearted Relationships

SEVEN

Clear-Hearted Service

Wounding and Survival

Wounding and Survival

Every child is born a genius.
— Buckminster Fuller

Y̲OU ARE A GENIUS.

The way Wolfgang Amadeus Mozart was born with the potential to make great music, you were born with the potential to create a happy, loving and fulfilling life. Mozart needed motor skills, opportunity and encouragement to manifest his genius. You needed certain emotional skills, opportunity and encouragement to manifest yours. Mozart got what he needed and created unequaled musical joy. You, like the rest of humanity, received information and instruction in life and loving of one kind or another. However, many of us are at least faintly dissatisfied with our lives and relationships; most would acknowledge that there is room for improvement. For most of us, life's curriculum didn't seem to teach us all that we needed to know.

With rare exceptions, parents love their children and do their best to raise them with love. But no one can teach what he or she was never taught. If you never had lessons in staying open and loving in the face of emotional pain, you can't teach someone else how to do that. If you have never been shown your own genius, you are not likely to recognize the genius of others. Think of the levels of intimacy and peace we could achieve had our tutoring in loving and life been of the caliber of Mozart's music lessons. His genius, combined with good instruction, produced magic. Our genius, combined with the right training, can do the same.

If you survived childhood more or less emotionally intact—
and the fact that you are reading these words proves that you
did—it was because you turned your genius to negotiating childhood's losses and hurts. Congratulations, and welcome. The
healing journey begins here, at the acceptance of your wounds. It
is at this point that you can begin traveling toward an ever more
perfect ability to love. You are ready to begin the work that no
one else can do for you: to recognize and nurture your genius for
life.

This section is a short course in our theories of how people
get to be the way they are—a sort of psychology primer or a
background reference for real life. In it, we outline our understanding of what happens to us as children, adolescents and
young adults that creates the blocks to feeling and succeeding as
we wish to. This information is essential to your understanding
of your own healing process.

ONE

Connection: The Foundation of Your Emotional Well-Being

With children, the secret is to be sensitive to any need or opportunity for communication.

— Henry Rabin and Ben Weininger

ONCE UPON A TIME, *(maybe last week and maybe a thousand thousand years ago), in a land just around the corner from here, there was a stream.*

The stream flowed through the land, sometimes swiftly bounding over rocks and sometimes quietly gliding through flat green meadows. Watching over the stream was the stream spirit, a young creature with much to learn. The spirit had only recently been given its own stream in its own land; he was still learning the ways of water. For the first few days, the spirit played and watched.

One day the stream spirit had visitors. Two older spirits appeared near a clump of willows and introduced themselves, explaining that they

*were the little stream spirit's neighbors and
guardians. "We're here to help you learn the ways
of water and land," they said. "We've been
around for a while. We have a lot to teach you."*

*The stream spirit was overjoyed, and threw
himself into the lessons with great enthusiasm.*

*"The first thing you must do," one of the
older spirits said, "is to tone down the noise. Your
stream, being new, is too loud. It disturbs us and
probably disturbs the neighbors, too. Go get some
big rocks."*

*The little spirit rolled three boulders over to
the willow grove. The elder spirits showed him
how to place them in the stream to block the flow
of the water. The stream's raucous flow was
reduced by half. A pond began to spread out over
the flat meadow behind the rocks.*

*"There!" the older spirits said. "You've made
a good start."*

The little stream spirit felt weak and dizzy.

*"Don't worry," the older spirits said. "You'll
get used to it. And anyway, it's better than being
buffeted about and deafened by all that
unrestrained flowing water."*

[1] Throughout this book, we use the term "spiritual resources." It is a sort of shorthand to refer to the many spiritual frames of reference people use. Feel free to mentally substitute, as you read, whatever term works for you (for example, Higher Power, Greater Power, God, Spirit, Natural Law, Higher Self, True Self, the Tao, Krishna, Guide, Mother Nature, Gaia, Holy Spirit, the Cosmic Christ, Jesus, the Buddha, the Cosmos, personal Truth, the Force, etc.).

THE FOUNDATION for a child's emotional health lies in the state
of his relationship with his caregivers. To understand the effects
of this first relationship, we need to understand what children
need to thrive.

Connection

connection—The experience of being joined with
another person, ourselves and our spiritual resources.[1]
Also called bonding.

Children need connection. From the time they are born, infants seek to connect with their caregivers. They respond to cuddling and cooing and other expressions of love and affection by becoming more and more expressive themselves.

In fact, connection is *the only thing that feels like love* to a child. During some of our presentations, we ask people in the audience to list things that caregivers can do for children that express love. Common items on their lists include:

- Regular medical and dental care
- Food, clothing and shelter
- Hugs
- Education
- Consistent rules
- Changing diapers
- Childproofing the house
- Providing good baby-sitters when necessary

Then we ask audience members, "What do you remember receiving from your caregivers that *felt* like love?"

Invariably, the second list is different. Where the first list tends to be wide-ranging in character (everything from hugs to dental care, for example), the second list is more narrowly focused, with all items on the second list having the same feel. For example:

- Hugs
- Long talks
- Making cookies together
- Walks on the beach
- Comfort during crises

People remember these as special times, in which their caregivers gave of themselves. What these items have in common is *connection*—a sense of an emotional joining between two people, a sense of mutuality, respect and openness.

That's what we mean by connection. From the moment of birth, children reach for their caregivers like flowers for the sun.

It is essential to their well-being, and they will do whatever they think it will take to create and keep the connection. In the presence of steady, consistent connection, they thrive. When the connection is broken, they shrivel.

In addition to making him feel acknowledged and validated, connection teaches a child to keep company with his feelings.

Connection, Keeping Company and the Feeling-Grieving-Healing Cycle

Being connected with your caregivers teaches you to keep company with yourself—a precious skill that provides the foundation for emotional good health.

> *keeping company*—The art of being a tender-hearted witness who listens attentively and compassionately to your own or someone else's feelings without saying how to feel or what to do.

If you know how to keep company with your feelings, you hold the key to healing any of life's pains and moving through the process we think of as the feeling-grieving-healing cycle.

"Feeling-grieving-healing" describes the process that allows us to move through strong feelings. With this process intact, we deal with a feeling much as a healthy body deals with food: we taste it, take it in, experience its flavor and texture, metabolize it into life energy, then allow what's left over to flow through and out without leaving residue. What drives the feeling-grieving-healing process is company keeping.

Although children have an innate ability to feel, grieve and heal, they need company to do it. If they get the connection and company-keeping they need, they eventually learn to do it for themselves. As a result, they learn not to fear their emotions, no matter how intense those emotions become. Imagine the natural, unassailable self-esteem that would come from not being afraid of any of your feelings.

Broken Connections

However, when caregivers break the connection, the feeling-grieving-healing process stops, and children don't learn how to keep themselves company.[2] It is this disconnection that creates wounds. Without it, wounding doesn't occur. With it, wounding always occurs, even when life appears to be otherwise pleasant.

> *disconnection, broken connection*—Emotionally withdrawing tender-hearted company-keeping from another person because your wounds have been triggered and are drowning out your love.
>
> Even in the most loving, most emotionally connected families, parenting sometimes falters. Parents and other caregivers all have unhealed wounds of their own, and as a result, they sometimes lose patience, get distracted, or react irrationally to situations. In those instances, the emotional connection is lost. Caregiver and child disconnect.

No matter what kind of family you came from, you experienced emotional disconnection. If your family was consistently loving and connected, the disconnections may have been subtle or infrequent. In a less healthy family, disconnections are often more dramatic, or simply unremitting. In either case, they are painful. Let's take a look at the forms disconnection can take and how it feels when a disconnection occurs.

[2] Fortunately, whatever you weren't taught about company-keeping as a child, you can learn as an adult. We explain more about company-keeping later in this book.

Four Ways to Disconnect

When a disconnection occurs, it feels as if you've had the wind taken out of your sails. You might feel that you're adrift and all alone, or that you've stumbled into an emotional desert. You feel profoundly lonely, hurt and afraid of your feelings. It can hurt so bad that you might think you won't survive the pain.

There are scores of ways for a caregiver to behave that will create the pain of a disconnection. However, we have found that disconnection behaviors fall into four general categories:

• Abandonment

• Attacking

• Spoiling

• Stealing the attention

Abandonment Breaks the Connection

If your caregivers disconnected with you by abandoning you, they may have simply ignored you or your feelings. Abandonment disconnections occur when caregivers:

• Leave an upset child alone, without follow-up conversations about these feelings.

• Ignore a child's feelings by rushing into problem-solving before she's ready.

• Change the subject when a child needs to talk about something upsetting.

• Offer philosophy (*"That's the way the cookie crumbles!"*) when a child is upset.

• Pretend to pay attention.

• Do not allow a child to affect them emotionally.

• Keep a poker face around a child, or act emotionally flat or distant.

Attacks Break the Connection

Sometimes caregivers disconnect more aggressively, by actually attacking a child either emotionally (by shaming or criticizing) or physically. If your caregivers disconnected by attacking you, the message you received was, *"Your feelings, reactions or preferences are wrong or don't count."* For example, caregivers disconnect by attacking when they:

• Tell a weeping child, *"Big kids don't cry!"*

- Tell an excited child to quit acting foolish or to quit showing off.

- Tell a frightened child that there's nothing to be afraid of.

- Say, *"Shame on you!"*

- Say, *"You shouldn't feel that way."*

- Hit a child.

- Touch a child in inappropriate ways, or in ways the child dislikes.

- Touch a child because *they* need to, whether or not the child wants it.

- Tell a child it's her fault she was abused (*"I wouldn't have to hit you if you were good"*).

Spoiling Breaks the Connection

This is a particularly insidious form of disconnection because it can look like support. If your caregivers disconnected by spoiling you, they may have:

- Always maintained that your feelings were "right" and you were an innocent victim, precluding the need to look at the part you played in painful incidents.

- Said, *"Who needs them?"* when you complained about a conflict with friends.

- Promised revenge on whoever caused your strong feelings.

Many of our clients have trouble at first distinguishing between spoiling and keeping company. It is a crucial distinction. In keeping company, you simply acknowledge the fact that the feelings exist; you don't pronounce judgment on the feelings or the people or circumstances that triggered the feelings. Company-keeping is what people (both children and adults) usually need first when they are having strong feelings. It is completely appropriate, however, to move from company-keeping into problem-solving at a certain point, especially for caregivers guiding children. Company-keeping becomes spoiling when a caregiver never moves into problem-solving with a child.

Spoiling encourages an attitude of irresponsibility. When a caregiver offers a spoiling response (or never moves into problem-solving), he diminishes the importance of the child's part in creating the situation that's causing the upset. A spoiling response blames other people, places or things for causing *all* of the upset. Spoiling does not encourage the child to solve the problem or to seek creative solutions.

In high doses, spoiling creates narcissists—people who simply can't give attention to any feeling, event, topic or activity that doesn't concern them directly. Such people, while often charming, tend to see themselves as completely faultless and to see others as either tools for, or obstacles to getting what they want.

Stealing the Attention Breaks the Connection

Stealing attention away from a child is another way to disconnect. Your caregivers may have stolen emotional attention from you when you needed it by:

- Telling you that your feelings were too much to handle (*"Don't tell your father about this—it would kill him"*).

- Reacting to your account of a problem or conflict more dramatically than you did (weeping and exclaiming over a story you told in a matter-of-fact tone).

- Deriving status from your accomplishments. (For perfect—and perfectly painful—examples of this disconnection, read or see *The Joy Luck Club* by Amy Tan. In her novel and in the movie, four mothers compete with each other for status using their daughters' achievements. Although they brag to each other about their girls, the girls themselves obviously do not feel that they have been praised. The glory of their success has been appropriated by their mothers.)

- Telling you that you ruined his or her life.

- Going into paroxysms of guilt, self-recrimination and apologies when you confronted him or her about an aspect of his or her behavior that hurt you.

- Becoming defensive and focusing all the attention on himself or herself when it was you who needed to be attended to.

We think of this type of disconnection as a theft because of its unique dynamic. All forms of disconnection produce the feeling of loss we described above. But when a caregiver disconnects by stealing the attention, he not only cuts the connection between him and the child, he requires the child to respond to *his* feelings. The caregiver, in effect, steals the child's life energy (that is, the emotional power of the child's original set of feelings) and re-directs it. The child's process is stopped in its tracks and forced to make a U-turn. From the emotional desert of disconnection, the child is asked to supply attention and caring for the caregiver. Some of our friends compare this to a vampire stealing the blood of his victims.

A Note of Compassion to Parents

By this time, readers who are parents may be sinking into despair as they recognize how often they unwittingly break their connections with their kids.

Before you resign yourself to a lifetime of the bad-parent blues, consider this: Because you are human and wounded, you will disconnect from and wound your children. However, you can equip them to heal the wounds they will inevitably receive *by healing your own.* (Remember, you only disconnect when you begin to feel the pain of one of your own unhealed wounds.) In this way, not only will you keep their collection of wounds to a minimum, you will model for them the skills you learn as part of your healing. Furthermore, as you learn to keep company with yourself, you will be better able to keep company with your children. Having learned from your example, they will heal their own wounds in their own time.

Children are educated by what the grownup is and not by his talk.

— Carl Jung

Besides, it is never too late to heal a wound. You can always help your child heal a wound created by a single disconnection—such as an angry outburst in a stressful situation—by re-connecting with him later on.

And even if that re-connection doesn't happen, you can take some comfort from the knowledge that *occasional* disconnections are not likely to create serious wounds. It's only when emotional disconnection is more consistent than connection that a child's natural ability to feel, grieve and heal his losses is thwarted. He doesn't finish his grieving when loss occurs; instead he carries this unfinished business around with him. The slings and arrows of daily life gradually accumulate to create painful, unhealed wounds (more about this in the next chapter).

Another important point to remember is the unconscious nature of disconnection. It's not a disconnection when you explain to your child that you need time out to be alone or be with others. (This is easier to do if you're not caught up in the cultural lie that says parents are there for their children all the time.) If you can be lovingly honest with your child about needing distance or temporarily not feeling close to him, you can take time-outs without disconnecting. It's only when parents insist that they are loving even when they are being abusive or unloving that the child's sense of reality is threatened and disconnection occurs.

Another Note of Compassion, to the Newly Aware

If you have just begun to understand how deeply wounding your childhood was, the last few paragraphs may have made you bristle—as will any expression of compassion for the people who hurt you. You may be vacillating between rage at your parents and guilt about your rage.

Our message to you is this: Yes, your parents may have made big mistakes, and yes, you are angry and hurting. We believe that, if you decide to heal those wounds, you must take responsibility for the healing work yourself, and that might seem unfair. *"I want them to understand how bad they hurt me!"* you may be thinking.

When you take responsibility for your wounds, it does not mean your parents are given some kind of cosmic absolution from spiritual responsibility for damage they may have done you. But it does mean you absolve *yourself* from the responsibility of bringing your parents to justice (to say nothing of freeing yourself of the burden of remaining damaged to prove their guilt). Hang in there through the feelings. Your anger is valid, and allowing yourself to have it is extremely important to your healing. If you remain committed to feeling your feelings, you'll find that after a while, the anger fades, emotional residue melts, and a sense of wholeness replaces the emptiness. At this point, forgiveness usually appears effortlessly.

> *So long as I blame my parents, I remain a child.*
>
> — *Sam Keen*

EXERCISES
Discovering Your Broken Connections

What broken connections created your wounds? All of us were wounded as children, even when our caregivers had the best of intentions. Identifying your wounds, the circumstances that created them and the conclusions about life you drew from them are the first steps to healing them. You can't heal what you don't know is there.

It is important to know that remembering is not about getting a *factually* accurate picture of what happened to you back then. The only reason you need to know the facts is to know who to blame, and healing is not about blaming. Healing depends not on knowing all the facts but on feeling all the feelings you felt back then and tried to bury.

1. List the primary caregivers in your life. A primary caregiver can be a parent, grandparent, older brother or sister, hired baby-sitter, neighbor, family friend, uncle, aunt—any person who tended to your needs on a regular basis.

2. Now list the ways in which you and your primary caregivers were able to be connected. For example, Deanna and her dad used to go to the dump together every Saturday morning to unload the family's trash cans. Deanna loved this time alone with her father. It was their special time alone together, and it made Deanna feel cared for. (What feels like love to a child is connection.)

Connection happens when the caregiver:

• Plays when and what both the child and the caregiver want to play.

• Expresses interest in the child.

• Has reasonable expectations of the child's constantly changing abilities to think, feel and act.

- Helps the child learn about the world, the creatures in it and herself at her own pace and in her own way.

- Helps the child learn to set boundaries by honoring his (the caregiver's) own boundaries in loving and appropriate ways.

   And especially:

- Keeps company with the child while he experiences feelings (fear, grief, anger, joy and so on).

What felt like love to you when you were a child? For each caregiver you listed in #1, write down at least one time that you felt connected and loved. These times might have been special outings, certain play times, traumatic events when your caregiver was able to comfort you, private jokes or times that your caregiver taught you to do something like drive a nail or crochet a pot holder. Connections may have been special rituals or spontaneous, once-in-a-childhood events.

3. When Deanna's brother turned four, their Saturday morning dump runs ended. Her dad abruptly began leaving seven-year-old Deanna at home and taking her brother instead. Deanna was shocked, hurt and angry, and concluded that her father liked her brother more than he liked her. The change was never discussed, and neither were Deanna's feelings about it.

Refer to the list you made for #2. Were there any connection rituals on your list? Did one of these rituals end? If so, how and when? How did you feel? What conclusions did you draw?

4. Besides connections that ended, how did your caregivers disconnect? List incidents you can remember in which you felt shamed, ignored, misunderstood or neglected.

5. Look back over your list of broken connections. Categorize them according to the four kinds of disconnections presented in this chapter (abandonment, attacking, spoiling, stealing the attention). Is there a pattern?

6. If you have trouble identifying the disconnections you experienced, think about the times you misbehaved. How were you disciplined or punished? How did you feel when you were disciplined or punished? (Ashamed, angry, hurt, glad, relieved, scared, sad?) Do any of these incidents fit into the four categories of disconnections presented in this chapter?

TWO

The Genesis and Power of Wounds

The events of childhood do not pass but repeat themselves
like seasons of the year.

— Eleanor Farjeon

Perhaps in an ideal world, there would be no disconnections. All children would grow up surrounded by unflagging support. If disconnections did occur, they would be followed by reconnections.

But in this world, as we saw in Chapter One, caregivers do disconnect from their kids. It doesn't take beatings or sexual abuse or a war to create a disconnection. In fact, you don't even have to be raised in an especially dysfunctional family to experience disconnections. Dysfunctional families are better at disconnecting than healthy families, but simply being alive is circumstance enough for these breaks. They happen on a daily basis. As a result, to one extent or another, we all grow up wounded—carrying the burden of painful, unmourned-for losses and uncertain that we really belong.

Two Examples

[3] Examples used in this book are composites based on the lives and experiences of real people. Names, histories and personal traits have been altered to protect privacy.

Mike[3] grew up with a physically abusive father. He knew his childhood had damaged him, and he knew this was no way to raise a child. He vowed early in life that he would be his father's opposite with his own children.

By the time he came to Rebecca for help, Mike was in serious pain. Despite his determination, Mike's relationship with his kids was not good. He never struck his children, but the challenge of fatherhood continually threatened to send him over the edge into an apparently bottomless pit of rage. In fear of losing control, Mike withdrew from his children. His wife accused him of being cold, distant and uninvolved, and he knew she was right. Mike's wounds were directing his relationships with his kids.

Ellen, a successful thirty-year-old real estate agent, showed up in David's office one day, also in pain and also looking for help. She was isolated and lonely. She found it impossible to create an intimate relationship with anyone and struggled with recurring depression. Worst of all, she berated herself for being unhappy.

"I can see how someone is wounded by yelling or violence," she said. "But my home was always quiet. My parents were never loud or abusive. In fact, they were proud of the stable home they maintained. They paid the bills, worked hard, made sure we kids were clothed and taken to the dentist regularly, and generally followed all the rules for creating a 'happy' family life. So why am I such a mess?"

Ellen answered her own question by assuming she was somehow defective. It was difficult for her to fully accept that her cool, disconnected family had damaged her just as much as it would have had it been more obviously dysfunctional. Like Mike, Ellen was wounded. And like Mike, her wounds were running her life.

How could two such different families both produce wounded people?

Anatomy of a Wound

> **wound**—A strong feeling or set of feelings (fear, anger, grief) that have frozen in place instead of being allowed to flow through you and out.
>
> Nothing can inoculate us against all wounds. But where the emotional connection between a caregiver and a child is unbroken, the chances of severe wounds are diminished. Good connections between a child and caregiver give the child the resources to heal his own wounds, and the child grows up trauma-resilient.

The stage is set for wounding when the connection breaks. Broken connections don't always create wounds. They do wound us, however, when:

- They are combined with trauma
- They are chronic, even if trauma is absent.

Trauma Plus Disconnection

A *trauma* is simply any difficult experience for a child—any experience that creates a strong negative emotional response or a state of shock. A trauma can be as trivial (from the adult's perspective) as the loss of a favorite toy or as significant as witnessing the violent death of a loved one. Other examples of traumas include:

- Illness
- Injury
- Bad scares
- Physical, emotional or sexual abuse
- The birth or death of a sibling
- Disappointments
- Social snubs
- Divorce
- Bankruptcy

- The death of a parent

- Loneliness

In fact, any of life's pains can be traumatic.

However, trauma alone doesn't create a wound. Being in pain or frightened is not, in and of itself, a serious problem for a child. Life is full of mistakes, accidents and scares. The most loving, attentive parents can't keep all hurt out of the lives of their children. And even the worst traumas can be processed and left behind if a child has the necessary emotional support. Trauma alone isn't the problem.

The problem is trauma that is coupled with disconnection.

Traumatic events create strong feelings. As we saw in the last chapter, feelings are meant to be processed and completed, and children need company to learn how to thoroughly process their feelings.

But sometimes a caregiver breaks the emotional connection at the time the child needs it most—while trying to deal with his reaction to a trauma. Then the child is left alone with more feelings, or more intense feelings, than he can handle alone. As a result, he simply stores the feelings, unresolved, as emotional residue. The residue hardens, and the child carries it with him into his future.

Mike's childhood was filled with trauma. His father often hit his mother and his siblings. Although he never struck Mike, the boy was terrified and enraged by the violence he witnessed, powerless to stop it and utterly alone with his overwhelming feelings. He had less difficulty than Ellen seeing how his upbringing had wounded him, simply because the craziness and trauma of his home was so obvious.

Whether a traumatic incident actually creates a wound that gets carried into adulthood depends on many variables, including:

- How often similar incidents occur

- How sensitive or happy-go-lucky the child is by nature

- Whether other caregivers or friendly adults can offset the experience with their own loving company-keeping

- Whether Mom and Dad come back later to mend the broken connection

Isolated traumatic incidents (unless they are *extremely* traumatic) generally have little power over our emotional development. If the *predominant* emotional tone of your growing-up years is loving and connected, you usually have the skills and the support to deal with the occasional trauma. Furthermore, wounding itself is not permanent *if* caregivers come back later, reconnect, and help the child process the stored feelings.

Chronic Disconnection Alone

For trauma to create a wound, it must be combined with disconnection. But just as trauma doesn't necessarily create a wound, neither does it form an essential element of a wound. Wounds can be created even without trauma, if disconnection occurs on a regular basis.

The way trauma and disconnection work together is similar to the way that dynamite and blasting caps work together—and apart. A stick of dynamite is relatively inert; by itself, it is not likely to cause an explosion. To do any real damage, it must be used in conjunction with a blasting cap. Blasting caps, however, are dangerous all by themselves, even without dynamite.

In the same way that a stick of dynamite may or may not produce an explosion—depending on whether a blasting cap is present— trauma may or may not produce a wound—depending on whether disconnection is present. But chronic disconnection, like a blasting cap, is dangerous all by itself.

A single incident of disconnection usually isn't, in and of itself, enough to cause lasting damage. But when disconnection is chronic—that is, it occurs consistently over a long period of time—wounding is inevitable.

That was how Ellen was wounded. She describes her childhood as "quiet, uneventful and benign"; she couldn't understand how it might have wounded her. But as she looked more closely at the dynamics of her family, she began to realize that her well-meaning but wounded parents were consistently unable to keep company with her feelings on a day-to-day basis. They disconnected mostly with low-level attacks (*"you shouldn't feel that way"*) and abandonment (no discussions of feelings at all). Ellen learned to ignore her feelings—the very things that, honestly and compassionately shared, bind humans together. Her consistently unmet needs for emotional connection were enough to wound her.

Similarly, if an adopted child grows up in a family that always heads off his questions about his origins with a pat on the head and an assurance that he is better off with them (disconnection by abandoning), he will almost certainly grow up with an unhealed wound.

Caregivers who disconnect from our feelings when we are children help us develop a lifelong habit of disconnecting from our own feelings.

The Power of an Unhealed Wound

Some people, confronted with evidence of the inevitability of wounding, react with a shrug.

Okay, they say, *my childhood may not have been perfect; I have wounds. So what? That was then, and this is now. I'm an adult, I make my own choices. What's past is past. Besides, I can't even remember being wounded.*

Our answer is one of the principles of the healing journey that we discovered:

We live our lives out at the level of our wounds, not our wishes.

Childhood wounding is serious. Unhealed wounds permanently alter a person's life. Like powerful magnets, they pull in precise duplicates of the people and circumstances from earlier experiences we have not mastered.

The fact is, unresolved feelings are never buried dead; they are always buried alive. Like zombies in a horror movie, our undead wounds reach out to us from the grave and take control of our lives. Even if we don't remember the events that caused them, they come with us into our future. Our wounds remember, whether our consciousness does or not.

Proof that your wounds still exist and are affecting your life today can be found in a couple of phenomena: the repetition compulsion and triggering.

The Unconscious Repetition Compulsion

Have you ever known a woman who was desperate to find a partner who would never abandon her? After much searching, she finally finds someone who seems rock-solid, but then, inexplicably, he turns out to be ever so slightly cold and distant whenever she needs him.

"But he seemed so nice," she protests. *"How could I possibly have seen this?"*

Or perhaps you've known a man who ended his first marriage and then remarried someone who was, emotionally and often physically, the spitting image of his first wife.

"I was so sure I was making a different choice," he says. *"Maybe it's just that all women are alike."*

Who has never seen an example of this phenomenon in ourselves or others? We all tend to attract the same types of people and circumstances over and over again. It's no accident—it's called the repetition compulsion, and it is driven by unhealed wounds.

Sigmund Freud identified the repetition compulsion. He defined it as an *unplanned, unconscious and unintentional* recreation of past experiences in the present. It means that the demands of old patterns and unhealed wounds take precedence over today's willpower and good intentions. These unhealed parts decide, without our conscious consent, which people and circumstances we are attracted to. Our wounds, not our positive thinking, control whom we pick as friends and lovers and how much we allow our lives to match our dreams. Even when we think *we're* in

It took me a while to learn that your relationship to your father and your mother has nothing to do with whether they're in the room or not. You're going to meet them everywhere, so you might as well confront whatever problems you have with them.

– Val Kilmer

control of our lives, it's actually this old programming that runs the show.

Ellen found herself the victim of her own repetition compulsion. She said she wanted a warm circle of friends, and decided to go out and find them. However, although she carefully selected people who seemed warm and caring, she invariably discovered that they dealt with conflict with angry outbursts. The blowups created distance and scared Ellen off, so that she ended up alone again.

Triggering

Much of the pain of adult life is due to re-experiencing childhood wounding through an experience we call *triggering*.

> *trigger* (as a verb)—To re-open an unhealed wound through events, words, sounds, behavior (or any other stimulus) that somehow reminds you (either consciously or unconsciously) of the original wounding event. When you are triggered, you behave as if you are back in the wounding event, and you tend to act to protect yourself from the pain. "When my supervisor shakes her finger in my face, it triggers an unhealed wound I have around critical women, and I am flooded with rage."
>
> (as a noun) The stimulus that causes an unhealed wound to re-open. "Ambivalent men are a real trigger for me—they remind me of my dad in a way that makes me pursue them even when I know they are not particularly interested in being with me."

Unhealed wounds resurface when events trigger a response in us that is out of proportion to the event itself. When triggered, people are often confused by their reaction precisely because they *have* forgotten the original incident. Being triggered is proof of an unresolved—and perhaps forgotten—wound from the past infecting the present.

Mike had not forgotten the incidents that wounded him, but his children's (perfectly normal) antics made him flash back to his childhood. His unresolved rage and fear surfaced each time this happened and kept him from responding appropriately.

Ellen, unaware of her wounds, was triggered each time someone tried to get close to her. At the first sign of friendliness, she became coolly polite and remote. Usually, she was so good at this drill that no one invited her anywhere. If someone did get past her icy barrier, she either declined the invitation, or accepted, then left early. She had learned to fear closeness from her parents' unwillingness to be close to her.

We're All Wounded

Eventually, all children are wounded, even those with careful, aware and loving parents. This is a given. No one comes away from childhood without wounds.[4] If you have tormented yourself with the idea that there are unwounded people and wounded people, and that your goal is to become unwounded and to raise unwounded children, please stop. It isn't possible. What is possible is healing—not all of our wounds, and possibly not even in one lifetime—but healing in a measure that will make a difference in our lives and the lives of the people we touch.

Wounds are a lonely burden for a child. Wounded children must figure out, all by themselves, a way to get through the pain as well as possible. In the next chapter, we'll see how a child makes it possible to survive his wounds.

[4] Indeed, we suspect that no soul comes into a body without wounds. It seems to be the nature of this place that the souls here are wounded. We think that may be what incarnation is for: to heal spiritual and emotional wounds. For more information and ideas about wounding and the soul, read Gary Zukov's *The Seat of the Soul* (Simon & Schuster, 1989).

EXERCISES
Identifying Your Wounds

1. Sometimes it's obvious what the traumas were in our young lives. Sometimes it takes some digging to recognize what was significant. In either case, most people benefit from writing them down. Complete the following sentences:

> The biggest loss in my childhood was…

> The most frightening thing that happened to me as a child was…

> The most humiliating event of my childhood was…

> I was terribly disappointed by…

> The worst betrayal of my childhood happened when…

2. Chronic disconnection takes many forms. Use the list on these pages to identify the forms chronic disconnection may have taken in your family. If you don't find one that fits, write your own.
In my family…

> ☐ My parents divorced or fought constantly.

> ☐ We moved a lot.

> ☐ My mother/father was distracted with problems of her/his own and was not able to really notice me or attend to my needs.

> ☐ I was told that my birth was an unwelcome accident.

> ☐ Someone important to me died when I was young, and his/her death was never discussed.

> ☐ I was yelled at a lot.

> ☐ A family member was chronically ill.

- ☐ I was given the silent treatment when I misbehaved.

- ☐ I was blamed or criticized for things that were not my responsibility or were out of my control.

- ☐ I was blamed for things my siblings did.

- ☐ I had an embarrassing or debilitating illness as a child.

- ☐ My mother/father was disappointed that I was not a boy/girl.

- ☐ My mother/father told me women/men could not be trusted.

- ☐ We never had enough money for important things like food, clothing or school supplies.

- ☐ My siblings and I did not get along.

- ☐ Our family worshipped a God that was vindictive, demanding and angry.

- ☐ My mother/father had affairs.

- ☐ My parents used me as a go-between whenever they fought with each other.

- ☐ I was molested.

- ☐ My step-parent hated me, and my birth parent did not protect me from him/her.

- ☐ I was hit a lot.

- ☐ I grew up in a war zone or a high-crime area.

- ☐ I played alone.

- ☐ My family was controlled by the addictions of one or more family members.

- ☐ I wasn't hit, but I regularly saw others in my family beaten.

☐ Our family looked good to the world, but behind closed doors, we were very different.

☐ I was a poor student.

☐ I was the family _____ (bad child, good child, brain, idiot, rebel, responsible one—any label that obscures who you really are).

☐ No one taught me how to _____.

☐ My divorced parents discussed their criticisms of each other with me.

☐ I was told that being abused was my fault.

3. Look at the statements you selected or wrote for the previous exercise. Think about what effect each one has had on your thoughts about yourself, others and the world. Then complete the following sentence for each one: *I concluded from these experiences that…*

4. One sign of an unhealed wound is the flashback: when one of your unhealed wounds is triggered, you move into your emotional state when the wound was inflicted, as if you were experiencing the wounding as a child (or yourself at whatever age it occurred), rather than an adult experiencing a similar event years (perhaps decades) later.

   For example, Lisa, a new psychotherapist, was yelled at in a therapy group by an angry, critical client. She said later the experience paralyzed her with fear. She felt like she was seven years old again, being yelled at by her drunken father. It was all she could do to keep from bursting into tears and running from the room.

   However, not all triggered wounds produce fear. You may be overcome by rage, shame or grief when someone talks to you in a certain tone of voice. One of the clues to look for is the disparity between the intensity of your reaction and the apparent significance of the event that triggered it. Usually, your reaction will be all out of proportion to the event itself. For example, Mark, a 26-year-old travel agent, changed channels when any one of a series of sentimental long-distance telephone service TV commercials came on to avoid the intense crying jags they triggered. Through his support-group meetings, he realized that they touched his unexpressed grief over his family's inability to express their caring for one another. Similarly, many people (women especially) are triggered by the romantic fantasies that appear in movies. Did *Pretty Woman* send you into a days-long fit of passionate yearning for a love affair that would transform your life? Did *The Bridges of Madison County* make you weep for the lost, perfect love you never had? There's a difference between enjoying a movie simply for its entertainment value and being triggered by its message. Deep reactions alert you to wounds.

What exposes your wounds? People can be triggered by:

• Rejection	• Authority figures
• Weddings	• Being ignored
• Being told what to do	• Being rushed
• Saying good-bye	• Criticism
• Sarcasm	• Drunk people
• Arguments	• Being misunderstood
• Compliments	• Parties
• Disapproving looks	• Other people's impatience

Write down the specific incidents that trigger your unhealed wounds. Beside each description of the event, write a description of your feelings. Were you panicky? Deeply sad? Enraged? Resentful? Try to identify what you were afraid of, sad about, angry about.

It's important to note that your triggers are defined by *your* perceptions. If you are triggered by criticism, and your friend says something that sounds critical to you, you will be triggered even if your friend truly was not criticizing. Learning to deal with this apparent contradiction involves a concept called self-responsibility, which we describe in detail in the next section.

5. Another way to locate your wounds is to identify the times when you disconnect emotionally from others. We always disconnect to protect an unhealed wound. Signs that you have disconnected include:

• Defensiveness

- Withdrawal, emotional shut-down, feeling emotionally numb

- Feelings of shame or embarrassment (also known as "shame attacks")

- Strong, nearly overwhelming feelings of rage that are out of proportion to the events that stimulated them ("rage attacks")

- Anxiety or panic

- Sudden difficulty in paying attention or understanding what is being said

- Cynicism

What kinds of events make you disconnect from another person? What form does your disconnection take?

6 Another indicator of wounds is repeating patterns in your life—the repetition compulsion. For most people, this means repeating certain kinds of relationships with certain types of people. Others find themselves working for the same kind of abusive or critical boss, no matter how often they change jobs. Some people repeat the same kind of argument or power struggle with a variety of authority figures, from landlords to instructors to older relatives. A number of our clients repeatedly get themselves into romantic relationships that follow a particular pattern: their partners are abusive, clingy, critical, distant, or addicted.

What patterns do you repeat in your life? If none come immediately to mind, think about the last argument you had with a friend or your partner, or a conflict you had with anyone. Was there anything familiar about it? Were you tempted to say (to yourself or out loud) *"They're all alike! Why don't I ever learn?"* Those are good clues that you're following the trail of a repetition compulsion.

THREE

The Survival Plan: An Overview

*[From a child's perspective] there is no fixing a
damaged childhood. The best you can hope for is to
make the sucker float.*

— Pat Conroy (with qualification by the authors)

§ § §

OVER THE NEXT FEW YEARS, *the little stream
spirit continued to take the advice of his
neighbors. He added more and more boulders to
the dam, until no water at all flowed below it.
The meadow became a huge, stagnant lake.
Below the dam lay a dying, dried-out wasteland,
emptier than a desert. The reservoir began to
stink. The little stream spirit complained to his
older neighbors, who had stopped over to see how
the stream spirit was managing its water. They
looked at each other in surprise.*

*"Why, this is how it's supposed to be," one
said.*

"This is how **ours** *are," said the other, "and
we worked hard, without the kind of help you've*

had, to make them that way. For goodness' sake,
what more do you want?"

The little spirit said he would like more
greenery below the dam and less odor above it.

"We can fix that," the older spirits said. They
reappeared the next day with a dozen buckets
and a bag of paint brushes. They opened nine
buckets of green paint and divided them among
the three of them, then set to work painting the
rocks below the dam. They even painted some of
the dead trees. When they had used the last of the
paint, the older spirits opened the three remaining
buckets with a flourish.

"These are the latest products developed for
just such a situation as yours," they said. "The
liquid in the first bucket will kill all that stinky
algae that have grown in your reservoir. The
powder in the second bucket will cover the smell
created by the chemicals in the first bucket. And
the third bucket is a pleasant blue dye to make
the water look pretty."

They emptied the three buckets in the
reservoir and left.

The little stream spirit sat on the shore of its
empty blue lake, disconsolate. He watched a dead
fish float past, pushed along by a hot breeze
blowing up from the desert below the dam. He
wandered down into the desert, sat on a green
rock in the sparse shade of a sickly little green-
painted tree and sifted sand through his toes for
a while. It didn't seem right, somehow. But his
older, wiser neighbors had insisted that this is how
the land and the water should be managed. The
stream spirit sighed and lay down for a nap.
When he awoke, the landscape was just as
forbidding and uncomfortable as it had been
before. The spirit wished he had stayed asleep.
He began taking longer and longer naps.

*The stream spirit became a skilled sleeper. He
found many ways to get himself to sleep, and he
had lots of nap spots. There was a cool, shady spot
for hot days, and a cozy, sheltered cave with lots
of dead leaves for days when cold winds blew.
One day, he found a ravaged clump of bushes
clinging to the shore of his lake. The stream spirit
nibbled the shriveled berries and discovered that
they helped him go to sleep faster and stay asleep
longer. He tended the bushes carefully after that
and hoarded the dried berries.*

*When he wasn't sleeping, the stream spirit
learned to pretend. He convinced himself that the
green trees were alive and the green rocks were the
animals that used to live near the flowing stream.
He invented games to play with his imaginary
friends.*

*Of course, he could no longer swim in the
poisoned water, and the only shade he could find
was in a hollowed-out cave in the bank. He
visited with his older neighbors often, though. He
began to think of them as his teachers. They gave
him advice about caring for his lands, and they
pretended with him that the trees and animals
were still alive. The stream spirit often felt lonely
when he was with the older spirits, but he didn't
call it that, because he didn't know that's what it
was. He just ate more sleepberries, and told
himself that playing made him tired.*

GIVEN THE LIST OF CIRCUMSTANCES under which wounds
accumulate, it's easy—and accurate—to conclude that everyone
on the planet is wounded to one degree or another. Some people
have numerous deep wounds that destroy their ability to connect
with others and lead to misery and pain. Their wounds are
obvious.

Others seem to be almost wound-free. They create apparently loving relationships, successful careers and happy, useful lives. Yet even these people have unhealed wounds.

We are not meant to carry around unhealed wounds. Given the support and guidance to heal them, that is what we will do. But when we're little, we don't have that option if our caregivers are too wounded themselves to help us. We can't do it alone. The only thing we can do is protect ourselves from the pain.

Life as we find it is too hard for us; it entails too much pain, too many disappointments, impossible tasks. We cannot do without palliative remedies.

— Sigmund Freud

That's the job of the survival plan. Everyone with unhealed wounds—meaning *everyone*, including those who wrote and those who now read this book—has a survival plan.

> **survival plan**—A defensive structure or pattern of thoughts, beliefs, behaviors and habits you create to shield yourself from the pain of emotional disconnection, created when you have insufficient support to feel the pain of disconnection and heal your wounds.

The Choice: Survival Plan or Death

Children can tolerate some disconnection and wounding without too much damage because of their survival plan. It keeps them from feeling the hurt, makes some sense of the way their lives are constructed and provides hope for change.

In fact, creating a survival plan is an act of creative genius, for which you have our hearty congratulations. You made a decision at a crucial point in your life that allowed you to grow up. You could have, instead, been among those children who chose a far darker path.

When a Survival Plan Isn't Enough

For some children, the pain of disconnection becomes unbearable. The point at which this occurs is different for every child and depends on individual temperament as much as it does on external circumstances. However, pain is bound to approach unbearable levels for virtually any child when too many of his experiences are one-sided, disconnected, dysfunctional or abusive.

Some children experience such deep, unremitting pain that not even a survival plan can save them. These children respond to their despair by dying. Some literally commit suicide. (In fact, we've seen evidence that many suicides are mislabeled accidental deaths.)

Other children die emotionally, spiritually and socially. They are such severely unbonded souls that they have no conscience; they are known as sociopaths. Symptoms of childhood sociopathy include chronic, destructive fire-setting, torturing animals and brutalizing or killing others—all without remorse or concern for their victims. Therapists still don't know how to treat this condition successfully without early intervention (before about age twelve). Even then, the only treatment is controversial, long-term and difficult, and involves forcing the children to face and experience the severe pain of parental disconnection that always accompanies this condition.[5]

What Happens to Kids Who Die Emotionally

People often are confused when children who seem to come from good families develop severe problems. You can read about this phenomenon almost daily in any newspaper. Recently, our local paper carried the story of a fourteen-year-old boy accused of shooting a pizza delivery man to death. The article questioned how such a nice kid—active in his uncle's church, doing well in school and well-liked by his teachers—might have been able to do such a terrible thing.

The reporter named various societal influences, but left the question unanswered. At the end of the article, though, the writer included the following facts, almost as afterthoughts:

- The boy's father abandoned the family when he was two.

- He was beaten by his stepfather.

- He had been involved in an auto theft to which he casually referred as "joy-riding."

[5] For more on how children become sociopathic, read *High Risk: Children Without a Conscience*, by Dr. Ken Magid and Carole A. McKelvey (Bantam, 1987).

- His older brother was involved in a gang.
- An uncle had been convicted of burglary and rape the year before.

Not once did the story suggest that these influences had anything to do with the cold-blooded murder the boy was accused of committing. The reporter seemed baffled. The people he interviewed seemed baffled.

We wanted to scream, *There is no mystery here!* Whether he is found guilty or innocent of the delivery man's murder, this boy has been mortally wounded by his upbringing. The death of his soul should have come as no surprise. In fact, what is surprising is how many kids survive a similar childhood without descending into sociopathy.

Our culture's ignorance and disregard for the power of chronic disconnection appalls us. Disconnection hurts children. It hurts us. And it hurts society.

Who Dies?

Beyond obvious damage due to disconnection, the way a particular child comes to choose death over survival, or survival over death, is a mix of many factors. They include (but are undoubtedly not limited to):

- Genetics
- Family dynamics
- The depth of his wounds
- The presence or absence of some nurturing somewhere in his life
- His basic temperament and physiology
- Hope

We have come to believe that the ability to generate some form of hope deserves a place near the top of the list. It is the primary component of the survival plan. We believe it is the loss of this hope for a better way (or at the very least, a safer way) that is largely responsible for skyrocketing crime rates among older children and adolescents. Hope, combined with emotional connection with caregivers, is the one thread that keeps a child connected to his spiritual resources and to his own soul.

Who Survives?

How do children who stay alive develop their survival plans? We have seen that:

- Humans need love
- Being emotionally connected to another human being fills the need for love
- Because life is what it is, all humans experience emotional disconnection.

Emotional disconnection hurts. The earlier in life it occurs, the less equipped we are to deal with this pain.

A mature, healed adult, faced with disconnection, can say to herself, *"The contact and love I need are not available to me from this person because he/she is wounded, but I'm fine anyway; I know how to give myself enough love and contact and company-keeping to stay whole and genuine."*

A child facing the pain of disconnection can't talk to herself this way. Her very existence depends solely on her caregivers; she doesn't have the perspective of years of life to help her conclude that the problem does not lie in her own worth; she hasn't yet learned how to give herself love, contact and company-keeping. She can't heal her wounds without the emotional support of her caregivers. She can't remain whole and genuine in the face of her pain. Instead, she manages her fear and pain and fulfills her need for a sense of control and predictability by creating a survival plan.

Survival plans vary from one person to the next. Children from highly dysfunctional families develop highly dysfunctional, complex survival plans. In healthier families in which pain is less pervasive, children form survival plans that are relatively more functional, and they develop them relatively later in life—sometimes not until early adulthood.[6] Their survival plans usually

[6] In a family that produces little pain to protect against, a survival plan may not be necessary until early adulthood, when people begin to confront the insanity of the world on a regular basis. As of this writing, there aren't enough of these kinds of people around to really begin to understand their processes.

look "normal," and may even keep them fairly healthy, happy and secure until the ends of their lives.

Sooner or later, everyone creates a survival plan, because, to one degree or another, everyone experiences emotional disconnection. By our late twenties, most of us have developed a complex and richly woven belief system impenetrable to contrary information. This survival plan provides the security every human being needs.

Elements of the Survival Plan

The survival plan is like a tripod consisting of three supports: a happy-ending fantasy, rules and anesthesia. When the three legs of the survival plan tripod are perfectly balanced against each other, we can balance on top, protected from the pain below. A closer look at the construction of this tripod follows in the next three chapters.

The Elements of the Survival Plan

Pain

Happy-Ending
Fantasy

Rules

Anesthesia

FOUR

Leg One: The Happy-Ending Fantasy

*Among the most harmful, irrational ideas in our
culture are these: any danger, failure or other stress is
catastrophic; whatever has affected one markedly must
continue to affect one in that same way; every person
should have someone stronger than himself on whom
to rely; it is better to avoid than to face difficulties and
responsibilities; unhappiness comes from without and
is wholly beyond one's control; happiness can be
gained by sheer inertia.*

— Albert Ellis

THE HAPPY-ENDING FANTASY forms the core of the survival
plan. It is the first of the legs of the tripod to go up, and the last
one to come down.

How the Happy-Ending Fantasy is Born

Psychologist Robert W. Firestone, Ph.D., developed extensive
theories on psychodynamics in family relationships. He says that
infants arrive with a strong need to bond with something, prefer-

ably with a living, consistently loving, flesh-and-blood member of its own species. However, Firestone says, in the absence of an ideal parent, an infant bonds with whatever is available and pretends it is everything he needs.

Firestone illustrates his theory with the infant's increasingly sophisticated ability to comfort himself when hungry. A baby starts out responding to its own hunger by crying; he stops when he tastes milk. Gradually, he learns that Mom's arrival means food is coming, and he quiets down when he sees her. He has associated her presence with the comfort of being fed. Gradually, his associations become more and more specific. He begins to associate her voice with hunger relief; at this point, she can call to him from another room when he cries in hunger, and he will settle down and wait for a little while. The baby learns to comfort himself with memories of his mother feeding him. He creates a fantasy to tide him over until the reality arrives.

This ability to comfort himself while waiting for his needs to be met is crucial to a baby's growing into emotional maturity. When Mom and food are consistently, predictably available, the baby uses the fantasy of comfort to ward off the pain of his separation from mom. However, his main bond is with Mom.

No person can live, no ego remain intact without hope and will.
— *Erik Erikson*

But if Mom and food are unavailable or inconsistent, the baby spends more and more time in his mental images of comfort. As a result, he bonds with his comforting fantasy of his mother, instead of with Mom herself.

When a child bonds with his fantasy of comfort instead of the provider of the comfort, Firestone says, he becomes locked into a self-defeating cycle. He can't break the bond he has formed with his fantasy, because that would mean feeling the overpowering pain of disconnection. But to maintain the fantasy bond, he must continue to perceive Mom (and other caregivers, as he forms relationships with them) as more loving, more available—or less damaged—than she really is. This inaccurate perception creates its own burden, because, according to a basic principle of psychology, *we pay for our idealized versions of others with our perception of our own lack of value.* So maintaining a bond with a perfect fantasy of his caregivers sets the child up for low self-esteem.

No parent is capable of being available one hundred percent of the time. Therefore, according to Firestone, to some extent all infants bond with a fantasy of their caregivers.

Firestone's groundbreaking and profound work on the fantasy bond provided a springboard for our own thoughts about the way people seek love and comfort in life.[7] We believe that, as a child grows up, he creates a more sophisticated, complex version of his original fantasy bond. We call this the "happy-ending fantasy."

> *happy-ending fantasy*—An imaginary relationship you create with a goal or a person to give you hope that you'll be okay someday.

Like the fantasy bond, the happy-ending fantasy provides comfort and helps shield us from pain. But the happy-ending fantasy goes a few steps further than the infant's rudimentary fantasy bond, as we'll see.

False Hope and the Happy-Ending Fantasy

The original happy-ending fantasy that you formed as a child went something like this: *These people—my caregivers—are normal, whole, healthy people who can love me. I just haven't found the way to unlock their love. But I will.*

The hope that you could do something to make people love you the way you needed to be loved was based on your inaccurate conclusion that your pain was your fault. You believed that the disconnection between you and your caregivers had something to do with *you*. That gave you a cause for optimism. After all, if the problem was you, there was every reason to believe that you could solve the problem and create the love and comfort you needed. This hope is as close as you could get to feeling powerful.

This hope, of course, was false. There was no magic formula that, when found and applied, would make the significant people in your life love you. You could not get what you needed by trying to change yourself or your caregivers. In fact, if there had

[7] We recommend his books to therapists of any theoretical persuasion, and his videotapes to anyone interested in personal growth. For more information, contact the Glendon Association in Santa Barbara; the address is listed under *Healing Resources* in Chapter Twenty-Six.

Refusal to hope is nothing more than a decision to die.

– Bernie S. Siegel

been a magic formula, you would not have needed a fantasy to sustain you. When your caregivers connected with you, it was because they were able to do so. When they did not, it was because of their own unhealed wounds.

Even so, your false hope contained an element of truth—just enough truth so that it made some sense. For example, if you grew up getting lots of attention when you told jokes, you may have experienced this attention as love and approval. If you connected most successfully in your family when you were unhappy and less successfully when you were carefree, you may have concluded that people will care about you only if you have problems to discuss with them. If you connected most successfully in your family when you were a caretaker or extra-good or extra-mature or extra-quiet or extra-responsible, you may have concluded that people would care about you only if you were codependent with them.

Hope is independent of the apparatus of logic.

— Norman Cousins

So, over the course of your childhood, you developed the sense that the love you received depended to some degree on something you did. You may have believed it was necessary to accomplish certain tasks in certain ways, or behave in certain ways. Regardless of the form, your false hope became tangled up with those conditions. Even if your caregivers were relatively unwounded themselves and were consistently open and loving, you may have done what children frequently do—drawn inaccurate conclusions about their availability and your power to elicit it.

For example, Allen nearly always feels resentful and angry when someone he is talking with appears to take comfort from a hot cup of coffee or a frosty beer. He was able to piece together the reason recently after a conversation with his father. Allen's dad confided that he thought he and Allen's mother drank too much during some trying times when Allen was a boy. Allen thinks his parents were probably not alcoholics—"drinking too much," in his dad's dictionary, meant a couple of cocktails each evening—but he remembers knowing that his parents were not available to him while they drank.

Allen's conclusion was, *"A person cannot take comfort or pleasure from a beverage and maintain a connection with me at the same time."* Thirty years later, the sight of his wife cupping her hands around a mug of hot coffee can leave him feeling like an eight-year-old competing with glass full of liquid for his parents' attention. In the past, Allen nagged his wife about her "caffeine addiction." Now he realizes that he felt the pain of that childhood abandonment whenever he saw Carolyn "involved" with a cup of coffee. (*"I would think, 'Now I have to compete with **that**.'"*) He responded by trying to get her away from her magical beverage since, according to his eight-year-old self, *that* was what created the disconnection. (Incidentally, this is a classic example of an old, unhealed wound being triggered by a present event, which in turn activates an aspect of the survival plan. Allen's fears of abandonment had nothing to do with current events. Carolyn was happy and committed to their marriage.)

Good Observers, Bad Interpreters

Like all children, Allen was great at noticing what was happening around him. However, all children are handicapped by a number of factors in their ability to draw accurate conclusions. These factors are:

- **They don't know the details.** In Allen's case, that means he didn't know what was in the glasses. Also, he could not have any idea of the emotional forces that drove them to use the alcohol in the first place or that part of what made his parents unavailable was the numbing effects of the alcohol.

- **They are egocentric.** Whatever happens, happens to or because of them.

- **They think in black-and-white terms.** Being able to perceive the shades of gray comes with physical and emotional maturity. In the meantime, their caregivers are either loving and supportive or coldly abandoning. There are no shades of gray.

As a result, children, although they are excellent observers, are poor interpreters. Keenly sensitive to broken connections, a child will tend to mistakenly conclude that such a break means something bad about *his* intrinsic value. (This is, incidentally, how shame is born.)

The Staying Power of False Hope

False hope is tenacious. Even when forced (by outright physical abandonment, for example) to face the fact that their caregivers cannot give them what they need, children often will simply switch the object of their happy-ending fantasy to someone they invent: imaginary friends or "real" parents who will return someday to take them home. In that case, their happy-ending fantasy might look something like this: *These people—my caregivers— can't/won't/don't love me. But that's not so important, because my **real** family will be back to get me as soon as they can, and they love me the way I need.*

Some children, faced with the hopelessness of getting the love they need, transfer their hope to real people—friends, romantic interests, other relatives, teachers, gangs—and revise their happy-ending fantasy to: *These people—my caregivers—can't/won't/don't love me the way I need. But that's not so important, because my boyfriend knows me better than anyone, loves me the way no one else does and will always be there for me.*[8]

It is important to note that false hope focused on a person has nothing to do with whether that person is *actually* capable of loving you. The aim of the false hope—whether with a person, behavior or substance—is to bring about the *sense* of connection and safety that *feels like love to a child*. Many people may be capable of loving you as an adult, but no one in the present can provide the sense of well-being that you needed and didn't get as a child. Often, people living under the terms of their survival plan give up relationships with truly loving people because they are still looking for the "perfect" love of childhood.

Children who give up on people may transfer their hope to material goals, work, philosophies, hobbies, television, computers,

[8] This is why teenagers (or adults who have an intact survival plan, for that matter) can't be forced to "just say no" to drugs or sex; survival plans *always* have veto power over common sense.

chemicals, food, music—anything that seems to fill the hole for a little while. Their false hope may be: *These people—my care-givers—can't/won't/don't love me. But that's okay, because making the honor role does it for me.*

False *Hopelessness* and the Happy-Ending Fantasy

Some children are disappointed so many times in trying to fulfill their false hope that they switch to false *hopelessness.* They come to believe that they simply can't get the love and connection they need. For them, hope lies not in achieving love, but in avoiding pain. The best happy ending they dare hope for is safety, invisibility, and making it through the day.

If false hope is a pair of rose-colored glasses, false hopelessness is a pair of dark glasses, tinted by despair, that make every day cloudy. Children wear the glasses of hopelessness so they won't suffer the pain of one more crushing disappointment. Life is no fun this way, since the hopelessness glasses block out the glow of love, affection and sincere appreciation, but at least you can feel safe from the hurt of unrealistic expectations. If you assume that the people you care about most won't love you back, you can dull the ache of that loss.

Cathie is a good example of how children come to false hopelessness. Her dad, embittered by a career-derailing layoff when he was forty-three, told her repeatedly, *"Cath, the world is full of bastards."* She grew up believing that she had to protect herself from people by being clever, quiet or good enough, by deciphering the rules and following them to the letter or by tricking people into giving her what she wanted. It wasn't an optimistic way of looking at life, but it made Cathie feel that she had a method of avoiding the terror of being controlled by people who didn't care what happened to her.

One of the seductive aspects of false hopelessness is that, like false hope, it contains an element of truth. There *are* people in the world like the ones who laid off Cathie's dad. Wayne's dad *was* a workaholic, and it *was* true that there was no way for

Wayne to get his attention. Toni's divorced mom *was* happier when she was alone than when she had a boyfriend, since all her boyfriends were abusive.

So if the hopelessness is based in reality, what makes it false? It becomes false when children, being what they are, generalize. Wayne constructed an emotional syllogism something like this: *There is no way to get through to my father; My father is a man; Therefore, there is no way to get through to any man.*

Wayne was right about his dad, but inaccurate when he lumped one hundred percent of the rest of the male population of the world in the same category. This false conclusion, however, was essential to his survival. It allowed him to believe what all children must believe: that his father was as whole and loving as he could expect any man to be. It protected Wayne from the devastating knowledge that, in fact, his father was unreachable because of his wounds. Toni's false hopelessness (*All relationships are painful and abusive for women*) protected her from knowing that her mother was too wounded to choose loving boyfriends. Because of her false hopelessness (*The world is full of bastards*), Cathie could blame her father's misfortune and his subsequent bitterness on a cruel, uncaring world. She didn't have to face the fact that her father was too wounded to overcome the rage and pain he felt when he lost his job.

To render ourselves insensible to pain we must forfeit also the possibility of happiness.

— Sir John Lubbock

False hopelessness creates a negative, self-defeating lifestyle. It acts like a pair of psychic blinders, shutting out all evidence of hope, love or change for the better. In our therapy groups, we have watched people attached to false hopelessness *fail to hear* positive comments and feedback from others. These folks don't just ignore positive remarks or brush them off with, "*Yeah, but....*" If asked, they will faithfully repeat, word for word, everything *except* the positive content. They actually don't seem to hear or remember the words being spoken. That's how powerful false hopelessness can be.

Your Happy-Ending Fantasy Today

Today, your happy-ending fantasy may take any number of forms. Usually, it can be expressed as an *"if...then"* statement:

> *If I eat just one more piece of chocolate cake with Rocky Road ice cream on top, then my bad feelings will go away and I won't feel so alone.*

> *If you would just express yourself more fully, then our relationship would be better for both of us.*

> *If I have children, then I will be content.*

> *If you would quit drinking, then we could be a happy family.*

> *If I act as if I know what I'm doing, then people will treat me as if I belong here.*

> *If I can just find the right relationship, then I will be happy.*

> *If I learn to play the piano, then I will be fulfilled.*

> *If God really loved me, then I wouldn't be so lonely and scared.*

> *If I get that promotion, then I'll have it made.*

However, this *if...then* form does not define a happy-ending fantasy. Many *if...then* statements are true and helpful. *If I manage my time more efficiently and work more diligently, I will have more clients and therefore more money* is a good example of a business goal founded in reality and focused on a narrow, tangible and achievable result.

What does define the happy-ending fantasy is the second element of the *if...then* form. The *"then"* portion of a fantasy carries the promise of living happily ever after—a broad sense that *"life itself will be okay"* if the condition is met. The goal of a happy-ending fantasy is both intangible and worthy: feeling approved-of, safe, powerful, sexy, happy or worthwhile. But it is based on the assumption that the source of our pain is external and therefore can be remedied by changing external circumstances. As a result, happy-ending fantasies place responsibility for your happiness on someone or something else, or require you to make an unrealistic assessment of your own responsibility or capabilities. When a goal is part of a happy-ending fantasy, it is also a substitute for what you're really looking for: love and connection.

For example, the business goal described above becomes a fantasy if it ends with something like "...*and then my relationship with my spouse will be okay.*" While it may be true that your spouse will gripe less about the bills if there is more money around, it is unlikely that working more and having more money will solve problems in your relationship that make you feel inadequate, lost and alone.

Happy-ending fantasies wear all kinds of respectable disguises. You may want to have children, and having children may bring you great joy and satisfaction. But having children is not the Holy Grail. It will not give you endless fulfillment, eternal happiness and peace of mind if your real problem is unhealed wounds. Neither will finding the right job, getting your spouse to quit drinking, losing thirty pounds, getting married, getting divorced or finding the perfect type of therapy. Outside solutions never fix inside problems.

Unless the actions described in the *"if"* portion require you to drop your walls and be authentic with yourself or others, and the effects described in the *"then"* portion are realistic, attainable and observable, you are dealing with a fantasy. Even if you succeed in fulfilling the *"if"* condition, the effects of your success will be fleeting; you will need to repeat them or rewrite them, usually in larger and larger forms, to feel their effects. Furthermore, they support your false hope that someone will love you in precisely the way you needed to be loved as a child, and so they become self-perpetuating.

◆

Symptoms of an Active Happy-Ending Fantasy

1. Anesthesia use

2. A vocal inner critic

3. A tendency toward gullibility

4. Chronic overachieving (that is, pursuing goals in a driven way, achieving them, then finding that you don't feel better for more than a little while)

5. Chronic underachieving (that is, aspiring toward appealing goals, but never achieving them)

6. A pattern of regular "closeness-shutdown cycles," in which you seek closeness, but unconsciously withdraw as soon as you achieve it (for example, by picking a fight, becoming very busy with work or finding something to criticize)

7. A tendency toward compulsivity

8. A tendency to rescue others, engage in "caretaking," turn people into improvement projects or become involved with people who have great hidden potential that somehow never manifests

9. Often believing in someone or something, then feeling hopeless, victimized and betrayed when your hopes in that someone or something are dashed

10. A tendency to practice "image management," in which you present to others a carefully coached and edited version of yourself in the hope that you will gain their approval—or at least that they won't see you as negatively as you see yourself

11. A tendency to insist on being right, even when it means sacrificing your happiness, peace of mind or ability to love

Happy-Ending Fantasies for the Falsely Hopeless

If your happy-ending fantasy is founded on false hopelessness instead of false hope, your *if…then* statements may look more like one of the following:

> *If people could really be trusted, then I wouldn't be so lonely (but they can't be trusted, so I'm doomed to loneliness; but at least I won't make the mistake of getting close to one of them and really getting hurt).*

> *If relationships were anything other than painful, then I would have one (but they're not, so I'm going to stay safe by not taking a chance on any relationship).*

> *If people were really considerate, then I would be more loving (but they aren't considerate, so I'm not going to waste my energy learning to love them, and that way I can be safe from their hurtful ways).*

If false hope encourages a "happily ever after" point of view, false hopelessness prepares you for an "*unhappily* ever after" sort of world. The best happy ending you can hope for under these circumstances is usually to simply avoid getting hurt. So hopelessness adherents strive for safety. *"Love and connection are impossible for me, so I won't even think about it. I will adjust to the idea that it isn't available."*

Such a conclusion is likely to leave you feeling angry and resentful. False hopelessness is dangerously close to the line between survival and emotional or physical death. People on the false hopelessness end of the scale often are chronically depressed or are underachievers, or both. Some step over the line into suicide. Hopeless people tend to turn their anger into blame; they blame themselves for being too defective to create the love they need, or they blame others for being too defective to provide it. People who build their happy-ending fantasies on false hope tend to find it easier to open up to healing, since they are usually more willing to maintain relationships with others. Relationships provide the raw material we need to heal our wounds.

False Hope
Happy-ending fantasy
is focused on **people**
who can make me
feel better: parents,
children, spouses,
friends, bosses, lovers,
therapists, etc.

Misery
Death

Healing

False Hopelessness
Happy-ending fantasy
is focused on **things**
that can ease the pain:
institutions, substances,
religions, activities, etc.

Identifying Your Happy-Ending Fantasy

The happy-ending fantasy that supports false hope takes many forms. However, it nearly always includes two parts: *Something I can do*, and *something I will get as a result* that I accept as a substitute for love and connection. For example:

> *If I stay out of romantic relationships, then I will be safe from hurt.*

> *If I find the right romantic relationship, then I will be safe from hurt.*

> *If I make $50,000 this year, then I will feel worthwhile.*

Sometimes the formula involves something you think someone else can (or should) do:

> *If other drivers were more considerate, then I wouldn't come home in such a bad mood.*

Use one or more of the statements below to describe the forms your happy-ending fantasy takes.

> If I...then I will....
> If you...then I will...
> If they...then I will...

FIVE

Leg Two: Rules

The first step to freedom is to reject absolute rules.
They're part of the tyranny of the should.
— Henry Rabin and Ben Weininger

WHETHER YOU BASED YOUR HAPPY-ENDING FANTASY on hope-lessness or hope, it was founded on a lie—an unsteady foundation at best. As a result, your happy-ending fantasy threatened to fall apart on a regular basis. Therefore, you needed to add a second component to your survival plan tripod to help keep this fantasy within reach: A set of rules.

Rules. We've all got them, whether we think of ourselves as free spirits or by-the-book engineering types. That's because the happy-ending fantasy by itself, although extremely powerful, usually isn't enough to completely shield you from your pain. Real-life evidence constantly threatens the fantasy. So you invented rules to provide a sense of logic and consistency, along with an inner critic to enforce the rules.

The Rule Book

Your parents may have rewarded you for getting good grades and punished you for getting bad grades. If so, you probably filed that information under "rules." You may have equated the attention and approval you received for getting A's with love and emotional connection, and the punishment with disconnection. The rule became: *Performing well brings love and acceptance.*

But things rarely stayed that simple. As you grew up, you probably added shades of meaning, exceptions and interpretations to the rule. If your family was violent or inconsistent, there were probably all kinds of complicated cross-references in your rule book.

For example, your parents may have had a house rule: kids in bed by 9:30. Gradually, you may have noticed that the rule didn't apply on holidays. Then you may have figured out that it also didn't apply if Dad was babysitting because Mom was out for the evening. But one night, Dad's babysitting and he's in a bad mood because he would rather be bowling, and suddenly the rule *does* apply. Right there, you've got four separate, cross-referenced entries in the rule book.

Keeping them all sorted out was the job of what we call the inner critic.

The Inner Critic: Keeper of the Rules

The same marvelous faculty that drives us along the road to morality often acts as a sadistic slave driver, a self-accusing fury, and a tireless jobber in guilt.

— Joshua Liebman

We all have an inner voice, created from three sources:

- **Direct input:** the encouragement, criticism and other messages we receive from caregivers and others

- **Indirect input:** an exasperated tone of voice, raised eyebrow, warm smile or hesitant voice; children nearly always assume these unspoken messages have everything to do with them

- **Invention:** whatever we used to fill in the gaps when there was no input

Your inner voice is there to advise you. You tune in to this voice to discover your feelings and needs, to help you choose a course of action, and to check your personal book of rules.

If you grew up in a healthy, loving family that generally provided comfort and gentle messages about yourself and the world, your inner voice became a source of comfort and wisdom.

But for most of us, the voice—at least part of the time—is far from gentle. Its tones are harsh and judgmental. Its main job is to fix blame. (People with backgrounds in twelve-step programs usually call this voice The Committee.) Like people with wise, comforting inner voices, you also tune in to this voice to help you choose a course of action. However, your voice presents a distorted vision of your feelings and needs based on, of course, your happy-ending fantasy.

As you can imagine, the inner critic's role of finding and keeping track of all the rules becomes essential. The fact that (as we discussed in the previous chapter), children are excellent observers but poor interpreters makes this job even more complex.

The Inner Critic Interprets

For example: Say Dad came home from work one day when you had just cleaned your room. He complimented you on your neatness and seemed pleased and happy. You interpreted his reaction to mean that neatness was an important prerequisite for his attention. What you didn't know was that Dad got a raise at work that day. He was so happy he would have complimented you on how precisely you tracked mud in the house. His compliments were a function of his good mood, not your lovability.

Similarly, your inner critic may have explained that it was your fault Mom was mad at you, because you were too noisy. But maybe it was because she was depressed that day and any stimulation from anyone would have been too much for her.

The Inner Critic Helps Maintain Hope

Your inner critic assured you there was, indeed, a set of rules for getting "love," (or for getting the closest thing to love that you could find, or at least for staying out of pain) and let you know when you were beginning to violate them. The inner critic told you how to act, to think, to feel.

Today, perhaps it tells you that you don't have a date for the company holiday party because you are ugly and boring and you dress wrong. When you fill out a job or school application, it whispers, *"No way are you going to get this."* And when you do get the job or when the school accepts you, it is your inner critic who says, *"Wait till they find out you don't know what you're doing."* The critic also finds fault with others—criticizing your co-workers, friends, family, even strangers.

Cathie's Critic

Take Cathie, for example. Her survival plan consisted of keeping all men at an emotional arm's length because, according to her father, they were all "bastards." She married a nice, relatively uncomplicated man who sincerely loved her. This was a severe violation of her rules for safety, since it provided evidence that there was at least one man who wasn't the kind of person her father told her to expect to meet. Within a couple of years, Cathie's inner critic found her husband boring. She divorced him and began dating a series of distant, unemotional men with a slight tendency toward cruelty. Their behavior, while it triggered a great deal of pain for Cathie, better suited her rules for reality. Cathie wasn't happy, but she was comfortable in this predictable environment.

Ed's Critic

Ed created a version of the happy-ending fantasy that continues to assure him that achievement and busy-ness will make him feel worthwhile and protected. However, his wife has begun to complain about his working hours, and he has begun to notice that his children virtually ignore him when he is home. The evidence is mounting against the distorted vision of his happy-ending fantasy. Ed's inner critic, in response, is beginning to suggest that the reason for this discord is that his wife is jealous and his children are ungrateful. It also whispers that perhaps Ed is simply not trying hard enough; he should continue to work hard and also find time to spend with his wife and be involved with the kids. *"Then no one would be mad at you, and you would feel that you are worthwhile,"* his inner critic whispers.

What possible value could such a harsh voice have for a wounded child? Why would an already-hurting child invent yet another source of pain?

Not Pain, But "Love"

The answer is that the child did not invent more pain. Our quest to discover the rules doesn't produce a harsh inner voice right away. We start out looking for ways to please others, be loving and make those around us happy. Our happy-ending fantasy gives us the answers. In turn, we search our world for clues about how we must behave in order to make our happy ending come true. We create the inner critic to observe these clues, convert them into rules and remind us of those rules in the future.

If your parents preferred their children to be seen but not heard, and punished you for speaking out, it was your inner critic who took note, opened the rule book and wrote, in permanent ink, Be Quiet. Keeping quiet brought greater safety and approval, and thus, "love."

If your caregivers believed that their own misfortune or bad feelings could be blamed on other people's actions, your inner critic learned to focus its criticism outward. By trying to change or control the behavior of others by cajoling, shaming or intimidating, you maintained the illusion of connection to them, chasing away the specter of abandonment, and feeling "loved."

If one of the rules in your family was "don't feel that way," you learned to ignore the feelings that made your parents uncomfortable. But because it is painful for a child to suppress powerful feelings, you had to find something even more powerful to help you keep your feelings hidden. Your inner critic knew the power of shame, and knew that being shamed in the middle of having feelings is an extremely effective method for cutting the feelings off. So your critic stepped in at the appropriate moment with comments like, *"You shouldn't feel that way! Look at all you have to be grateful for! Many people have it so much worse than you! I can't believe you're this upset over such a little thing!"* These messages stopped you from feeling—the first step in the natural process of feeling, grieving and healing. However, they also allowed you to stay out of trouble and get the approval you craved—again, "love."

So your inner critic's value lay in its ability to help you, as a child, create consistency and the closest thing to love that you could get, and make it through painful circumstances in your young life. Unfortunately, a side effect of the critic's work is guilt.

Guilty, Guilty, Guilty

Lisa is a good example of how one woman's inner critic found fault with virtually everything she felt.

At fifty-five, Lisa knew that her marriage of twenty-seven years was dead. The love between her and her husband was strong, but not strong enough to stand up to a destructive combination of emotional residue, unwillingness to forgive and a preference for blame rather than self-responsibility. They agreed to divorce.

Lisa dreaded breaking the news to her deeply religious family but discovered that their reactions were unpredictable. Many were sympathetic and supportive. However, an uncle brushed off this significant change in Lisa's life by saying, "Don't worry, you two are great together. You'll get back together, you'll see."

Her uncle's response angered Lisa. However, at the first glimmers of anger, Lisa's critic attacked. *"What right do you have to be angry? They practically raised you! You know they love you. Just let go of it. What's wrong with you anyway?"* it roared.

When Rebecca pointed out that her uncle's remark had sharply invalidated Lisa's feelings and ignored her pain, she realized that she had a right to feel angry. But what really amazed her was that, within minutes of deciding to ignore her critic's input and accept her anger, it disappeared.

Later, when Lisa noticed that she was having a good time living on her own, her critic chastised her for feeling too good.

According to her critic, she should be miserable while in the throes of the divorce. "I can't wait to see my therapist this afternoon so she can tell me what's wrong with me," she told a friend. She was surprised when Rebecca told her the only wrong thing was her critic's continual insistence that her feelings—positive and negative—were wrong.

The Inner Critic's Limitations

This is the genealogy of your inner critic: Your happy-ending fantasy needed rules to support it. Since it *was* a fantasy, you couldn't look inside yourself, where the truth lies, to find this guidance. You had to look outside for rules—substitutes for your own inner sense of what you feel and want and what your boundaries and true needs are. These rules had to be sturdy enough to brace up the fantasy and overrule your inner guidance. To find them, you had to disconnect from your own authenticity. You created the inner critic to help you carry out this search.

EGO:
Edging God Out.
　　　– Anonymous

Your critic started life as a friendly guide, keeping you out of the swamps of your emotional pain. But, like an underqualified employee in a high-stress position, it gradually turned into an impossible, screaming taskmaster. It always advises you to sacrifice your authenticity in the interests of achieving that happy ending. It has no choice—it was created in the image of your own self-betrayal. When your inside truth and the outside rules conflict, it will decide in favor of the outside rules.

The fact that it is outer-directed rather than inner-directed is your inner critic's strength and flaw.[9] Being outer-directed, your critic can distract you from your pain—which is, of course, internal. But because it *is* outer-directed, it is poorly equipped to keep you from feeling this pain indefinitely. Eventually, it and your happy-ending fantasy fail, and your pain surfaces again. This is why your survival plan tripod needs a third leg: *anesthesia*. The next chapter describes anesthesias and how they help support the survival plan.

[9] The spiritual implications of this strength/flaw are staggering: the inner critic gradually takes the place of your spiritual resources and your conscience. It becomes God. This is the source of the spiritual crisis most people undergo when their healing begins to free them from their inner critic's control.

EXERCISES
Describing Your Inner Critic and Its Rules

These exercises will help you codify, possibly for the first time, the rules by which you *really* run your life. They also give you a chance to meet your inner critic face-to-face.

1. You created your inner critic from three sources: Direct input, indirect input, and the material you used to fill in the gaps when there was no input.

    For most of us, the inner critic was not formed of equal parts of the three. One source dominates. If you were neglected, you filled in the blanks a lot. If your caregivers interacted with you verbally most of the time, you used direct input. If your caregivers were relatively non-verbal but were physically expressive, you used indirect input. Of the three sources, which formed the mainstay of the information you received? Was it more negative or more positive? What were some of the specific forms it took?

2. What is your critic's mission in life? Draft a mission statement for your critic that addresses, from the critic's point of view, such issues as how it/he/she:

    • keeps you safe from criticism

    • helps you handle or avoid conflict in your life

    • talks to you about failure and success

    • views the values of honesty, courage, faith, etc.

    • views the dangers and joys of connecting with others

    • assesses your lovability and the lovability of others

    • regards your wounds

    • regards pain

3. Describe your critic's physical or personality characteristics.

- Is it quiet or loud?
- Male, female or androgynous?
- Tall or short?
- Old, young or middle-aged?
- Fat, thin or in-between?
- Is it a snob?
- A slob?
- Subtle and sneaky in its criticisms, or overtly critical?
- Attractive? Ugly?
- What does it wear?
- How does it walk?
- Does it speak with an accent? (Perhaps it doesn't speak at all.)
- What kind of facial expressions does it wear?
- Does it carry anything, such as a book or a briefcase?

Try drawing a portrait of your critic (nothing fancy—a stick figure will do). If your mental image of your critic is more felt than seen, try painting an abstract impression of its presence. And consider the possibility that your critic has more than one personality or face. Carrie's inner critic turned out to be a potted plant with three blooms: one with the raging face of her father, one with the closed eyes of her uninvolved mother, and the third with the sneering face of her sister.

4. Caregivers pass on to children their own ideas about life and their roles in the world. As children, we tend to absorb these beliefs uncritically, incorporating them into our own frame of reference as if they were as true for us as they were for our parents. Identifying them brings them out of the closet of your unconscious, provides clues to your unhealed wounds and gives you an opportunity to choose new rules.

Your caregivers may have passed on their beliefs in the form of advice or in unspoken attitudes. For example:

> Marvin's father's advice to him about sex was, *"Screw women with big boobs, and don't ever tell your mother."*

> Jerry has no memory of his mother actually saying anything about the value of staying silent, but he realized that one of her unspoken rules about relationships was *"Some things are better left unsaid."*

Each of these people, in identifying the information they had received from their parents (or other caregivers) about what to expect of themselves, the world and other people, felt they had been given important clues to the nature of their own wounds. In addition to caregivers, we learn about the world and our role in it from teachers, magazines and newspapers, television and movies, church, friends and other societal forces.

For this exercise, write the names of each of your major childhood influences at the top of separate sheets of paper. You might have several sheets—for example, one headed MOM, one DAD, one for an older sibling, one each for THE MEDIA, ELEMENTARY SCHOOL TEACHERS and THE CHURCH. On each sheet, write about what you learned from that influence about:

Life	Men	Women
Love	Work	Sex
Emotions	Food	Time
Society	Conflict	Children
Health	School	Marriage
Friendship	Family	Fun
Beauty	Career/Job	God
Money	Religion	Other (list your own)

Which of these statements do you currently believe are true? Which ones do you believe are false, but live as if you thought they were true? How do these beliefs affect your life right now?

5. Many families have unspoken (or, sometimes, explicit) rules about what can or can not be talked about. For example, Mallory's mother used to say that

"In this family, we talk things out." However, whenever Mallory tried to discuss feeling afraid of a new challenge (such as going off to college or taking a long trip by herself), her parents simply told her that there was nothing to be afraid of and that Mallory was strong enough to accomplish whatever she set her mind to. Although their remarks sounded reassuring, it seemed to Mallory that their discussion ended too quickly, leaving her with a backlog of unexpressed feelings.

Were there topics that could not be discussed in your family, or could be discussed only in limited ways? What feelings? What events? What people or relationships? What ideas?

In what ways do these rules influence your life today? Have you rebelled and gone to the opposite extreme? Or do you still follow the rules set out by your caregivers? Are there certain situations in which you follow the rules and others in which you flout them?

SIX

Leg Three: Anesthesia

To spare oneself from grief at all cost can be achieved only at the price of total detachment, which excludes the ability to experience happiness.

— Erich Fromm

anesthesia—A way to hide one's feelings from oneself.

NO MATTER HOW LOUD your inner critic's voice, no matter how strong your happy-ending fantasy, your survival plan is shaky at best. When it threatens to collapse, you begin once again to feel the pain. This is too much for a child or a teenager to bear. You need something to shield yourself from this pain— an escape. You found anesthesia.

The Function of Your Anesthesia

Anesthesia relieves the pain of:

- Your (necessary) abandonment of yourself in favor of your survival plan.

- The failure of your survival plan.

- The unhealed wounds that are exposed when your survival plan falters.

Anesthesia shields you in two ways: It numbs the pain itself and it distracts you by getting you high.

When you were a child, you could lose yourself in activities like drawing, building model planes, reading, sports, eating candy. *Those were not necessarily anesthesias.* Everyone needs time out to recharge, and nearly everyone can lose himself in the passionate pursuit of something. However, anything can be used as anesthesia, even healthy pursuits.

The difference between anesthesia and a healthy activity is in its function and its effect on your life. Does your practice clear your head and help you discharge and resolve strong feelings? Does it make you more able and willing to deal assertively and compassionately with the people in your life? Or do you use it to try to forget strong feelings such as grief or fear? Does your family consistently complain about the amount of time or money you spend in your pursuit? Does your practice cause problems for you at work or in your relationships?

Nick, Anna and Janice

Nick volunteers for the local humane society. He helps out at the shelter for two hours a couple of times a week. He is quite committed to this time and rarely allows anything to interfere with it. In addition, he usually spends several hours a week with one or more of his humane society friends, discussing specific animals, community outreach, fundraising and other animal-oriented topics. His volunteer work relieves stress for Nick. His interactions with animals and other volunteers provide him with many uplifting illustrations of love and selflessness in action. Nick finds that a couple of hours at the shelter clears his head and allows him to return to work and family refreshed and calm.

Anna takes a similar approach to her meditation practice. She meditates at home at least once a day for twenty minutes at a time, reads books and magazines about meditating and attends group meditation once a week.

Janice is training for a triathlon. She runs seven days a week and works out with weights four days a week. She and her partner have worked out a schedule that allows her to temporarily work half time instead of full time. While she is in training—and by mutual agreement—their lives revolve around her schedule.

Anna, Nick and Janice have healthy relationships with their pursuits. Their practices enhance their lives. All three report that their practices often help them find the clarity and courage they need to confront and solve problems in their work and personal lives. They find inspiration and release in their pastimes.

Adam's Anesthesia

Adam is a runner. His running takes precedence above all other life activities. If he oversleeps, he gets to work late rather than miss his morning run. His physician has told him his knees will give out if he continues to run, but Adam runs anyway. He's discovered that taking over-the-counter anti-inflammatory drugs before and after running keeps the pain down. When he feels depressed, he runs an extra five miles; after that, he is too exhausted to feel anything. When his girlfriend began to complain that he never had time for her anymore, he broke up with her and began running more. Adam's solution for any life problem is the same: run more.

For Adam, running is an anesthesia. He runs instead of spending time in other pursuits, ignores danger signs like physical pain, and relies more and more on runner's high or exhaustion to numb his emotional pain. His life revolves around running, not because he made a conscious decision to put it first in his life for a while, but because it numbs his pain.

People we have worked with have identified their anesthesias as:

• Compulsive reading (up to five novels a week)

• Charity work

- Organizing and re-organizing every closet, drawer and storage space in the house
- Collecting stuff until every surface in the house is covered
- Pet care chores for too many pets
- An obsessive interest in eating the right foods
- Working constantly to earn sales achievement awards
- Religious practices and beliefs

There is nothing wrong with any of these activities. None of them are, in themselves, inherently destructive (or, for that matter, inherently constructive). Practiced in moderation and for healthy reasons, they can be beneficial. Our clients identified them as anesthesias because of the way they used them.

Especially Dangerous: Addictive Substances

If your anesthesias are physically addictive substances, you are at grave risk of gradually losing your ability to choose whether or not you will use them. Alcohol, cocaine, caffeine, marijuana, nicotine, heroin, amphetamines, sugar (to name a few) all eventually tend to take control on a biochemical level.

The survival plan is very good at keeping you from feeling the pain. However, like a gangster who offers protection from his own violence, it exacts a steep price for its services. In the next chapter, we'll take a look at exactly what that price is.

Unmasking Your Anesthesias

For most of us, abstaining from our anesthesia of choice is the first step on the road to healing. Before you can take this step, you need to know what it is you need to abstain from. These exercises can help you pinpoint the substances, activities and mind games you use to numb out.

1. What substances and activities did you use (or do you use now) to shield yourself from pain? How did these strategies evolve to become your anesthesias? Use the list below and the definition of anesthesia you read earlier in this chapter to help you identify your anesthesias.

       ☐ Projects (crafts, hobbies, home improvement, etc.)

       ☐ Trying to help other people who are hurting themselves

       ☐ Religious practices

       ☐ Work

       ☐ Sleep

       ☐ Self-improvement activities

       ☐ Cleaning

       ☐ Volunteer work

       ☐ Computer or video games, "surfing the net"

       ☐ Spending money

       ☐ Drinking

       ☐ Smoking

       ☐ Sex

       ☐ Gambling

       ☐ Obsessive relationships

       ☐ Coffee

☐ Reading

☐ Gardening

☐ Television

☐ Isolating yourself

☐ Sports

☐ Drugs

☐ Procrastination

☐ Other

2. Describe how and when you use your anesthesias. For example, Claire responds to a fight with her husband by cleaning the house top to bottom; Earl escapes the tension in his family by burying himself in a novel; Harry avoids conflict with his brother by spending his time with him watching televised sports.

3. How does your anesthesia use specifically affect your relationships with other people? How does it affect your relationship with your feelings? With money? With your spirituality? Your sexuality? Your work?

   If the effects of your anesthesia use are not apparent to you, ask the people in your life.

SEVEN

The Survival Plan Takes Its Toll

The adolescent may begin the "life behind a mask"
that tends to characterize numbers of our urban
denizens. The mask, however, requires so much energy
for its successful maintenance, that personality growth
is apt to end with its successful construction.

– Harry Stack Sullivan

THE SURVIVAL PLAN HELPS YOU DECIDE what you do and do not control. (Of course, the more dysfunctional your upbringing, the more distorted your conclusions about who controls what.) In this way, it gave a sense of logic and consistency to your life.

Every survival plan comes with a price tag, however. The price of your survival plan's benefits is so high that you must borrow to pay it. As a result, your authenticity suffers: the debt creates in you an inescapable sense of low self-esteem, blunts the depth and breadth of your emotional responses, locks you into limited and destructive relationship patterns, makes you dependent on others changing for you to be okay and prevents you from creating healthy boundaries.[10]

Your survival plan accepts as legal tender your most valuable resource—life energy.

[10] One of our friends calls this condition "psychic cancer."

How Your Survival Plan Uses Your Life Energy

Life energy is the reservoir of raw power each of us possesses at birth. We focus this life energy on our physical, emotional and spiritual pursuits, divvying it up according to how much each pursuit draws our attention.

If our life circumstances allow, we choose these pursuits based on ability, passion and a universal imperative to explore who we are. For example, a twelve-year-old boy who discovers a passion for music might pursue piano lessons if his caregivers provide an atmosphere of interested approval. However, if his family ridicules his interest and praises him only when he pursues sports, he is less likely to put life energy into his music. He is more likely to put energy into a survival plan that helps him go against his natural strengths to find ways to get their approval. If he stubbornly insists on taking piano lessons instead of going to football practice, his need for a survival plan to protect himself from his family's disapproval is even greater. It will take a fair amount of his life energy to create and maintain one.

What Is the Price?

How much you pay for your survival plan depends on how complex and dysfunctional it is. High-maintenance plans, designed to protect against extreme pain, require a great deal of life energy to keep them going. In healthier families, children create simpler, easier-to-maintain survival plans.

Regardless of how much or how little your survival plan costs you in life energy, the diverted life energy will compromise your:

- Self-responsibility
- Authenticity
- Ability to feel, grieve and heal your losses.

Let's look in detail at these compromises.

Compromised Self-Responsibility

We make a distinction between responsibility and *self*-responsibility. Lots of people are responsible. They get up and go to work each day, pay their bills, drive safely, keep their promises and take pride in being considered reliable. Fewer people are *self*-responsible.

> *self-responsibility*—Understanding of, and acceptance of, the fact that your interpretations, not outer circumstances, determine your ability to respond to people and situations, your feelings, your awareness of choices available to you, and, ultimately, your behavior. The opposite of a self-responsible attitude is victimhood.

One of the first things you give up when you develop your survival plan is the possibility of being fully self-responsible. Your survival plan is built on the premise that you aren't good enough as you are. According to your survival plan, what the "true you" needs and wants is not as important as getting a sense of safety or love. In fact, pursuing what you need or want actually *prevents* you from getting your survival plan's version of safety or love, since this pursuit very likely violates some of its rules.

So you learn to focus your attention *out there*, on the people or circumstances that seem to hold the power to make you feel loved, or at least safe. You sacrifice your self-responsibility to your prime directive, which is to feel safe or loved.

A non-self-responsible attitude asserts that something about others or the world must change for you to:

- be okay

- feel peaceful

- feel valid and worthwhile

- be happy

- get your needs met.

We also make a distinction between self-responsibility and self-blame. When you take responsibility, you don't take blame. Blame is founded in shame and carries a punitive sense. Taking self-responsibility means reclaiming the power to make yourself happy and whole. (In Section II, we examine in detail how this reclamation project is the key to healing your wounds.)

Lost Authenticity

We all developed our survival plans because we concluded that it was too painful and scary to risk being fully authentic and vulnerable. To one degree or another, we realized that having our own thoughts, feelings and boundaries meant being alone or in pain—or both.

> *authenticity*—The capacity, in a child or adult, to have one's own feelings, thoughts and boundaries; the absence of a need to hide feelings, thoughts and boundaries. In an adult, the ability to choose when, with whom and how to convey one's feelings, thoughts and boundaries in a self-responsible, non-defensive and respectful manner. The capacity to feel safe being vulnerable rather than through self-protections.

To the extent that you sacrifice authenticity, you lose access to those qualities that depend on authenticity: creativity, emotional vitality, joy, curiosity and the capacity for intimacy and a healthy spiritual life.

Lost Ability to Feel, Grieve and Heal

One of your natural skills is the ability to feel, grieve and heal your losses. However, the imperative that drives the creation of the survival plan makes it impossible to give much energy to this skill. The survival plan's purpose is to *keep* us from feeling. The ability to feel, grieve and heal is anathema to the survival plan.

Other Costs and Pitfalls

You will pay and pay for the privilege of being safe. In addition to the losses described above, your survival plan also:

- Requires you to block out real love—or anything else that would threaten your happy-ending fantasy

- Keeps you repeating old patterns—because you're convinced that they will someday work

- Puts pressure on your relationships to provide you with the sense of safety and well-being you missed as a child

- Requires you to use more and more anesthesia

- Keeps you running back and forth between feeling frantic and feeling hopeless

- Makes you rightness-addicted, in which being right becomes more important than being happy.

Besides all that, your inner critic eventually develops a life of its own and becomes harder and harder to control. It starts to run your thoughts. You either become self-defeating and depressed or relentlessly critical of others.

All survival plans, fortunately, are inherently weak. In the next chapter, we'll examine how survival plans begin to fail, and the choices you have each time they do.

EXERCISES
Determining the Price of Your Survival Plan

What have you paid for your survival plan? This knowledge will help bolster your willingness to heal, because it provides a reminder that living within your survival plan just isn't worth it.

1. How does your survival plan...

> ...keep you from being authentic?

> ...keep you from being self-responsible?

> ...keep you from healing wounds?

Be as specific as you can, including such information as dates and people with whom you are particularly inauthentic or un-self-responsible.

2. How else does your survival plan make you pay?

EIGHT

The Survival Plan Falters

Desperation is the raw material of drastic change.
Only those who can leave behind everything they
have ever believed in can hope to escape.

— William Burroughs

ৡ ৡ ৡ

ONE DAY, THE STREAM SPIRIT *woke up with the*
sun in his eyes and saw two figures striding over
the ridge beyond the lake. He thought they were
his teachers, but as they drew closer, he realized
they were strangers.

The strangers introduced themselves: they were
grown-up stream spirits who lived two ridges over.
They had heard about the little stream spirit from
the teachers and decided to call. The stream spirit
watched them carefully. Although these spirits
were the same size as his teachers, it was hard to
tell their age; they seemed both older and younger.
They laughed more, and yet they seemed quieter.
The stream spirit decided he liked them, and
invited them back.

Gradually, he grew to like and trust his new friends. When they invited him to come visit their lands, he excitedly packed up his things. They stopped him, though, when he started to pack a box of sleepberries.

"We prefer that you don't use those while you visit our place," they said. "Besides, you might find that you don't need them. Being awake is more fun."

The stream spirit shrugged, and left the sleepberries behind. Later, he wished he hadn't.

The place where his friends lived was magnificent—everything that the stream spirit's lands used to be but now were not. The stream spirit had forgotten how beautiful the land could be, how intense the colors, how cool and wet the water. His friends' land had birds and squirrels and lizards and too many other kinds of animals to count. The trees were huge and offered acres of shade.

He was excited and dismayed at the same time. How could this place be so beautiful? How could his be so awful? He lay awake at night, jumpy and alert, wishing for the comfort of a sleepberry-induced snooze. He hated to leave, and yet was relieved to get home.

Once he was home, though, the reality of his situation became excruciatingly painful. He sat in the unrelenting sun and longed for the shade and cool breezes of his friends' lands. He drank the brackish water and remembered the sweet liquid from his friends' streams.

Worst of all, the sleepberries quit working. He couldn't sleep.

THE SURVIVAL PLAN is like a paranoid delusion. A paranoid person's delusion is a filter that suggests an ever-present threat. Eventually, his distorted vision of the world cripples his ability to respond to the real world. He operates out of a narrow repertoire of possible behaviors.

We view the world through the filter of our survival plans. We may think we are objective and that our vision is clear and true, but, like the paranoid, we see only what we expect to see. After a while, we can no longer respond creatively and positively to life circumstances. Like a delusion, the survival plan can appear convincing and powerful. However, because it is built largely on false information, it is actually fragile. It adapts life to its assumptions and so cannot adapt us to life.

As if this inherent weakness were not enough, one of the survival plan's three legs—anesthesias—is continually in danger of failing. When one leg of a tripod threatens to collapse, the entire structure trembles. It is often the anesthesia leg that is responsible for the survival plan's failure.

And of course, there is the core weakness of the survival plan: its failure to address the real problem—our unhealed wounds. Instead, it covers them up, like a Band-Aid placed over a gaping, infected cut. Unattended, the infection gets worse and worse, eventually causing blood poisoning and weakening limbs and organs. Like neglected infections, our wounds will eventually kill us (emotionally if not physically) if we don't seek treatment.

Wake-Up Calls

Fortunately, life doesn't give up so easily. The tripod of the survival plan doesn't quietly fold up into itself. Something happens to get our attention, like evidence of infection oozing out around the edges of a bandage. We call this a wake-up call—an alarm that brings our attention to the pain and mess of our unhealed wounds and offers us a chance to heal them at last.

The positive aspect of the wake-up call is lost on most people. Almost without exception, people view wake-up calls with

Despair lames most people, but it wakes others fully up.

– William James

terror. They do everything they can think of (usually more of what hasn't worked before) to prop up their survival plans, because their failure looks like the end of the world.

In reality, the wake-up call portends the death of the *survival plan*, not the death of the person. For the wounded person, it represents the opportunity of a lifetime. He can now take out a bigger Band-Aid and patch up his survival plan, or he can abandon mere survival in favor of true healing and vivid life. We'll describe the way these choices line up in the next couple of chapters. For now, let's take a closer look at wake-up calls.

Custom-Designed for Your Needs

Wake-up calls appear in a variety of forms and degrees, from catastrophes such as auto accidents or getting fired, to a simple loss of inner peace.

Regardless of form or degree, all wake-up calls have several attributes in common: They always point up the fact (whether you acknowledge it or not) that a pattern in your life is not working; they indicate that your anesthesia is failing; and they often consist of increasingly destructive side effects of your anesthesia use.

In anesthesia failure, whatever you've been using to numb yourself quits working quite so well. No matter how much you use or how frequently you use it, you can't numb your pain with your anesthesia anymore. This exposes the futility of any patterns you tend to repeat in hopes of eventual success, such as relationships with certain types of people.

As your anesthesia fails, you get hit with the other element of the wake-up call: worsening side effects. Alcoholics begin to have worse hangovers, overeaters outgrow the last of the clothing in their closets, overspenders begin receiving dunning notices and calls at work.

Sometimes, as in Tina's life, the anesthesia failure and the worsening effects can be subtle. Her anesthesia was criticism. By finding fault with others, she convinced herself that she was superior to them. This false sense of superiority shielded her from the pain of a total sense of inadequacy and unworthiness.

Her wake-up call came when people in her new therapy group confronted her about her critical ways. For the first time in her life, Tina heard a clear, powerful and consistent message about the effect of her behavior on others. When she tried to protect herself from the pain of the feedback by using her anesthesia again (by criticizing group members or discounting their feelings), the facilitators and the group members confronted her again. In doing so, they kept her anesthesia from being effective and they kept the effects of her anesthesia use before her.

Brad's Wake-Up Call

Wake-up calls are as loud as you need them to be. Our friend Brad grew up in a fairly functional family and is relatively unwounded. He is good at recognizing his wake-up calls. Brad responded to an escalating series of conflicts with a colleague with increasing rage and, finally, nightmares.

He made an appointment with a counselor. Conversations with the counselor gradually led him to an important insight: the colleague looked like the man who had exposed himself to Brad on a playground when he was about eight years old. He realized that his extreme emotional discomfort was a wake-up call to attend to this wound.

The Volume Rises

When pressed, most people admit that they have received their current wake-up call before—sometimes even years before—in a milder form. Wake-up calls rarely change in content. If you ignore them, they just become louder, more urgent, and more dramatic. Their intensity increases until they are loud enough and painful enough to get your attention and maintain your motivation to change. The higher your denial and oblivion to pain, the louder the call. The louder, more dramatic the call, the more change required on your part.

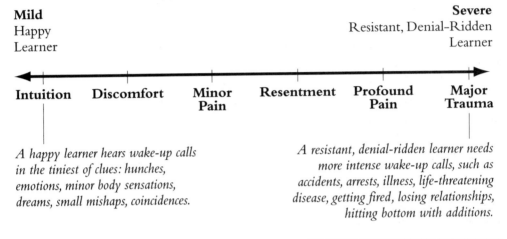

♦

How Intense Must Your Wake-Up Calls Be to Get Your Attention?

Mild
Happy
Learner

Severe
Resistant, Denial-Ridden
Learner

Intuition Discomfort Minor Pain Resentment Profound Pain Major Trauma

A happy learner hears wake-up calls in the tiniest of clues: hunches, emotions, minor body sensations, dreams, small mishaps, coincidences.

A resistant, denial-ridden learner needs more intense wake-up calls, such as accidents, arrests, illness, life-threatening disease, getting fired, losing relationships, hitting bottom with additions.

The forces that affect our lives, the influences that mold and shape us, are often like whispers in a distant room, teasingly indistinct, apprehended only with difficulty.

— Charles Dickens

The more advanced your healing, the quieter your wake-up calls will be, because you have learned to pay attention sooner.

You don't have to wait for your survival plan to completely fail to start healing. Some people, like Brad, recognize intense feelings as wake-up calls. They can respond to relatively subtle signals and begin to examine and dismantle their survival plans, heal their wounds and take a closer look at the meaning and purpose of life.

In our experience, these people are in the minority. Most of us need painful and dramatic wake-up calls.

Paradoxically, people with particularly deep wounds often start their healing journey relatively early in life, simply because their survival plans are so destructive and self-sabotaging that the wake-up calls are too painful to miss. People with relatively functional survival plans (or those who are thoroughly cut off from their emotions) can go an entire lifetime without confronting the ways their unhealed wounds keep them from being fully alive.

Wake-Up Calls I: Survival Plan Failure

These exercises will help you understand how your survival plan is starting to fall apart (or has fallen apart). This understanding can help you face courageously the end of your old way of life.

1. What indications do you have (or did you have in the past, if you are starting to break free of living under the terms of your survival plan) that your survival plan is falling apart? Use the list below to help you.

☐ I lie to myself and others about how involved I really am in my anesthesia use.

☐ I'm hiding my anesthesia use from others.

☐ I am increasingly anxious.

☐ I'm feeling more and more guilty.

☐ I need more of my favorite anesthesia to get the same effect.

☐ I'm beginning to realize that I can't get quite as numb as I used to.

☐ I'm taking more risks to get my anesthesia.

☐ I'm starting to try out new anesthesias.

☐ My anesthesia use is costing me more—financially, emotionally, or both.

☐ I'm spending more and more time thinking about my anesthesia.

☐ My important relationships are becoming more distant.

☐ I think I'm starting to lose control over the amount of anesthesia I use, or how often I use it.

☐ I'm spending more and more time alone.

☐ I hang out more and more with people who use the same anesthesia.

☐ My physical health is beginning to be affected by my anesthesia use.

☐ My work or my schoolwork is beginning to be affected by my anesthesia use.

2. What other signs of survival plan failure have you noticed in your life? Review Brad's and Tina's stories from this chapter for ideas.

NINE

Avoiding Wake-Up Calls

Most people change not because they see the light but because they feel the heat.

— Anonymous

Pᴇᴏᴘʟᴇ ᴅᴇᴀꜰᴇɴ ᴛʜᴇᴍsᴇʟᴠᴇs to their wake-up calls by:

- Trying to fix their survival plans
- Retreating to a window of willingness
- Sliding into what we call *purgatory*

Let's take a look at each of these methods.

Fix the Survival Plan

Some people ignore their wake-up calls by patching up, improving or expanding their survival plans.

Since it is the anesthesia leg of the survival plan tripod that tends to fail first, this usually means increasing anesthesia use or finding a new, better anesthesia. For example, a workaholic faced with a wake-up call may expand her survival plan by getting a second job or taking on an additional project. A jogger might add more miles to her daily workout.

If these measures don't work, the person may add a new activity or substance. The jogger may begin weight training. The alcoholic who always stuck to beer may start drinking vodka, or may start drinking in the morning. The compulsive gambler may add compulsive routines—such as taking a certain number of steps to get to the car from the front door, performing morning chores in a rigid sequences—in an effort to influence her luck.

If a person's anesthesia and the object of his false hope are identical (as they are in relationship addiction), he may also redirect his false hope onto someone or something new.

Take the example of a woman who depends on the emotional high of the early months of a relationship to shield her from her pain. She might improve her survival plan by finding a new, better and possibly more potent anesthesia (that is, a new boyfriend) and, simultaneously, a new focus for her false hopes (the new boyfriend).

For a person whose anesthesia/false hope is possessions, a new purchase (or flurry of purchases) may stave off anesthesia failure. When staying busy keeps the pain away, taking on a new project, putting in lots of overtime or setting a new goal can do the trick. This is what twelve-step people call insanity—doing more of what already isn't working in hope it will produce a different outcome.

How Elaine Fixed Up Her Survival Plan

Even people without obvious addictive practices have survival plans they can improve. The mother of one of Rebecca's clients is a good example of a woman with a life that appeared to be healthy and successful. Elaine had devised a practical, functional survival plan centered on success in business through perfectionism, logic and single-mindedness about career goals. She married Jack, a business executive twenty years her senior with a similar, success-oriented survival plan. They agreed not to have children. Elaine built a career in the advertising industry and eventually founded her own agency.

Several years into the marriage, Elaine accidentally became pregnant. She and Jack dealt with this intrusion into their joint survival plan by including the child in their lives as if he were an adult companion—an arrangement that worked fairly well for all three. When Donna (now Rebecca's client) was born seven years later, Elaine hired nannies and still kept her career on track and her survival plan intact.

It wasn't until years later, when Jack fell into a coma following a stroke, that Elaine's survival plan threatened to fail her. Elaine had always relied on a detailed set of unconscious rules to guide her decisions regarding career moves or family logistics. However, her rule book had nothing to say about what to do with the intense grief, anger and fear she felt when Jack fell ill. When he finally died a year later, Elaine responded by kicking her survival plan into high gear. If career, logic, goal-setting and efficient scheduling got her through the first fifty-seven years of her life, then it ought to get her through the rest. She became even more driven, busier and more distant emotionally. Her children, now grown, noticed that she changed the subject constantly, especially if it began to veer uncomfortably close to emotional topics. Where she was controlling and rigid before, she now began to insist on having even the smallest of details her way.

Two years ago, just before Christmas, Elaine came down with pneumonia. She was too ill to prepare her usual gourmet Christmas dinner. The children volunteered to cook. Elaine agreed, but insisted that the cooking be done in her kitchen, and be done exactly the way she had always done it. She sent Donna and her brother all over town gathering spices from special markets, getting chicken from a particular butcher, buying vegetables from the only organic market she trusted, and tracking down a special pan she used for her traditional Christmas chicken dish. She sat in the kitchen while the children cooked. She coached their vegetable-chopping, managed the timer and criticized their mixing techniques until the whole family was frazzled, resentful and tired.

According to Elaine's survival plan, life still functions pretty much the way it always has. You just have to stay busy and clear about your goals, and make sure people do things right. Her survival plan still has not failed her.

Or so she thinks. Her children openly resent her and are becoming more and more unavailable. For the most part, Elaine is still fit enough to stay busy, so she hasn't really noticed the shortened family visits or more superficial conversations. She hasn't noticed her daughter Donna's life is moving forward—without Elaine.

The Downward Spiral

Attempts at improving a survival plan usually become cyclic, gradually evolving into a downward spiral. The spiral is characterized by more control and rigidity, more emotional numbness or explosiveness, and more compulsive behavior with less control over it. Anesthesia use makes you oblivious to painful wake-up calls, but also creates more pain (and louder wake-up calls). The more you try to escape your wake-up calls by improving your survival plan, the louder your wake-up calls will become, and the more you will need your anesthesia to block your pain. Eventually you will lose track of your original objective—to find love and safety. Your prime directive is now to avoid pain. The distinction between false hope and anesthesia fades as your hope becomes founded on simply staying numb.

◆

The Downward Spiral

I've found it! *This* will make me feel loved.
It failed me; I'm hurting.
   This will make me feel better.
      I've found it! This time, for sure.
         It failed me; I'm hurting.
            This will make me feel better.
         I've found it; this is really IT.
      How could I have been so wrong? I'm hurting.
   This will make me feel better.
This is the answer.
   It failed me! I'm hurting.
      This will make me feel better.
         I've found it. *This* will make me feel better.
            It failed me; I'm hurting.
         This will make me feel better.
   This will make me feel better.
      This will make me feel better.
         This will make me feel better…

Enter a Window of Willingness

Some people turn the volume down on their wake-up calls by taking refuge in what we call a window of willingness.

> **window of willingness**—A response to a wake-up call in which you temporarily become willing and able to discontinue your anesthesia use.

Rebecca recently talked with a woman who was in a window of willingness. Jeannie had never met Rebecca, but was so anxious that she paged her on the emergency beeper, and left a message saying "I just *have* to get in to see you."

When Rebecca called back and suggested an appointment time, Jeannie found it inconvenient. Rebecca offered an alterna-

Insanity is repeating the same actions over and over and expecting a different outcome.

– Anonymous

tive; it was equally unsuitable. Rebecca came up with a third time; Jeannie thought she could manage that one. Rebecca gave her directions to the office; Jeannie said, "That's awfully far for me to drive." Rebecca quoted her fee (which was set below the county average); Jeannie thought it was too high.

In the course of the conversation, Jeannie confided that she had tried counseling several times before but never stuck it out. As it turned out, this time was no different. A few days after she spoke to Rebecca, she left a message on voice mail canceling her appointment and explaining that "things are much better now."

Attributes of Windows of Willingness

A window-sitter's goals are to:

- Reduce her pain by:
  - developing better or more sophisticated anesthesias.
  - bringing under temporary control what she thinks of as her bad habits.

- Get others off her back by convincing them of her sincerity.

True willingness (which we describe in detail in the next chapter) is non-ambivalent and unconditional. A window of willingness, on the other hand, is marked by a lot of pre-conditions—convenience being the favorite. If pre-conditions seem to be absent, the unconditional openness (*"I'll do anything it takes..."*) dries up shortly after, like a flash flood in the desert.

People usually enter a window of willingness after receiving a wake-up call in the form of pressure from someone else to change. An alcoholic may get an ultimatum from a spouse. A workaholic may start getting intense complaints from neglected family members.

To the inexperienced eye, someone in a window of willingness looks as though he is truly willing to change. He sounds sincere. He takes action and makes apologies and promises. He even seems to begin addressing his wounds honestly. Under the best of circumstances, he may actually do so—but only for a little while.

Ed's Window

Our workaholic friend Ed's response to the heart attack that was his wake-up call is a good example of a window of willingness. He is a wealthy, successful commercial real estate broker with a deep need to win at everything he does. One day when Ed was fifty-four, his heart gave out and put him in the local hospital's cardiac unit. His cardiologist told him that, if he wanted to make it to his sixtieth birthday, he would have to change his way of life. Knowing that sailing was Ed's favorite source of relaxation, the doctor prescribed at least one day of sailing per week. He set about filling his prescription with a vengeance. Ed was enthusiastic and committed—but not to healing.

We went sailing with Ed several months after he left the hospital. From the beginning of the day, his old cutthroat attitudes colored his (and our) experience. "See that boat off the starboard side?" he would say. "Mine's a foot shorter than that model, but we're going to beat him to the channel." Or, "Notice the varnish on the boats moored next to mine? Poor job. I use the best boat-care company in town to do mine, and it shows." Or, "None of these guys really knows how to sail. You want to see how to pop a spinnaker and do it right, watch me." Ed couldn't relax; the same overriding need to compete and win that made him a financial success had depleted his ability to enjoy a day of sailing. His attempts to fulfill his physician's prescription paint a clear picture of someone trying to do something different, but whose actions were in reality the same old stuff.

Ultimately, the actions of a person in a window of willingness reveal that:

- He wants to change for someone else—usually a lover or spouse.

or

- He thinks it's the right thing to do.

or

- He believes that changing will improve his public image

or

- He really does want to change, but only if changing is convenient and comfortable...

...or all four. As a result, he obtains only temporary relief from his pain. As soon as his goal is accomplished—the spouse has stopped complaining, he has proved to himself that he can control his behavior, his boss has patted him on the back for improved attendance—his downward spiral resumes. The next wake-up call, of course, is louder and more painful.

Typical Window-Sitting Activities

Window-sitters frequently work at improving their survival plans by devoting attention to their anesthesias. They may attend stress management classes, increase exercise schedules, begin meditating (or meditate more), read more self-help books, attend more support group meetings, join social clubs, take up new hobbies, or re-organize closets, the garage, files and Christmas card lists. Or they may simply do the equivalent of drying out for a while. They'll go on a diet, stay away from the slot machines, resolve to be celibate for the rest of their lives, even resolve to control their need to control other people's behavior. Sales people may set new sales records. Those who use multi-level marketing companies as an anesthesia will attend another rally, sign up more associates or push harder to make more sales. A chronically depressed individual might resolve to increase his endorphin levels by starting an exercise program or taping up affirmations all over the house.

Sometimes these efforts alone are enough to relieve the pressure from others to change. If not, a window-sitter will add whatever activities seem necessary to do the job. Window-sitters who are addicted to drugs or alcohol or to such processes as gambling or shopping sometimes continue practicing their addictions in secret while telling their family or friends that they have quit.

Regardless of the particulars, window-sitters will try to reduce pain with willpower. To that end, if they think it will help, they will do anything—except identify, explore and heal their wounds.

Window-Sitting and Positive Thinking

A popular window-sitting activity for many people is positive thinking. These folks unconsciously adopt a false hope that says, *"If I stay motivated and think positive thoughts, I will be spared having to face my wounds."* They begin to use motivational techniques, positive affirmations and inspirational slogans as anesthesias.

These techniques are a trap when used in this way. They are so powerful, it is easy to use them to hide from your wounds for a long time, while assuring yourself you're doing something good and life-enhancing. For a while, it can look as though you are actually healing and evolving.

But what you've really done is adopt a more sophisticated survival plan. This merely delays the inevitable; it extends the time it takes for your survival plan to fail completely. Some people will do exactly this for many years. Some do it for the rest of their lives.

David, one of this book's co-authors, was this type of window-sitter for years.

In the late seventies, he dove headfirst into metaphysical thinking, eastern philosophies and altered states of consciousness. Meditation got him higher than any drug could have. "Thinking I was profound and wise, I spouted metaphysical drivel that made even my sympathetic friends retch," David remembers. He says he continually disregarded his friends' feedback no matter how often they told him, *"Beam back down to earth, David."*

It wasn't until years later, after he started to dismantle his survival plan and face his core wounds, that David understood what his friends had been trying to tell him. As his wounds healed, he was able to put his knowledge to use in healthy ways and to quit using it as an anesthesia.[11]

Fred, a thirty-five-year-old computer programmer, was a growth seminar junkie. He convinced many people in his life (including himself) that he attended weekend intensives because he was committed to healing. It certainly looked that way; Fred

[11] *What Really Matters*, by Tony Schwartz (Bantam, 1995) provides an in-depth examination of the need for a balance between spiritual practices and emotional healing.

completed workshops in anger release, grief release, dysfunctional family dynamics, sexuality, work-related issues, creativity, self-hypnosis, healing the inner child, drumming and past-life regression. Eventually, he realized that each workshop represented a window of willingness in which his true goal was to get high and convince himself that he was actually doing something about the feelings he was afraid to feel. Healing his wounds was not on the agenda.

These Things Have Their Place

Many of us have known people like Fred and David—people who have used motivational techniques, positive thinking or metaphysical practices to shore up their survival plans or to hide from their feelings and wounds. We can't begin to tell you how many people we've treated who have been driven into therapy in despair over their inability to make these methods work, often in spite of long, dedicated practice.

If you are one of these people, don't throw the baby out with the bath water. You can use the best of these techniques to serve your healing rather than to hide from it. The trick is to not use them as substitutes for dismantling your survival plan, feeling your feelings and addressing your core wounds. We've never seen affirmations, positive thinking or motivational techniques alone work when unaddressed wounds are the real issue. As one of our clients says, *"You can put a ribbon around a bag of manure, but it still smells like manure."*

Until a significant portion of your healing work is behind you, these techniques, although attractive, will not have much effect. In fact, you may end up feeling frustrated, shamed and hopeless when they don't work. But when you reach Stage Five (which we discuss in detail later, along with all the other stages), they become invaluable.

Slide into Purgatory

A person who is determined to stay numb, to stay in control at all costs, to defend her rightness at all costs, will ignore even the loudest wake-up calls and slide into purgatory as a lifestyle.

> *purgatory*—A state of dead disconnectedness. People in purgatory don't know that's where they are. In fact, they usually think they have the corner on reality and the rest of the world is living in a naive fantasy. People who choose purgatory are convinced that there is no other place to be, even though it may be cold, lonely, frightening or just boring.
>
> A choice for purgatory is a choice for some form of death. Sometimes people in purgatory join the physically dead by committing suicide, being fatally injured in an accident or overdosing on drugs. More often, they join the living dead by becoming:
>
> • emotionally and spiritually empty
> • chronically (sometimes severely) depressed, or
> • obsessed with their beliefs or goals, sometimes to the point that they are willing to destroy whatever or whoever gets in their way.

People stuck in purgatory (we call them purgatorians) would rather die than admit that they might be wrong about life, or that they might need some help to change.

Once chosen, purgatory tends to be permanent. It usually takes a wake-up call in the form of a catastrophe devastating enough to propel a person into the worst pain of his life. Even then, a purgatorian may simply enter a window of willingness until life is more or less back to normal, then go back to survival-plan living. Occasionally, a catastrophe will propel a purgatorian into a genuine, lasting state of willingness. Don't count on it, though. For most people, purgatory ultimately brings death.[12]

The newspapers are filled with stories about people whose choice for purgatory destroyed them: the habitual criminals, those with long-term gang or drug-dealing involvement, those

[12] For an excellent discussion of what it takes to leave purgatory, we recommend *Beyond the Darkness* by Angie Fenimore (Bantam, 1995). A good description of the emotional bleakness of purgatory can be found in *Waking Up, Alive* by Richard A. Heckler, Ph.D. (Grosset/Putnam, 1994).

who continue their criminal careers from behind bars. Purgatory is the adult version of the choice for death that some children are forced into.

The destruction of a purgatorian is not always dramatic, however. One of David's clients realized recently that his parents are purgatorians. After fifty years of marriage, Ned's mother and father live in separate rooms of their home, each bitter and angry at the other for ruining their lives. They have no friends. By their own choice, they rarely see their children. Conversations are pleasant and superficial, but their underlying blaming rage tends to break out in jabs at each other. The emotional atmosphere of their home is so heavy and tense that most of their children refuse to spend even a single night with them. Ned has the feeling that they are waiting around for their bodies to die, because their spirits already have.

Ned's parents' story won't make it into the papers because it's not dramatic enough. But, no matter what form purgatory takes, it moves a person very far away from his spiritual resources.

You don't have to ignore your wake-up calls. In the next chapter, we describe what happens when you decide to answer one.

Wake-Up Calls II: Past and Present

Understanding this chapter is important because it can help you see why your healing cannot really proceed in a meaningful and lasting way until you stop trying to bolster your survival plan. If you're not one-hundred-percent sure that you have made a commitment to dismantle your survival plan, be sure to complete these exercises. They will help you clarify this issue for yourself.

1. Identify your current wake-up calls by writing a description of any situation that is bugging you or that is making you feel angry, scared, frustrated or just plain stuck.

2. List the wake-up calls that you have experienced in the past. Are any of them the same as those on your current list?

3. How did you respond to the past wake-up calls? How are you responding to your current wake-up calls?

4. Why might you be afraid to dismantle your survival plan?

TEN

How to Answer a Wake-Up Call

> *Tolerance for pain may be high, but it is not without limit. Eventually everyone begins to recognize, however dimly, that there **must** be a better way. As this recognition becomes firmly established, it becomes a turning point.*
>
> *— A Course In Miracles*

THERE IS ONLY ONE WAY to truly answer a wake-up call: surrender.

When you are ready to finally admit that none of your anesthesias work anymore; when even you are no longer fooled by your windows of willingness; when you finally stop, turn and face your wounds squarely; then you have reached surrender. This is what addicts call hitting bottom. It is what we call willingness.

> **willingness**—An attitude of genuine openness to input from a source entirely outside of your programming that promotes the healing of your wounds. We think of programming as unhealed wounds and self-protections.

Most of us reach willingness only when we become thoroughly tired of living through our survival plans. And it is usually only when we are completely beaten down by the recurrent and devastating effects of ignored wake-up calls that we become exhausted enough to give up.

Surrender to Healing

Our culture promotes a belief in self-sufficiency. According to this belief, to seek help is to acknowledge weakness, and to acknowledge weakness is to admit failure. Rather than admit failure, we are encouraged to flex our willpower, keep a stiff upper lip, think positive and try, try again.

Healing requires you to turn these ideas on their heads. Undertaking your emotional and spiritual healing is not an indication of weakness—far from it. Nothing takes more courage. Trying again and again only digs you deeper into your survival plan. The paradox of emotional healing is that, to bring about your healing, you must let go of your own efforts.

Nature does not require that we be perfect; it requires only that we grow, and we can do this as well from a mistake as from a success.

— Rollo May

You do not have to wave a big white flag to be willing. A little one will do. You have only to be willing *to consider* the *possibility* that *maybe...*

...I'm addicted, or

...I've been faking it, or

...I can't control my feelings, or

...I didn't have the idyllic childhood I thought I had, or

...My life is out of control, or

...My best thinking got me into this mess and won't get me out, or

...I really need help, or

...Life doesn't have to be this way.

Such admissions are a form of surrender, an acknowledgment of the depth of your pain. In making this kind of admission, you begin to consider that your way of doing things may be flawed. You concede the race—or at least a portion of it—and agree that you don't have the power or ability, all by yourself, to accomplish what you thought was your responsibility to accomplish.

Brad's Surrender

Remember Brad? In the last chapter, we described Brad's wake-up call: some intensely emotional reactions to a colleague. When Brad examined his feelings with the help of a counselor, he realized that the man reminded him of the man who exposed himself on the playground when Brad was a boy.

The insight itself represented something of a release, but Brad didn't stop there. He worked with his counselor at physically releasing his rage about the incident (in safe, non-destructive ways), and he healed the wound that was getting in the way of his relationship with his colleague.

As a result, Brad now works with his colleague more comfortably and productively. He feels more relaxed about being himself around the man, and has noticed that conflicts simply don't occur as often as they did. Brad says he is glad he used the discomfort as a springboard for his own work. "Much better than belting the guy," he said.

Brad answered his wake-up call. He could have stuffed his anger, blamed someone or something else for it or let his colleague have it. He could have stopped with the initial insight. Any of those responses might have made him feel better temporarily, but they would have done nothing to heal the wound.

Eli's Story

Right around the time Rebecca heard from Jeannie (the reluctant would-be client we described in the last chapter), she received a call from Eli. His circumstances were similar to Jeannie's, although his attitudes couldn't have been more different.

A relationship breakup had left Eli feeling suicidal. He paged Rebecca in great distress one day, and after some crisis management, made an appointment to see her the following day.

Like Jeannie, Eli lived an inconvenient distance from our office. He didn't consider the drive to be a serious problem, however, and actually arrived early for his appointment. His pain and confusion were intense; perhaps because of this, he was willing to do whatever he needed to do to heal his wounds. In any case, he read the books Rebecca recommended and joined a support group. Eli's insurance covered only a small portion of the cost of therapy, but he said, "I can't think of a better way to spend my raise than getting my head on straight." Over and over, Eli continues to confront his pain, even when it seems to him that it will never end. But his willingness continues to grow, and it is taking him steadily through the healing process.

Tina's Response

Tina, whose wake-up call we described in the previous chapter, also surrendered. (She was the woman whose anesthesia was criticism; her wake-up call came from her therapy group, which confronted her about the effects of her criticism.) Although her experience in group was extremely painful, she decided to stick it out. Her life was not working the way she wanted it to, and she knew she didn't have any more answers.

With the help of a supportive therapist in group and in individual work, Tina became willing to *consider* the *possibility* that *maybe* she didn't have all the answers—that maybe she had something to learn from the group members about herself and her wounds.

Ultimately, she was right. After several months of gritting her teeth and showing up at group each week, Tina had a break-through. With a sudden stroke of clarity, she understood what people had been telling her about the effects on them of her hypercritical attitudes. She could see their pain, and even more important to her healing, she was finally aware of her own. She saw how she used criticism to hide from and mitigate her pain. Tina began working to heal her wounds that day.

The Purgatory About-Face

Sometimes, people who chose purgatory in spite of numerous catastrophic wake-up calls suddenly reverse themselves and surrender to healing for no discernible reason. Like Sharif and Scott.

Sharif's Story

Sharif was a forty-year-old stockbroker whose inability to control his rage was going to kill him. He got into fist fights in movie theater lines, couldn't keep a secretary and began losing clients. His two sisters refused to speak to him. He picked fights in bars, even though he never drank more than a beer or two at a time. He was arrested, ejected from several clubs, and lost a couple of teeth. In one extraordinary incident, when he screamed obscenities at a driver who cut him off in traffic, the insulted driver pulled out a gun and shot at Sharif's car. In the resulting accident, Sharif's shoulder was dislocated and he wound up in traction for several weeks. Remarkably, none of this convinced Sharif he had a problem with rage.

Finally, a friend asked Sharif to meet with her friend Alex, who had had similar problems with his temper before going into intensive therapy. The two men had coffee and Alex told Sharif his story. Something about the conversation got to Sharif. To this day, he can't say exactly what it was that captivated him. In any case, he got help. It has been a long, difficult struggle, but Sharif began a new life that week. He hasn't hurt anyone, destroyed property or even shouted at anyone in five years now. He doggedly continues to confront painful wounds in therapy.

Scott's Story

Scott is an example of an addict who wanted to choose recovery but remained in purgatory anyway until surrendering a few years ago. A self-made millionaire, Scott lost everything to his alcoholism. He hit bottom, got sober, and rebuilt his life, but ignored his underlying wounds. As a result, another problem surfaced: sex addiction. Once again, Scott came close to losing everything.

Once more, he hit bottom and entered recovery. He hung on to his wounds, however, and was known as an ego-driven, angry, mean-spirited user of people.

It wasn't until he fell in love with a woman he didn't want to lose that he finally got serious about emotional healing. Scott approached true willingness through a window of willingness. He started his healing work to keep his relationship. Once he caught a glimpse of what might be available to him, he committed himself to the healing journey. He's still on that journey.

People who surrender to healing have begun to give up their false hope that something outside themselves is going to make life all right. Their pain and the events of their lives have forced them to stumble across the only antidote to survival plan living: self-responsibility.

In Section II, we examine specifically how healing follows the track of reclaimed self-responsibility.

Wake-Up Calls III:
Lessons and Consequences

We think the information in this chapter will help you look at the bumps and failures of your life in a new way, and to take advantage of them instead of trying to overcome them. These exercises are designed to help you think about what you have to gain—and lose—by listening to your wake-up calls.

1. Begin to clarify for yourself what your wake-up calls are trying to teach you. Use the list below for inspiration.

   ☐ Wounds, grief or other unfinished business, particularly...

   ☐ False hopes and unrealistic expectations, especially...

   ☐ My need to always be right about...

   ☐ Parts of myself that I dislike, especially...

   ☐ Ways in which I invite other people to take advantage of me, particularly...

   ☐ Skills I need to develop, such as...

   ☐ My life purpose or goals, especially those regarding...

   ☐ My spiritual development, especially regarding...

2. What would the consequences be if you surrendered to healing for each of these wake-up calls?

3. What would the consequences be if you ignored your wake-up calls?

The Self-Responsibility
Solution

The Self-Responsibility Solution

Who owns your wounds?

Your survival plan required you to deed your wounds to other people, circumstances or events. Healing requires you to take back the title to your wounds. That is what it means to be self-responsible.

In this section, we will look at the elements of self-responsibility and the process by which people become self-responsible.

Once you succeed in dismantling large chunks of the first two legs of your survival plan (anesthesias and rules), your life is much happier and more fulfilling than it used to be. However, if you want even more from life, you must embrace the single most important key to healing: *the willingness to become unconditionally self-responsible.*

Here's why: In relinquishing your anesthesias and dealing with your inner critic, you begin to reclaim the self-responsibility you lost in creating and maintaining your survival plan. Abstinence and repeated applications of good self-care and contact with your feelings makes the first two legs of your survival plan tripod start to crumble.

Truly thorough-going healing, however, means you must dismantle *all* of your survival plan. And that last leg—the happy-ending fantasy—is vulnerable only to self-responsibility.

Understanding the concepts presented in this section, as well as the role self-responsibility plays in your healing will help you to:

• Monitor your own healing progress

- Accurately estimate the healing levels of prospective friends and romantic interests—and therefore what you might reasonably be able to expect from relationships with them

We offer some advice: Don't try too hard to rate your own level of self-responsibility as you read this section. If you're like most people, your inner critic will get into the act, and you'll end up feeling discouraged and ashamed. Just treat Section II as important background information. When you get to Section III, we'll look at self-responsibility again in the context of The Seven Stages of Personal Healing and of your own healing journey.

ELEVEN

Self-Responsibility as Growth Indicator and Growth Catalyst

Many modern psychotherapists have adopted as their credo Socrates' declaration that "the unexamined life is not worth living." But for modern man, that is not enough. We should pledge ourselves to the proposition that the irresponsible life is not worth living.

— Thomas Szasz

§ § §

THE STREAM SPIRIT *sat on a rock with his head in his hands. His friends sat beside him. The stream spirit sniffled. He hadn't slept in days. The glimpse he'd had of his friends' homes haunted him. He found his own surroundings bleak and depressing, so much so that he could hardly bear to open his eyes and look around. He wiped away another tear.*

"Why did this happen to me?" he whispered. "Why did they do this to me?"

One friend raised an eyebrow. "As I recall," he replied, "you did all this."

"Yes, but I **had** to!" the stream spirit said. "What choice did I have? I was little, and new. They were supposed to tell me what to do! They were supposed to help me!"

The other friend sighed. "All that is true," he said, "and yet it won't help you get your garden back."

"What do you mean?" the stream spirit said.

The friends looked at each other. One took a breath, then sat for a moment, gazing at his feet, as if considering what to say. When he looked up at the stream spirit, his eyes were soft.

"There are those who believe that each of us chooses our lives," he said. "We choose the people who are to help us. We choose our families and friends, our enemies, our teachers, our lovers, neighbors, bosses and employees. They say we choose before we are born, before we come to this planet. They say we choose based on what our souls believe we need to grow and learn."

"You mean, I **chose** those jerks, those stupid ones, those people that told me to destroy my garden?" the stream spirit cried.

His friend nodded.

"Ridiculous!" the stream spirit said. "Why would I pick people so destructive? And, if I did pick them, then that must mean that I'm a mess, too! Or else I would have chosen wiser, kinder teachers!"

"If one of the tasks your soul set for itself was to learn how to trust your own judgment," his friend said, "then you picked the right ones."

The stream spirit just stared at him.

"Because," his friend continued, "if you learn to trust your judgment under these circumstances, you will be able to trust your judgment forever, under any circumstances."

The stream spirit was silent for several moments. Then he squinted up at his friend. "So maybe I'm actually brave for choosing these circumstances," he said, "and not stupid?"

His friend nodded.

"I don't know," the stream spirit said. "That sounds far-fetched to me. I'm not sure I believe all that—about choosing before you're born."

"That's okay," his friend said. "You don't need to believe it for it to have value for you. Just behave as if it were true."

The stream spirit shook his head. "You lost me again," he said.

"Well, what would it mean if you did believe that you chose all the things in your life?" his friend asked.

The stream spirit thought. He thought about other choices, choices he knew he had made—like the time he chose to plant a sleepberry seedling in a sandy area instead of a loamy one. That choice meant the seedling had died, but it also meant that he'd learned a little about what sleepberries needed to thrive.

"Well," he said, "I guess it would mean that there was something for me to learn. That maybe it's not all a big mistake. That maybe it's nobody's fault that I'm miserable."

"Okay," his friend said. "And what would you do differently if you believed all that?"

"Well, I guess I'd quit sleeping so much," the stream spirit said. "And I guess I'd have to look around here and start doing some work to put things right. And I'd have to forget about trying to get them to fix it for me."

"That's it," his friend said. "That's how you'll get your garden back. We call it 'self-responsibility.'"

Now that you're an adult, your survival plan has outlived its usefulness. Where it once kept you emotionally alive, now it limits your capacity to live fully. Where it once served you by shielding you from the pain of your unhealed wounds, now it is a liability—and for the same reason. It has served its function.

Now, it is in the way. It still blocks your access to your wounds, and that prevents you from healing them—but not from feeling their effects.

So if you want more from your life than you have had, there is only one choice: the survival plan has got to go.

Dismantling Your Survival Plan

You begin dismantling your survival plan with your very first steps of emotional healing. As a rule, people start with the anesthesia and rules legs. They identify and abstain from their primary anesthesias, replacing them with healthy self-care habits and vulnerability. Then they tackle the rules leg of the tripod by examining their assumptions about themselves and the world and rehabilitating their inner critics. They begin to replace rules with feelings and boundaries.

This is no small task, and always brings a marked sense of restored happiness. But its benefits are limited. Many of our clients did a great job of replacing these parts of their survival plans, then continued to feel that there was still something missing in their lives.

As we worked together to discover that missing element, these seekers began to understand what they needed to do. They realized that, if they wished to reap the benefits of emotional and spiritual authenticity—joy, contentment, a sense of personal power and fulfillment—they would have to heal on a profound level. They would have to dismantle *all three legs* of the survival plan and expose their deepest wounds—the ones they protected with their happy-ending fantasy.

And the only tool that works on the happy-ending fantasy is self-responsibility.

Self-Responsibility and Healing vs. the Happy-Ending Fantasy and Victimhood

As children, we hid from our wounds when we didn't have the option of feeling and healing. We attributed the origins of our pain to other people and outside circumstances. As we saw in Section I, this handing-off of responsibility can be expressed in "If…then" statements. Unconsciously, we said to ourselves, *If I weren't this way, I wouldn't hurt. If I did this thing, they would quit ignoring me or hitting me or criticizing me, and I would feel okay. I will be safe if you…I will be safe if they…*

This attitude made us victims of circumstances, of other people or of our own emotions.

> ***victim***—Someone who believes that his happiness, integrity or capacity to love is in the hands of another person or situation.

Victims believe that they can not heal until other people—or the world—changes. Victims assign the power to determine whether they feel peaceful, whole and well to other people or circumstances. They depend on *external* changes to fix *internal* problems.

This is a common affliction in our culture. Most of us suffer from the delusion that we'll be happier if others quit annoying us, behaving badly or ignoring our needs. Under this delusion, changing ourselves is not an option.

An example: You know your mother always changes the subject when you try to tell her about exciting developments at your job. This hurts your feelings. You have gotten angry with her, you have explained what you would like from her and you have shared your hurt feelings with her. However, she continues to brush off your attempts to engage her interest. If you continue to try to force her to get it, and then feel angry and hurt each time she fails you, you have placed yourself in the position of being her victim.

To quit being a victim, you reverse the process that you used to build your survival plan and reclaim your self-responsibility. Just as you replace anesthesias with healthy self-care and rules with feelings, you must replace the happy-ending fantasy leg of your survival plan tripod with something healthier. This something is an acceptance of reality, and the tool you use to accomplish the replacement is self-responsibility. As a reminder, here's the definition of self-responsibility again:

> *self-responsibility*—Understanding of, and acceptance of, the fact that my own interpretations, not outer circumstances, determine my ability to respond to people and situations, my feelings, my awareness of choices available to me, and my behavior.

Self-responsibility and healing are virtually interchangeable terms:

> *healing*—The process of becoming emotionally and spiritually whole by gradually taking full responsibility for my own needs, feelings, thoughts and reactions. Healing is a lifelong process that ultimately becomes a way of life.

The two concepts are inextricably intertwined. Increasing self-responsibility weakens the happy-ending fantasy, which exposes unhealed wounds. Healing the wounds requires the willingness to increase your levels of self-responsibility. When a wound is healed, self-responsibility naturally, effortlessly increases a bit. This provides the emotional strength and willingness to expose another unhealed wound, which is then healed by deliberately increasing your level of self-responsibility. And so on and on.

The Benefits of Self-Responsibility

There's no getting around it: *responsibility* is a heavy word. It implies obligation, accountability, duty, dependability and reliability. To be responsible is to be subject to penalty in case of default. It is a serious, humorless, no-nonsense kind of word.

Try not to let this put you off. Because on the other side of taking responsibility for yourself lies a landscape whose beauty is beyond anything you've ever experienced. Once you enter this landscape, self-responsibility becomes a joyful, life-affirming occupation.

This is what self-responsibility and healing bring you:

- Less frequent disconnections from yourself, others and your spiritual resources

- More skillful, more rapid reconnections when you do disconnect

- Greater awareness of the presence of love

- More willingness and ability to extend love outward

- More willingness to honestly examine your part in any conflict between you and another, because you know it will bring you yet more healing.

More benefits of self-responsibility appear in the list below, side by side with the liabilities of *not* being self-responsible.

Non-Self-Responsibility Leads to Being:	Self-Responsibility Leads to Being:
Unconscious	Self-aware
Focused on solving other people's problems	Focused on solving your own problems
Self-absorbed	Attentive
Numb	Fully emotional
Resentful	Grateful
Whiny	Assertive
Controlling	Accepting
Pessimistic	Optimistic
Absorbed in finding the rip-off in life's circumstances	Absorbed in finding the gift in life's circumstances
Manipulative	Honest
Rigid	Flexible
Overly careful	Willing to take some risks
Judgmental	Compassionate

Pain is Inevitable

We don't want to mislead you; the benefits of healing are not easily obtained. The healing process hurts. After all, you can't expect to expose deep wounds without feeling the very pain you've shielded yourself from all these years. At some point in the healing journey, the likelihood of pain becomes apparent. That's when people get scared.

All of us are afraid of the pain—why else would we create a survival plan? We have found some comfort and strength for facing the pain by thinking about it in this way:

- **The pain of healing is no worse than what you're used to.** The sharp pain of healing is certainly no worse than the constant, dull ache of living within the restrictions of your survival plan.

- **The pain of healing is temporary.** But you can never finish with the pain that comes from living within your survival plan.

- **The pain of healing is productive.** When you're done healing a wound, you have something to show for it. Because the wound no longer blocks your life energy, you discover more joy, more fulfillment, more love.

- **You have already lived through the worst.** Exposing and healing your wounds is just a matter of returning to the scene of the crime—this time with the guidance, emotional tools and understanding you didn't have as a child.

Man must accept responsibility for himself... There is no meaning to life except the meaning man gives his life by the unfolding of his powers.

– Erich Fromm

As one of our clients concluded, "Your wounds are going to get you one way or the other. If you turn your back on them, they are going bite you in the butt. Better to just turn and face them and deal with them actively."

Sometimes doing this requires a huge leap of faith: that your spiritual resources will somehow see you through the profound transition from living under the rules of your survival plan to living with an open heart.

One Woman's Journey into Self-Responsibility

Once they understand the concept of self-responsibility, people want to know what it looks like in real life.

Aggie's relationship with Burt provides a good example of how a happy-ending fantasy breaks down over time with increasing self-responsibility. In the following pages, we look at how Aggie's happy-ending fantasy came apart bit by bit, in pre-, early, middle and advanced healing, as she developed self-responsibility and healed her wounds.

As a child in a family preoccupied with her mother's multiple sclerosis, Aggie learned that she was going it alone when it came to losses—no one was there to keep her company when she felt scared or sad. In fact, most of her scared and sad feelings *came* from being neglected by her family. So Aggie learned to ignore the feelings and the disconnection that triggered them.

The false hope at the bottom of her happy-ending fantasy took several forms:

> *If I pretend everything is okay, then it **will** be okay.*

> *Other people's behavior shouldn't bother me.*

> *How people treat me is my responsibility.*

She also developed a false hopelessness foundation for her fantasy that asserted:

> *Loving relationships happen to other people, not me, and*

> *The best you can hope for in a relationship is a man who is willing to be with you—period.*

But Aggie was largely unaware of the effects of her happy-ending fantasy until she began a serious relationship with Burt.

Aggie's Happy-Ending Fantasy Pre-Healing

Aggie's happy-ending fantasy ran her life. As a result, she was constantly disappointed in other people. Her happy-ending fantasy blinded her to their wounds as well as her own, so her expectations of them tended to be much higher than their capabilities. Relationships never seemed to work out, and she was certain that was because *there are no good men, all the good ones are taken,* and *I'm just not attractive/smart/rich/funny/skinny/healthy enough.*

This didn't keep her from putting herself in painful situations, however. She continued to enter relationships with people who couldn't meet her needs, and continued to be surprised (or annoyed) when they didn't work out.

Most of us want to feel not responsible for actions prompted by our own questionable impulses.

— Eric Hoffer

In the beginning of her relationship with Burt, Aggie was willing to ignore a great deal of pain and discomfort. The night they met, she noticed he was drinking quite a lot. On their first date, she noticed that Burt drank an entire liter of wine himself. Both times, Aggie noticed her own discomfort. Both times, she excused Burt's drinking and discounted her discomfort so she could continue to see him.

Aggie's Happy-Ending Fantasy in Early Healing

In early healing, people still tend to overestimate others' levels of healing and then feel disappointed or betrayed when they fail to live up to expectations. This allows them to preserve their dependence upon whatever false hope for love has kept them going all these years.

But once people admit they are wounded and start to heal, they begin to make small changes in their lives. They find support groups and start thinking about how they have gotten themselves into the scrapes in their lives. They become less willing to subject themselves to the pain of a bad relationship. They begin to examine their other relationships and the roles they play in them. They start thinking about what it would take to dismantle their happy-ending fantasy.

Here's how Aggie took responsibility for her early healing:

• She confronted her happy-ending fantasy in the twelve-step groups Codependents Anonymous (Co.D.A.) and Adult Children of Alcoholics (A.C.A.).

- She found friends and a therapist who could keep her company while she grieved the loss of her dream.

- From their compassionate caring, she learned to keep herself company.

Aggie stayed in her relationship with Burt, however, and continued to nurse her false hope. She figured she was beating the odds by having a relationship to begin with, because, after all, *Loving relationships happen to other people, not me.*

Aggie's Happy-Ending Fantasy in Middle Healing

In middle healing, people begin to feel the true grief of their losses for the first time. Gradually, they understand that they can trust their own feeling, grieving and healing process. This process, because it is founded in self-responsibility, is the enemy of the happy-ending fantasy. No happy-ending fantasy can long withstand the power of the feeling-grieving-healing cycle.

As people begin to release their happy-ending fantasies, they get braver about saying no and having realistic expectations of others. They become even more committed to their healing. They embrace self-responsibility.

As Aggie came to trust her ability to take care of herself and survive her grief, she became more realistic about Burt's abilities and limits. She understood more and more that there was a ceiling on the amount of intimacy she could have with Burt. Being sad about that reminded her of the deeper sadness of her emotionally absent family. She began to grieve both losses.

However, Aggie's happy-ending fantasy was still firmly in place. It showed itself during a trip she took with Burt one year during Aggie's middle healing stage.

She and Burt had made plans in September to drive to another state to visit Aggie's family for Christmas. Between September and December, their relationship had become quite tense. In fact, they hadn't seen each other at all between Thanksgiving and their departure date. In spite of her misgivings about the trip, Aggie believed she should keep the commitment

Today responsibility is often meant to denote duty, something imposed upon one from the outside. But responsibility, in its true sense, is an entirely voluntary act; it is my response to the needs, expressed or unexpressed, of another human being.

— Erich Fromm

she made (an indication that the rules leg of her survival plan was still in place, at least part of the time). She also rationalized that she wanted to see her family, it was too late to buy a plane ticket so she could go by herself, and she didn't want to make the three-day drive by herself. So she and Burt left as planned.

Along the way, Burt became angry with Aggie, but would not tell her why. He denied being angry at all, but his behavior toward her was cold and hostile. Aggie spent the entire two weeks trying to draw Burt out (*How other people treat me is my responsibility*). When that didn't work, she concentrated on having a good time in spite of his silent treatment (*Other people's behavior shouldn't bother me, If I pretend everything is okay, then it **will** be okay*).

She knew something was wrong and was fully aware of her feelings about it, but she didn't see that she had any choice other than to keep a stiff upper lip (*If I don't make waves, they will come around; The best you can hope for in a relationship is a man who is willing to be with you—period*). So she remained in the relationship and tried to make the best of it.

It wasn't until couple of years later that Aggie began to see alternatives to the way she had responded to Burt's withdrawal. She told him, "If you were to behave that way now, I would buy myself a plane ticket and fly back home without you."

...Responsibility means the awareness that we are capable of acting foolishly at times. When this occurs, it is advisable to learn from such experiences and accept them as stepping stones toward a higher degree of awareness and integration.

— Arthur Lerner

This was a huge leap forward for Aggie. She realized that she *didn't* have to sit still and be miserable. As she slowly dismantled her happy-ending fantasy and gave up the idea that she could turn Burt into the loving, self-responsible partner she wanted, she was learning to set boundaries. (However, like most people in middle healing, she could set them only if they didn't inconvenience anyone. She still had a long way to go in her boundaries work.)

Aggie's Happy-Ending Fantasy in Advanced Healing

By the time people reach the advanced healing stages, they are more committed to their authenticity than to their happy-ending fantasy. They are more interested in seeing the truth about the people and situations that surround them than in forcing their happy-ending fantasy to come true.

As a result, they are no longer controlled by their happy-ending fantasy most of the time. The are rarely disappointed by others. Their expectations are based firmly in reality. They don't believe quite so much in their old list of prerequisites to being happy. Certain events can still trigger the remnants of their happy-ending fantasy, plunging them into strong emotional reactions. However, now they quickly recognize these reactions for what they are, and are less likely to get seriously caught up in them. And because they tend to keep their feelings company instead of numbing out or attacking themselves for having them, they resolve and release them more rapidly.

After Aggie entered advanced healing, she rethought her Christmas vacation with Burt. She decided it would have been ridiculous to leave her own family at Christmas time. Why should she, Burt's host, be the one to go, when it was his refusal to talk to her that was making the situation tense? She told Burt that if the incident happened today, she would insist that he either work out his problems with her or leave.

About six months later, Aggie surprised herself with the realization that, given the tension level before the trip, she would never have made the trip with him, regardless of the plans they had made.

Recently, Aggie acknowledged that if she had really paid attention to her feelings during the early days of their relationship, she would have broken up with Burt three weeks after their first date. She thought a moment and then corrected herself: "Actually, I don't think I would have had a second date with him. I was terribly uncomfortable with his drinking that night, and today I would honor that feeling."

The last time we saw Aggie, she told us that her thinking had undergone yet another change. "If I met Burt at a party today, I would not give him my phone number," she said. "I noticed that night that he was drinking a lot and doing it fast, but I invented excuses for his behavior and discounted my own feelings. Today, I'd pay attention to how I felt and what I saw."

[13] Ultimately, as Burt's unwillingness to heal his wounds became clear to her, Aggie chose to end the relationship. Not all relationships fall apart when healing work enters the picture. Some become stronger—but usually only when *both* people are committed to deep healing. However, losing cherished relationships is definitely a risk. Sometimes, the prospect of this loss can hold us back from going all the way in our healing work.

Today, Aggie does pay attention to what she feels. Her relationship with Burt is in the past.[13] She turns down invitations from men when she feels uncomfortable with them, and finds that more and more of the men who appear in her life these days are also committed to deep healing. She no longer assumes that any relationship is better than no relationship. She notices that many other aspects of her false hope still influence her feelings, but she catches them and challenges them more often than not.

The Nine Indicators of Self-Responsibility

We have discovered nine measures of a person's level of self-responsibility. We call them indicators of self-responsibility. They are listed below, grouped in three main categories.

Categories	Indicators
Feelings Indicators: How Do You Deal with Hurt?	• Ability To Feel, Grieve and Heal • Response to Pain
Personal Power Indicators: Who's In Charge?	• Boundary-Setting Skills • Foundation of Self-Esteem • Investment in Victimhood
Connection Indicators: How Do You Join?	• Attitude toward Unfinished Business • Mission in Life • Quality of Relationships • Quality of Relationship with Your Spiritual Resources

Some people think of these indicators as landmarks. We like this analogy. In any road trip, you will see landmarks each day that you didn't see last week or last month. The view changes, and the landmarks give you an idea of where you are relative to where you came from and where you are going. It takes no special effort to see each new landmark once you have arrived. You are either standing on the edge of the North Rim of the Grand Canyon or you are not. You can't pretend the landmarks are there or force landmarks to appear today that you won't be in a position to see until next month. The landmarks simply show you where you are. Landmarks help you accurately determine where you are on your journey.

However, these landmarks behave differently than, say, the Grand Canyon. For one thing, the indicators are not always completely distinct. There is a great deal of overlapping and intertwining among them. For example, as your *Response to Pain* changes from avoidance to attention, your *Ability to Feel, Grieve and Heal* improves. *Boundary-Setting Skills* improve with changes in the *Foundation of Your Self-Esteem*. As your *Relationship With Your Spiritual Resources* improves, your *Mission In Life* changes.

In this way, all the indicators nourish each other, just as all are powered by the work you do to chip away at your happy-ending fantasy.

Another way to think about the indicators is as souvenirs. When you travel, you notice landmarks, take pictures of them and leave them behind. But souvenirs are things you collect and take home with you. The best souvenirs are unique—you can get them only in particular spots. The Nine Indicators are unique in that way. Even better, unlike souvenirs, they don't simply sit in a box in the closet, gathering dust. They become a part of who you are and they change your life.

In the following chapters, we describe how each indicator appears in pre-healing, early healing, middle healing and advanced healing stages.

In addition, the Appendix contains a chart called *How Self-Responsibility Grows Through The Seven Stages* (pages 410-11). This quick-reference chart will be most helpful to you after you read about the Seven Stages in Section III, but feel free to refer to it now as a visual representation of what you're going to read in the next three chapters.

TWELVE

Feelings Indicators:
How Do You Deal With Hurt?

Trust thyself: every heart vibrates to that iron string.
– Ralph Waldo Emerson

THE WAY YOU HANDLE YOUR FEELINGS is one of the first things that changes in the healing journey. (In fact, the journey begins because you become willing to feel the emotional pain you have been hiding from.) Everything to come builds upon your willingness and ability to feel everything you feel. The Feelings Indicators are a way to gauge how you deal with the uncomfortable emotions—the ones you have anesthetized yourself against.

Ability to Feel, Grieve and Heal

> *ability to feel, grieve and heal*—How well you recognize feelings, stay with them and work them through.

As you've seen, children and adolescents hurt by disconnection substitute their innate ability to feel, grieve and heal with a happy-ending fantasy. As you heal and begin to reclaim self-responsibility, this capacity is restored.

Ability to Feel, Grieve and Heal in Pre-Healing

In pre-healing, your ability to feel, grieve and heal is virtually nonexistent. You have little or no idea how to heal emotional wounds. When hurt, you take refuge in blaming others or yourself, or in numbing yourself with defenses and anesthesias, to shield yourself from having to experience the pain alone. As a result, you collect more and more pain, then use more anesthesias and blame to contain it within yourself. Those feelings don't get completed; they get buried alive.

If you were able to feel, grieve and heal, you'd have to face the truth about your happy-ending fantasy. Doing that too soon would be devastating, because before healing begins, you don't possess the skills, the support or the understanding of the process to get you through the pain.

Ability to Feel, Grieve and Heal in Early Healing

In the early stages, you begin to get an idea of how much there is to do, and accept the idea that feeling and grieving are the keys. These understandings are the precursors to developing your ability to feel, grieve and heal your losses.

Ability to Feel, Grieve and Heal in Middle Healing

You do the bulk of your feeling repair work in middle healing. You begin to recognize your feelings and express them. You develop the skills to feel them all the way through instead of running away by using an anesthesia, blaming others, blaming yourself or becoming overwhelmed by them.

Later in middle healing, you find that you can stay with your feelings and work through them to healing almost all the time.

Ability to Feel, Grieve and Heal in Advanced Healing

This process is easy and natural for you now; there is no feeling that is too scary to feel, no loss too overwhelming to grieve. In early advanced healing stages, you practice feeling, grieving and healing skills daily in terms of your own feelings. Later on, you use these skills to grow your relationships with others. You develop the ability to be there to help others feel, grieve and heal, sometimes even when your own needs are not being met.

Finally, you begin to create environments in which others can safely develop their feeling skills—in your family, at work, in your community, among your friends and spiritual groups.

Response to Pain

> **response to pain**—How you perceive and react to emotional or physical pain. Your view of the purpose of pain determines your response to it.

Philosophers, theologians and psychologists have struggled with the meaning of pain and suffering for centuries. Some new age practitioners have concluded that healing (or enlightenment) is always followed by prosperity, good health and the absence of emotional pain. According to this model, if you are poor, ill or hurting, you must be doing something wrong.

We don't have the answers to the paradox of pain or the riddle of suffering, but it is obvious to us that emotional healing does not necessarily eliminate pain. People with high levels of emotional healing still get their hearts broken, injure themselves in accidents, worry about their children and get scared when they lose their jobs. It is possible to be well along the healing road—and to be poor, ill and hurting. What changes on the healing journey is your relationship to your pain.

Of all the indicators, response to pain shows perhaps the most dramatic change over the course of healing. As you make progress, not only will your attitude and response to pain change, so will the distinctions you make between what you will and will not tolerate. Your ability to sweat out and learn from pain increases. (However, your willingness to stay in situations that are painful because they are abusive—or in pain created by your own actions—virtually evaporates.)

So we don't look for an absence of trouble and pain as proof of healing. Instead, we look for an increasingly refined ability to recognize and respond to smaller amounts of pain as wake-up calls. This new response to pain creates a growing capacity for love and a willingness to experience all circumstances as gifts—even the difficult ones.

Let's see how people make this transition.

Response to Pain in Pre-Healing

Pre-healing, your attitude toward pain is permeated by fear. You may be aware of your fear or not. Your fear of pain can take any number of forms: you may be afraid that your pain will never be healed, or that facing the source of your pain will propel you into a black hole or that you'll go ballistic and lose control.

You may also fear your pain simply because you have never learned what to do with it.

In pre-healing, you might not even notice pain. Physical clues to emotional pain (stomachaches, tightness in the chest, headaches) are ignored, denied or treated as solely physical problems. Emotional pain that makes itself felt more directly (for example, tears that leak out, lumps in the throat, undeniable anxiety) gets stuffed or masked by anesthesia.

You see pain as a call to avoidance, through denial (*It's not that bad*), anesthesia (see Section I) or blame (**You're the reason I am unhappy**). Your willingness to endure painful circumstances is astronomically high because you know how to keep yourself from feeling the pain. Numbed by your anesthesias, you accept neglect, or you tolerate (or dispense) emotional and possibly even physical abuse. Painful consequences of your anesthesia use often don't faze you until they become catastrophic—auto accidents, spouses leaving, or children banning you from their homes, for example. Even then, your anesthesia may still be working well enough to keep you from answering these wake-up calls.

Response to Pain in Early Healing

In early healing, your anesthesias usually have failed you and so your ability to walk oblivious through pain is severely compromised. You finally begin to respond to your pain as a wake-up call instead of a call to avoidance.

Once you choose healing, you tend to feel high with relief and newly awakened hope. This is sometimes called the pink cloud or honeymoon phase. You might see a long, painless future stretching out ahead of you. *"After all,"* you may think, *"what could possibly be more painful than fighting the collapse of my survival plan?"*

Later, you may discover that learning to live without your anesthesia can be more painful than keeping your survival plan patched up. For example, alcoholics often find that, after the initial period of euphoria, sobriety is excruciating. The circumstances against which they were anesthetizing themselves are still there, but their anesthetic is gone. Because they haven't yet developed something more healthy to take the place of their anesthesia (like good self-care habits), they are left raw and naked with their pain.

For people who are not struggling with a physical addiction, the situation may not be as dramatic. However, most people find themselves in similar straits when they give up whatever behaviors they were using to numb themselves. They usually find that their pain levels remain high while their pain tolerance continues to slide.

Response to Pain in Middle Healing

As you move into middle healing, you confront your happy-ending fantasy for the first time. (This is less the result of making a decision as it is a result of doing good early healing work; the issues emerge spontaneously.) This period can be even more painful than early healing stages, largely because your pain tolerances are almost non-existent by now, and your ability to keep your feelings company is still new and relatively undeveloped.

However, as you develop your ability to feel, grieve and heal, your skill in dealing with pain improves daily, which allows you to persevere. You have learned that healing requires sweating out your feelings. You begin to see pain as territory you must cross to get where you want to go. You develop a grudging acceptance of what you may see as a necessary evil.

By the middle of this period, pain levels begin to decline. As a result, you come through middle healing with a profound sense of your own ability to survive pain, no matter how bad it gets.

Response to Pain in Advanced Healing

By now, your attitude toward pain has become more detached. More and more, you regard pain simply as information. You begin to understand the maxim *Pain is necessary; misery is optional.* You realize that your pain is not caused by external events and that you determine your own pain levels by deciding what is and is not acceptable behavior from others. The world is no longer black and white to you. You recognize that there are few situations that fall into distinct categories called "bad" or "good."[14]

You tolerate very little pain before becoming willing to use it as a wake-up call. You have virtually lost your willingness to become caught up in other people's dysfunctional behavior. You recognize and deal with problems more quickly because you don't need to be in extreme pain before taking action; you have become a happier learner.

Your response to pain is closely linked to the ability to feel, grieve and heal. As you will see in the next chapter, it is also linked to your willingness to set clean boundaries.

[14] One situation that does fall firmly into such categories is being struck; it is *always* unacceptable.

How Do You Deal With Hurt?

The Feelings Indicators:
- **Ability to Feel, Grieve and Heal**
- **Response to Pain**

1. What incidents in your life have illustrated your ability to feel, grieve and heal and your typical response to pain?

2. In what ways could you increase your levels of self-responsibility in similar incidents?

3. What would you stand to lose by doing so?

4. What would you stand to gain?

THIRTEEN

The Personal Power Indicators: Who's In Charge?

Integrity simply means willingness not to violate one's identity.

– Erich Fromm

PSYCHOLOGISTS USE THE PHRASE *perceived locus of control* to talk about personal power. It refers to your tendency to believe the events in your life are consequences of your own action or are unrelated to your behavior. You can perceive the locus of control as internal (caused by you) or external (caused by the situation, by chance or by other people).

The Personal Power indicators reveal who (or what) you believe possesses this control: yourself, your internalized programming or other people, events and circumstances. As wounded people, we tend to assign our power to others. As we heal, we take more responsibility for being the bosses of our lives and stop allowing external forces to run us.

Boundary-Setting Skills

boundary—A personal limit that allows me to love you (or simply work with you) and to openly give to you and receive from you without resenting you or compromising my integrity or healing journey.

It is impossible not to have boundaries. Everyone has these internal limits that, when crossed, create resentment. You can try to conceal or deny them, but eventually they become apparent. Your choice is to be aware of them and set them directly and cleanly or deny them and let them leak out. When you choose to be aware of and share these inner limits, you free yourself from resentment, make your world safe to live in as a whole, authentic person and allow yourself to behave lovingly toward others—even though you're not fully healed, and even when they don't cooperate.

Boundaries range from the simple to the emotionally complex. Examples include:

- **Simple self-disclosure:** "I'm uncomfortable about what is happening between us"

- **Requesting something:** "I'd like a hug;" "I want you to stop teasing me"

- **Expressing a consequence of someone's behavior:** "Your choice to continue drinking is your choice for me to consider leaving this relationship"[15]

- **Taking action without discussion, such as moving out without notice.**[16]

[15] This particular form is harsh, and is effective only under extreme circumstances. Therefore, it should not be used lightly.

[16] See previous footnote.

Setting boundaries is extremely challenging work. As you will see, most people are well into advanced healing before they begin making real progress in their boundary-setting skills. It is only in advanced healing that boundary-setting skills become well-established and boundaries consistently graceful and compassionate.

Boundary-setting skills are closely linked with two other indicators: *Response to Pain* and *Ability to Feel, Grieve and Heal* (covered in the previous chapter). This is because your ability to sense and stay with your feelings (rather than anesthetize yourself against them) is the key to locating your own inner limits.

Boundary-Setting Skills in Pre-Healing

In pre-healing stages, boundary-setting skills are virtually non-existent. Instead of setting boundaries based on your own intuition, you use rules and "shoulds." You cite authorities and philosophies rather than simply stating what fits for you. Your focus is on the other person's behavior. Your message is, *Follow the rules or you will hurt me*—a setup for victimhood. You'd rather be right than happy. Your attempts to make rules produce guilt, fighting and shame.

We found an excellent example of rules substituting for boundaries in an Ann Landers column a few years ago.

Part of the emotional maturing process is to learn how to say "no" and mean it honestly with a minimum of fear, doubt, anxiety and guilt which may get into the psyche and help to distort it.

— Arthur Lerner

Dear Ann,

What is a "date?" When my husband, "Walt," and his pals go out on the town, they drop in at cocktail bars where there is music, meet girls and spend the evening talking, buying drinks and dancing. Good, clean fun, he calls it.

I call it dating. Walt says they are just being sociable and enjoying some innocent fun. He points out that they never take the girls home or make plans to meet them again. Occasionally, he admits, some of the same women do turn up in the same places, but nothing is ever planned.

I've told Walt that we wives can talk, drink and dance, and we wish our husbands would take us out instead of going alone, looking for other women. How about it?

— Trudy

Dear Trudy,

No good ever came of a pack of married men cruising cocktail lounges buying drinks and dancing with girls. Furthermore, the wife has earned the privilege of being entertained and those evenings aren't cheap. And tell Walt something else. His wife will never slip him a Mickey and lift his wallet.

Focusing on the rules is a way for Trudy to avoid taking personal responsibility for saying, *"I don't like this, and it's not okay with me."* By arguing about rules, she protects herself from the risk of setting a boundary that might turn out to be incompatible with her husband's—or setting a boundary and creating more intimacy with him than she is prepared to handle. Rules create power struggles and increase emotional distance. Boundaries reveal the truth about a relationship.

Boundary-Setting Skills in Early Healing

Resentment may spring more from a sense of weakness than from a sense of injustice.

— Eric Hoffer

Early healing produces no significant changes in boundary-setting skills. You still concentrate on the other person's behavior and how to control it or sidestep it. While support groups are usually wonderful resources, some of the more dysfunctional ones provide all-too-good examples of this lack of boundary-setting skills. These unfortunate groups tend to be riddled with rules (spoken or unspoken) against certain topics or behaviors, in attempts to make the meetings safe places to share feelings.

Your lack of boundary-setting skills does not prevent you from seeing your need for good boundaries. Therefore, in early healing you become willing to use "canned" (or borrowed) boundaries—scripts you learn from trusted advisors or therapists—that help you build the foundation you need to get on with your healing.

For example, Rebecca gave a client, Joan, specific sentences to say to an intrusive set of grandparents whose unannounced visits and criticisms of her healing activities were making it impossible for Joan to stick to a schedule.

"Let's say your grandmother drops in during your daily quiet time with your healing workbooks," Rebecca said, "and says, 'I think all this support group nonsense is poisoning the minds of young people.' I would suggest that you do not argue with her. Instead, say something like, *'I understand that you see it that way. Thanks for stopping by. This is not a good time for me to visit with you; I have a commitment to myself to keep right now. I will call you on Tuesday.'"*

Together, Rebecca and Joan wrote a script. They rehearsed Joan's lines and role-played responses and counter-responses. Joan was able to buy herself some time and space with these suggested phrases. Later, her healing progressed to the point that she could create her own responses in the heat of the moment.

Boundary-Setting Skills in Middle Healing

Sometime in early middle healing, it dawns on you that you've taken a lot of garbage and violated yourself for a long time. At this point, you may find that you are angry about the way you have allowed others to violate your boundaries. This anger shows up in the way you start setting boundaries. You tend to be uncompassionate, blaming and sloppy in conveying your wishes and preferences to others. For example, a store clerk who is unfortunate enough to snub someone in middle healing may find himself the object of a pointed, threatening speech delivered at high volume in front of other shoppers.

It's not a slam at you when people are rude— it's a slam at the people they've met before.

– F. Scott Fitzgerald

Frequently you don't recognize your own boundaries (or those of others) until after they have been violated. However, your boundaries are clearer to you than ever, which is progress.

When boundaries in the middle stages are not aggressive, they are tentative, apologetic and vague. You may be fearful of hurting others by setting boundaries and can be talked out of them by skillful manipulators.

Middle healing also tends to be characterized by honest confusion about the difference between self-protections (such as rules) and true boundaries. While you are less tempted to make rules about the way other people behave, you aren't always sure when you are setting a boundary and when you are simply trying to avoid dealing with a wound. The next chart contrasts the two.

Self-Protections	Boundaries
Result from denying my own wounds	Result from addressing my own wounds
Portray the other as responsible for my pain, so he/she must change	Portray myself as responsible for my pain, so the other is free to make choices
Are full of expectations and blame	Accept the other's choices, even though I know which outcome I'd most prefer
Attempt to shame and control the other	Express compassion and respect for the other
Are confusing and indirect	Are clear and direct
Are rigid and unresponsive	Are flexible and responsive
Diminish the capacity for loving behavior	Enhance the capacity for loving behavior
Feel awful in the long run	Feel liberating, enduring and powerful
Magnify conflict and power struggles	Promote collaborative problem-solving and creative solutions

Boundary-Setting Skills in Advanced Healing

It is in advanced healing that you really make progress in boundary-setting skills.

Early in advanced healing, you begin to set increasingly precise boundaries. As your shame and codependency recede, the quality of your boundaries improves. You feel less guilty about them, even if someone reacts negatively when you set one. In those cases, you begin to feel more and more comfortable allowing the other person to stew for a while; you are less likely to rescue him by giving in and changing your boundary.

However, your boundary-setting still lacks compassion. You are concerned more about how your boundaries affect you than how they affect others. You expect others to take care of their own boundary issues without your participation.

Later in advanced healing, you become more gracious about how you set your boundaries. Boundary-setting that used to be abrasive and unilateral becomes compassionate—but still unilateral.

As your defensiveness and anger begin to melt away, you become genuinely interested in the other person's reactions. Your boundaries are clean, responsible, more flexible and far less self-centered. In setting them, you strive to make or deepen connections with others. You begin to make boundary-setting a shared activity that you perform with an eye toward both of you getting your needs met.

For example, imagine you and your significant other want to spend an evening together. However, one person has been cooped up all day and wants to go to the stock car races, while the other has had a day of driving from one appointment to the next and wants to fall asleep on the couch watching *The Sound of Music*. In middle healing stages, this situation would be a perfect set-up for a standoff, if not a fight. You would both be aware of the importance of getting your needs met and setting firm boundaries so you don't create resentment, but you would not yet have the tools, understanding or self-confidence to get past apparently conflicting needs. In advanced healing stages, you work together to find something you can both do that meets the mutual need to spend time together *and* do something entertaining. This is not the same as compromise, in which each party sacrifices something and usually ends up feeling mutually ripped off. The mutual boundary-setting that you learn to do in advanced healing tunnels through superficial issues to underlying, shared intentions. When this happens, no one has to give up having these underlying intentions met, although the form of meeting those intentions may change.

Finally, you become able to honor others' boundaries even when they don't honor their own or yours. This does not mean that you tolerate being abused. You just don't retaliate by responding in kind. For example, the rude store clerk from a couple of pages ago would not receive the tongue-lashing we described if he snubbed someone in advanced stages of healing.

Rudeness is the weak man's imitation of strength.

— Eric Hoffer

Someone with advanced boundary-setting skills would certainly state his preferences and his objections. But while firm, the statement is likely to be calm and respectful.

We found a good example of the way people deal with boundaries at different stages of healing in Bonnie's story. Bonnie is a pretty thirty-two-year-old brunette who feels unattractive. At a birthday party a while ago, she was part of a group in which two male friends were discussing a woman they had met, also named Bonnie, whom they considered to be quite a knockout. One of the group said, "This Bonnie?" and pointed to our Bonnie. The men said, "Oh no, we're talking about *gorgeous* Bonnie."

Our Bonnie was understandably embarrassed and hurt by the remark. After the party, she expressed her pain to friends and connected her reaction to a childhood in which she was constantly compared to her more beautiful sisters. Later she spoke to the men[17] who had drawn the comparison with "gorgeous" Bonnie. "You should have been more sensitive," she said. "You shouldn't make remarks like that."

Obviously, her boundaries were clear. However, she expressed them in terms of what she thought the men should or shouldn't have done, which almost always sets the stage for shaming and power struggles.

Bonnie is in the early middle stages of healing. A year before, the same incident might have left her feeling ashamed and angry but unclear about her feelings and what triggered them. She probably would have felt humiliated, but pretended not to feel anything, and said nothing. A year or two from now, we expect that Bonnie's response to an incident like this one might be to fully accept her reaction to the remarks. She will probably be able to talk to the men about her hurt feelings in a spirit of vulnerability, rather than trying to correct their behavior. She might say, *"I have some deep unhealed wounds about not being pretty enough. Your comments seemed to compare me and 'gorgeous' Bonnie, just the way my family compared me to my sisters. It really hurt, and I would like those kinds of remarks to stop."* And that will bring her closer to healing the wound.

[17] Who were not only fairly close friends, but also fellow travelers on the healing journey. Bonnie knew she could safely talk with these men about her more tender feelings—that they would listen with respect and not laugh at her. Making wise choices about with whom, where and when to be vulnerable is an important aspect of developing healthy boundary-setting skills.

Foundation of Self-Esteem

The effort to maintain your happy-ending fantasy creates a drain on your life energy resources. Releasing your fantasy frees up this energy for other uses. As you spend less time and energy keeping your happy-ending fantasy alive, you have more time and energy to spend on your home and career and your reliability and effectiveness in the workaday world.

Initially, the foundation of your sense of self-esteem is tied to your performance, especially the way you perceive your success at meeting the prerequisites and following the rules of your survival plan.

As you heal, it shifts to your sense of personal competence—the abilities you know you possess, whether or not your performance on a given day demonstrates them.

> *personal competence*—How well you manage your time and energy to express your authentic self; your level of personal effectiveness in creating your home, career, financial picture, method of self-expression, etc., that reflect who you truly are.

Still later, you begin to value yourself for your ability to have your feelings without fear. Gradually, your self-esteem becomes rooted more deeply in your character—who you know yourself to be at the core of your being, regardless of what you can or cannot do.

Foundation of Self-Esteem in Pre-Healing

Pre-healing, self-esteem is derived through how well you execute the terms of your survival plan. For example, if one of the rules of your survival plan is *A worthwhile person makes a good living*, you may feel good about yourself because you make enough money to support your family. If one of your rules pertains to the value of loyalty, you may derive self-esteem from the fact that you have never committed adultery. If your inner critic tells you that self-sufficiency is the measure of a worthwhile person, you may take pride in your independence.

All of these are important, laudable values. However, as the foundation for your sense of self-esteem and personal competence, they are of limited value in helping you deal with many of life's challenges. In the face of pressing family problems or unexpected bills, you may be haunted by unfounded fears that you are not doing enough to earn your right to be alive, or frustrated that everything you can do will not solve the problems. If deprived of your ability to meet the conditions laid down by your inner critic—by a layoff, injury or illness, for example—you may lose your sense of self-worth entirely.

Foundation of Self-Esteem in Early Healing

Early in healing, your sense of self-esteem is largely non-existent—a result of finally acknowledging your unhealed wounds and their damaging effects on your life. You're likely to spend at least part of your early healing feeling like a failure. This is a normal part of recovery. Later in the early stages you'll get a taste of hope and beginnings of true humility.

As you begin to take responsibility for your own healing, you start managing the basics of your new life. You show up at self-help group meetings or therapy, or both. You restructure how you spend your time and energy to reflect your new commitment to healing. If you are a recovering addict, you maintain your abstinence, whether that means staying sober, calling a friend instead of your former boy/girlfriend or eating three meals a day at specific times. A new sense of self-esteem emerges, based on your ability and willingness to commit to your own healing.

Foundation of Self-Esteem in Middle Healing

In the middle stages, you expand your notions of your personal competence by taking new emotional risks. You try new ways of communicating or setting boundaries, or start speaking up more at your meetings. Your effort to change is now conscious. You develop the self-discipline to sweat out the uncomfortable feelings that come up. With each risk you take, your self-esteem grows. You become more confident in your own character, and begin to believe that you can trust yourself to choose growth over self-protection.

However, one especially difficult event of middle healing invariably vaporizes your new-found self-esteem: uncovering your core wounds. This new and devastatingly painful low is temporary, however. Paradoxical as it may seem, completing this work is precisely what builds self-esteem better than anything else.

By the end of the middle stages of healing, you no longer fear your wounds; you fully trust your ability to heal.

Foundation of Self-Esteem in Advanced Healing

People in advanced stages of healing almost can't help but develop a passion to manifest their potential. It is not unusual to see people change careers, go back to school, start businesses or begin that novel they always wanted to write. Their desire finally overcomes their fear. (The fear is still there, but they are less controlled by it.)

If your happy-ending fantasy tells you to expect people to leave you if you become successful, you deal with that now. Similarly, you begin to express yourself in other aspects of your life; being authentic comes more and more naturally.

Another source of self-esteem is your growing ability to resolve conflict with others. Consequently, you come to view conflict as an opportunity to build bridges rather than an indication that someone failed at something.

In later stages of advanced healing, you begin to base your self-esteem on how well you can extend love to others—even to people who are attacking you—without being self-destructive. Jesus and Gandhi are good examples of people whose self-esteem was probably founded in their ability to remain loving, even in the face of attack. (However, having compassion does not mean you fail to take action to avoid being abused or to prevent others from being abused.)

Investment in Victimhood

As you heal, you release your need to see yourself as the victim of other people, your feelings, or the circumstances of your life. You begin to whine less, the phrase *I choose* gradually replaces *I can't* and forgiveness replaces resentment against those who harmed you.

The commitment to victimhood is insidious. At first blush, most people say emphatically (and with a certain amount of indignation) that they are not victims. However, we believe that we are all very much more invested in our suffering than most of us are willing to admit. Many of us actually derive a sense of comfort from the familiarity of suffering and feeling we can't do anything about it.

It may be hell, but it's home.

— Anonymous

If you begin to see yourself as you read the next few pages, please know that you are in good company, and please abstain from shaming yourself. It takes great courage—and is tremendously liberating—to just acknowledge your attachment to suffering.

Investment in Victimhood in Pre-Healing

You are fully invested in victimhood, making victims of others, or both. Others may accuse you of whining a lot. You may believe that your parents ruined your life. You may think that your life would be wonderful *if only* your spouse would quit drinking, or *if only* your boss weren't such a jerk, or *if only* the administration were run by Republicans/Democrats again. You may be baffled by the way your life is turning out, since you are convinced either that your childhood was idyllic, that you have completely overcome (usually through willpower) the disadvantages of your upbringing or that the past has no bearing on your actions today.

Your attitude in pre-healing is likely to be *"I can't get on with my life until I get that which was denied me."* If so, you are addicted to the righteousness of your position: you would rather prove to the world that you were hopelessly damaged than feel your grief and get it over with. (This is partly because you simply don't yet know how to feel your grief.)

Investment in Victimhood in Early Healing

In the early stages of healing, you become willing to consider the possibility that you have been living as a victim and that there may be another way to live. In fact, life as a non-victim begins to look quite appealing. You can imagine a rosy future. At this point, you are no longer the victim of your primary anesthesias, although you may experience some slips.

However, most of your dysfunctional patterns (and some of your secondary anesthesias) are still in place, and they soon reclaim for you your sense of being a victim. You still function as a victim of your own feelings (especially of your fear of your own issues) and as the victim of other people and of certain situations. You tend to talk incessantly about your feelings, the people or the situations.

You also tend to be victimized by false hopelessness, if that is how you have constructed your survival plan. If your underlying belief is something like, *"You can't expect to be happy in this life; this is as good as it gets,"* you will see no solutions except to figure out what other people expect of you and then trying to meet their expectations.

When someone criticizes you, your reactions have the power to ruin your day. You are likely to continue to stay in abusive relationships, if that is your pattern, nurturing the hope that he or she will change. If you hate your job, you are likely to stay anyway, feeling trapped and hopeless. Your tendency is to shrug and say, *"That's just the way it is."*

Investment in Victimhood in Middle Healing

In early middle healing, you become more aware than ever before of your tendencies to feel like a victim. You learn to keep company with those feelings. However, you still lay the responsibility for them at the feet of other people and events. It is at this point also that you begin to be aware of the part you play in victimizing others, and begin to feel remorseful about it.

In late middle healing, you do the emotional work that gives you the power to finally stop living as a victim. You go deep into your wounds and begin the transition from blame to forgiveness. You begin to distinguish between how you were victimized as a child and the patterns you maintain to keep yourself victimized now. You begin to acknowledge the damage you have done to others out of your wounds.

Investment in Victimhood in Advanced Healing

Advanced healing represents the end of your role as victim. You begin to exercise the power you claimed in middle healing by delving into your wounds. You no longer feel like a victim of your past; in fact, the very idea of victimhood bores you. You find it easy to make amends for damage you have done. You are no longer being run by your happy-ending fantasy, and now feel comfortable letting go of its remnants. You occasionally succumb to the temptation to blame or feel sorry for yourself, but move out of it quickly and cheerfully. You release the need to prove to others that they have damaged you. You have moved from an attitude of *"I'm a hurt person and you are responsible,"* to *"You did this to me back then, but I am responsible for who I am today."*

In late stages of advanced healing, you take your sense of freedom and self-responsibility out into the world at large. You are able to fight for the rights of people who are being victimized without blaming anyone.

Who's In Charge?

The Personal Power Indicators:
- **Boundary-Setting Skills**
- **Foundation of Self-Esteem**
- **Level of Investment in Victimhood**

1. To whom or what do you tend to give your personal power?

2. Who sets your boundaries for you, and according to what internal rules you carry? What incidents in your life have illustrated your boundary-setting skills?

3. On what do you base your self-esteem?

4. How invested are you in victimhood? Who or what victimizes you? To whom or to what situations do you lose your peace of mind?

5. How could you increase your levels of self-responsibility in these areas? What would you stand to lose by doing so? What would you stand to gain?

FOURTEEN

The Connection Indicators: How Do You Join?

> We meet ourselves time and again in a thousand
> disguises on the paths of life.
>
> — Carl Jung

THE CONNECTION INDICATORS reveal how you join—or avoid joining—with your self, with other people and with your spiritual resources. All these relationships are profoundly affected by your level of self-responsibility.

Attitude Toward Unfinished Business

unfinished business—An emotional or logistical loose end; an incomplete. Unfinished business results when we leave a situation without a sense of peace about the adequacy of our actions in that situation. *Alcoholics Anonymous,* the bible of A.A., calls unfinished business "the wreckage of our past."

Not every unfinished project constitutes a piece of unfinished business. Unfinished business consists of those projects left undone because of your own blocks, not because they are still in the process of being completed. The key to determining an unfinished project's status is how you feel about it. If thinking about an unfinished project makes you feel anxious, tense or irritable, it counts as unfinished business. If the emotional weight of an unfinished project prevents you from doing things in the here-and-now, it's unfinished business.

As you heal, you become less and less comfortable with these "incompletes." You stop blaming your unhappiness on seemingly external factors that are actually within your control. *I really can't start therapy until I get this house organized; I wouldn't drink if I weren't so depressed; I can't look for a better job until I fix the car, because how would I get to an interview?, and I can't afford to fix the car* are all incompletes. As you become more and more self-responsible, you gradually lose these false prerequisites to happiness. You learn to be happy while you're in the process of completing tasks. You no longer believe that you must wait for them to be done before you can be happy; the ones you know you'll never finish, you unload—physically, emotionally or both.

Attitude Toward Unfinished Business in Pre-Healing

Unfinished business is abundant at this stage. You are far more comfortable living with incompletes than you are with the honest confrontations that would allow you to put them to rest. Your incompletes can be as innocuous as unfinished crafts projects or as overwhelming as unpaid debts or unresolved conflicts with relatives or former friends.

Attitude Toward Unfinished Business in Early Healing

As they begin the healing process, many people are overwhelmed by the sheer number of incompletes in their lives. They tend to freeze in confusion, indecision and fear. We usually suggest that they simply choose the biggest, most ruinous incomplete to deal with, then deliberately put all other, non-emergency incompletes on hold. This advice is based on the 80-20 rule: twenty percent of our incompletes cause eighty percent of our anxiety.

Later, in middle healing, they begin to address other debilitating incompletes one by one.

For example, when Marsha, a widow, came to see Rebecca, she was faced with a long, intimidating list of crises. Her twenty-four-year-old son had suffered permanent brain damage in a motorcycle accident. Marsha needed to make a decision about placing him in a special home. Her car was headed for a brake job, but she thought it might be better to trade the car in on a newer model. Her relationship with her boyfriend was rocky and she couldn't decide whether to break up with him or stick it out. She was unhappy with her job. She had begun binge eating late at night when she couldn't sleep and consequently had put on thirty-five pounds she wanted to lose. Her teenage daughter was dating a boy Marsha didn't trust, both dogs needed their annual shots and she had recently noticed a suspicious-looking mole on her calf.

Rebecca asked Marsha to write down all these claims on her attention. After she discussed her list with Rebecca, Marsha used the 80-20 rule to decide to concentrate on dealing with her mole and her binge eating and getting her son into a good group home. Later, she assigned priorities to the other issues, and placed some of them on the back burner. While they were all important, most of them didn't hamper Marsha's essential commitment to healing, so they could safely be deferred until a later time.

Attitude Toward Unfinished Business in Middle Healing

In the middle healing stages, you learn to deal with small emotional incompletes as they come up. This means that if a friend says something that hurts your feelings, you say so, rather than trying to let it go. In this way, not only are you keeping your friendship free of trust-eroding emotional baggage, but you are also training for bigger work to come.

In later middle healing stages, you will deal with large pieces of emotional incompletes—your core wounds. As you begin to deal with them, you'll also begin to address the backlog of emotional incompletes you've amassed over the years.

Attitude Toward Unfinished Business in Advanced Healing

As you enter advanced healing stages, you begin to deal with your backlog of logistical incompletes, from old debts to neglected chores to overflowing closets.

Gradually, you virtually eliminate this backlog, which makes it easier to live in the present. You begin taking care of issues quickly, so you do not create another backlog. Eventually, unfinished business is no longer an issue.

Lupe is a good example of a pre-healing attitude toward incompletes. She loves to sew. She used to have time to sew all her clothes, but gradually the demands of career and family and other interests made it impossible to find the time. Lupe continues to buy fabric and patterns, however. They're stacked up on the top shelf of a closet, and every time she looks at the boxes and bags from the fabric store, she feels irritated and anxious. Lupe's sewing projects are incompletes—millstones around her neck that sap her energy and joy and keep her from starting other new projects.

Lupe's friend Andrew has reached an advanced-healing attitude toward his unfinished projects. Andrew also enjoys a hobby—woodworking. He has several projects stored on shelves in his garage in various states of completion. But when Andrew looks at these bits of birdhouses, stools and cabinets, he feels excited about his next woodworking session. Several weekends a year, the rest of his family goes camping or skiing and Andrew stays home. He chooses a project and spends the entire weekend working on it. These times are a source of joy and replenishment for him. Andrew has found a way to accept the pace at which he can work on his projects. He thinks of his woodworking projects as works in progress.

Mission in Life

mission—Your prime motive; the driving force in
your life; your special task or calling.

What motivates a person is usually clear to the careful
observer. Your main motivator indicates whether you are committed to sustaining your happy-ending fantasy or have become
willing to heal your wounds. It represents your willingness to
join with or avoid your true needs, desires, talents and abilities.

Mission in Pre-Healing

At this point in life, your number-one priority is to avoid pain.
This means keeping your survival plan together no matter what
it takes, by maintaining your addictions or anesthesia use,
following your inner critic's rules and never questioning your
happy-ending fantasy. For some people, the mission is just to
make it through another day.

Nothing can deter you from your mission. If your spouse
threatens to leave if you don't quit gambling away the rent
money, you might agree to go to counseling, but you won't
stop gambling. Instead, you will try to hide it more efficiently
(a classic window of willingness).

Mission in Early Healing

Before you can do anything about your wounds, you have to
acknowledge they are there, seek help to heal them and arrange
your life so healing can take place. That's the early healing
mission: setting the stage for changing your life. For an addict,
this means going to support-group meetings and developing a
new group of non-addict friends. For others, it may mean
entering therapy, attending seminars in life-changing topics,
taking classes, or getting financial advice—anything that provides
a new structure and new input about a way to live life beyond
your survival plan.

This change in mission requires real effort. You must resist the survival plan imperative to simply do more of the things that didn't work before.

Mission in Middle Healing

Your mission in the middle stages is to learn how to feel your feelings. Later in middle healing, when you enter for the first time the most painful period of the healing process (healing core wounds) your mission is simply to survive the pain that confronting your inner forbidden territory brings, without returning to your anesthesias. (On return visits to heal other core wounds, you know that you will survive, so your mission becomes, once again, to feel the feelings. We'll talk more about this core wound stage in Sections III and IV.)

Mission in Advanced Healing

The life mission of a person in advanced healing centers on developing the self, then on deepening relationships with others, then on a deepening relationship with a power greater than the self.

In advanced healing, you periodically return to middle-healing stages as you continue to heal your core wounds. As we explained above, your mission on these return visits is no longer to simply survive the pain, but to feel the feelings. When you finish with a piece of middle-stages work, your mission becomes, once again, an advanced-healing mission.

Frequently people in advanced healing develop a sense of something special they want to do for the world, or at least some small portion of the world. When this happens, it becomes an important part of the person's mission in life.

Quality of Relationships

The character of your relationships changes dramatically as you become more self-responsible. Quality of relationships is a nearly foolproof indicator of healing, especially when you look at relationships with your primary significant others—boyfriends, girlfriends, family members and spouses. (All relationships, however, reflect your level of healing to some extent, even the most platonic friendships.) In fact, our experience as therapists has taught us that quality of relationships is the best indicator of level of healing and self-responsibility.

Taking responsibility for your own feelings and happiness allows your relationships to grow and allows you to grow in them. This does *not* mean that you have to have a good relationship with someone who is abusive or unwilling. It does mean that you learn to maintain your inner peace even when the other person doesn't change.

Relationships in Pre-Healing

Your relationships are more dysfunctional than functional. You may fight or argue a lot without resolving anything. In fact, you are clueless about the real issues. You may think that the fight this weekend, for example, really *is* about wet towels on the bathroom floor. You may notice repeating patterns in your relationship, but you feel helpless to do anything about them.

Especially in romantic relationships, sex role differences (*"I'm this way because I'm female, and you are that way because you are male"*) are very important at this stage. We use them as defenses and rationalizations for our behavior. People in dysfunctional relationships rely on sex-role differences the way non-self-responsible people rely on rules instead of boundaries.

Relationships in Early Healing

In the early stages of healing, you are focused almost exclusively on getting your new life stabilized and developing plans to deal with problems before they become crises. As a result, you usually don't have much energy to devote to romantic relationships and may feel scattered and divided when you try to have one.

At first, some relationships are infused with new hope as one or both people become willing to heal and seek help. However, this hope is quickly replaced by disappointment as you realize that the progress you make in early healing isn't enough to solve the problems, and there is still much work to be done.

Even in later stages of early healing, relationship skills (such as setting clean boundaries) are almost non-existent. You may find some relief in being able to take time-outs for the first time, and abstinence from addictive processes and substances certainly takes a lot of heat off the relationship. However, things haven't changed much since your pre-healing days.

In romantic relationships, people still use sex-role differences in much the same way they used them pre-healing.

In Alcoholics Anonymous, newcomers are advised to avoid romantic relationships for the first year of sobriety. Human nature being what it is, practically no one follows this advice. Even though we do believe it is a good idea to focus on yourself in that first year, we think better advice is: stay sober no matter whom you become involved with, treat your relationships as learning experiences and don't wallow in guilt.

Relationships in Middle Healing

Relationships are still difficult during the middle stages. However, you are beginning to figure out how to work conflicts out, and have begun to learn the importance of expressing appreciation and abstaining from criticism. You are better at expressing your feelings, although you tend to do it in a blaming way, which starts a lot of fights. You experience frequent breakups. For the first time, you understand how frightening it is to be as vulnerable emotionally as you need to be to build intimacy and heal your wounds. If you choose to risk being this vulnerable, your relationships are characterized by productive struggle and by more and more frequent glimpses of what relationships can be.

Later in middle healing stages, your primary relationship is threatened all over again while one or both of you begin to heal core wounds. It is at this point that many people learn their relationships are built upon self-protections they developed to shield them from the pain of these wounds. They realize that losing the self-protections and healing the wounds eliminate the foundation for the relationship. They are faced with a decision: end the relationship, stay in and build a new one (assuming the other partner is willing) or stay in and accept a low level of intimacy.

It is also at this point that people start to realize that their relationships were built upon a contract to protect each other from their wounds. Under this contract, this protection is synonymous with love; not protecting your partner from his/her wounds is called abandonment or at least uncaring behavior.

The use of sex-role differences in romantic relationships does not change from early healing.

Relationships in Advanced Healing

Partners—romantic or otherwise—who make it through the difficult territory of middle healing find tremendous excitement in the work of advanced healing.

As boundary-setting abilities improve, autonomy becomes an issue. You take joy in creating a new contract for a relationship built on trust and healing rather than on wounds.

You feel powerful in your ability and commitment to work out all conflicts. You no longer place any hope in conflicts blowing over. In fact, you gradually lose your fear of conflict and begin to see it as a gift to your relationship—an opportunity to build even deeper trust and heal even more wounds. Conflicts become opportunities for growth and for practicing understanding and compassion.

You now view relationships for what they are: projections of your own reality. This means that you take full responsibility for your own remaining unhealed wounds and the power they have to influence your perceptions and expectations. For example, when Dennis entered advanced healing, he began to clearly see the influence of unhealed wounds on his relationships with his wife, Becky. Dennis was wounded by his mother's harsh perfectionism and fault-finding. He was committed to healing his wounds, and had made a great deal of progress. But he realized that, until they were gone, he would still to tend to hear his mother's criticisms from Becky—even when they weren't there. As a result, Dennis was able to take a step back from his reactions, calm himself down, separate his wounds from what was currently happening between him and his wife and work his conflicts through with Becky.

Your relationships are characterized by a mutual understanding of the spiritual nature of your joining, and a sense of shared mission.

Early in advanced healing stages, as you discover autonomy, you each celebrate your emerging uniqueness. In romantic relationships, you begin to view sex-role differences as a strength and something to celebrate, rather than as a defense.

For example, as Jim entered advanced healing, he began to counter his girlfriend's requests for tenderness in their sex life with an insistence that, as a male, he needed and excelled at playful, animalistic sex—not the romantic, sweet sex Jackie tended to crave.

Of course, sex role differences are played out in all aspects of life, not just the bedroom. They influence everything from decisions about who takes out the trash to who makes travel reservations. A common division in sex roles in our culture is between problem-solving skills and bonding skills; men tend to take on the former and women the latter. In advanced healing levels, many women who had felt apologetic for their bonding skills begin to take pride in them. Men tend to become more matter-of-fact about their problem-solving abilities and start figuring out how to be better at bonding without losing their masculinity.

Later in advanced healing stages, the importance of sex role differences fades. People don't abandon their uniqueness, but find that blending their uniqueness becomes more important. The more balanced their male and female energies are, the more whole they feel, and the more they are able to join in their relationships without fear of being consumed.

For example, when Jim reached more advanced healing stages, he began to see that Jackie's archetypically feminine approach held treasure for him. Without abandoning his preference for (and skills at) wild, steamy sex, he began learning and appreciating Jackie's ways. His openness to her guidance allowed Jackie to drop her own defenses and learn from Jim as well. They each moved from, at best, simply tolerating each other's preferences to a willing exploration of each other's territory.

We compare this healthy merging to a popular ritual used in many modern wedding ceremonies. In this practice, the bride and groom each carry a lighted candle to the altar, where they use their two candles to light another, larger candle. Then they place their candles, still burning, beside the new one. This symbolizes the way their lives, without extinguishing themselves, join to create a greater life—a perfect picture of relationships in advanced healing.

Man is born broken. He lives by mending. And the grace of God is the glue.

— Eugene O'Neill

Quality of Relationship with Your Spiritual Resources

At the core of your spiritual resources is what we call your Higher Power.

> ***Higher Power***—A core frame of reference through which you interpret events and make choices; an advisor; the force and logic behind your spiritual resources.

One of our groups defined Higher Power as a *binding force that ties me to that which is larger than me, of which I am a part.* There are many synonyms for Higher Power; refer to the first footnote in this book for a partial list. In this section, we will use Higher Power, which is one of our personal favorites, to refer to this core frame of reference.

A Higher Power can be anything—another person, a group, an inanimate object, a substance or process, an idea. We all have one, even if we don't believe in a deity. How you view your Higher Power—as loving, murderous, indifferent, absent—

depends on which of your wounds remain unhealed. As people become more self-responsible, they tend to adopt a Higher Power that reflects a more loving, more joyful life.

Spiritual Resources in Pre-Healing

Your Higher Power consists of your anesthesias and false hopes. It is critic-infested and either provides no sense of caring about you, or provides a highly conditional sense of caring (*Do this and I'll spare you my wrath*). You may feel alone in the universe, very much on your own, and often feel that you are doing battle against malevolent forces. There are no allies in your life.

If you do pray to a deity, you tend to ask for *things*—parking places, jobs, lovers—without taking responsibility for all the blocks you use to deflect the help of a Higher Power. Your relationship with your Higher Power is characterized by fear, anger, distrust, guilt, paranoia, grievances (*You didn't come through for me with that promotion, God!*) and projection. For example, if you are vengeful and blaming—or your parents or childhood clergy were—you imagine your Higher Power is, too.

Spiritual Resources in Early Healing

For most people in the early stages, the principles and effort of getting a new life into place is their new Higher Power. For example, their Higher Power might be simply the belief that there is a better way. Their relationship with their Higher Power is marked at times by desperation and at other times by hope. Usually by this point, they have tried everything they can think of to get their lives into shape, and are out of ideas. The possibility of a relationship with a Higher Power is, for people in early healing, a court of last resort.

People begin to take responsibility for the first of their blocks between them and their Higher Power in these early stages. They spend less time asking for things and more time asking for help in maintaining their new life. Because they have taken a chance on healing, they are beginning to change their ideas about the Higher Power they created. Their attitude is cautiously optimistic. They think there might be the possibility of establish-

Personally, I am overwhelmed by the spiritual evidence of a greater intellect. Call it God, but a word is just a direction and so utterly inadequate to capture the meaning of this one hundred percent efficient, eternally unlimited integrity.

— Buckminster Fuller

ing some kind of diplomatic relationship with this Higher Power. This relationship is marked by an attitude of bargaining: *Okay, I'll learn to meditate (or go to church, or join A.A., or have a daily quiet time) if you will please just help me change my life.*

Spiritual Resources in Middle Healing

In middle healing, you begin to trust and even like your Higher Power, often for the first time. Your perception of your Higher Power shifts. Where it was once heavily influenced by your inner critic, it now begins to be influenced more by your feelings, or what some call your inner child. The relationship is marked by a tentative—and rather surprised—trust.

Because you are more willing to find a personally meaningful way to pray, you are more willing to pray. If this is not your first experience with prayer, you find at this stage that your prayers change. Paradoxically, you begin asking for *more*, but in *less specific terms*. Instead of creating a wish list for your Higher Power to fill, you tend to pray that your life fulfills the will of a loving Higher Power. You are excited about the possibilities of this relationship, about which you feel less fearful and more curious, inspired and positive.

Later in middle healing, when you come to the difficult work of healing your core wounds, you may for the first time confront a hatred and resentment of God that you didn't know you carried. This is the time when you are most likely to resolve these feelings. Ironically, you will probably lean more heavily than ever on your Higher Power to get through this work.

By the end of middle healing, this trust deepens. Your Higher Power becomes your certainty that you will be better off for having gone through your pain to heal your wounds.

Spiritual Resources in Advanced Healing

In advanced healing stages, you begin to see your Higher Power as a truly beneficent, loving presence that you can connect with in order to discover the gifts in all situations—even the most tragic.

It is self-evident that a belief in a super-meaning —whether as a meta-physical concept or in the religious sense of Provi-dence—is of the foremost psychotherapeutic and psychohygienic impor-tance. As a genuine father springing from inner strength, such a belief adds immeasurably to human vitality. To such faith there is, ultimately, nothing that is meaningless.

— Victor Frankl

Your relationship with your Higher Power is now characterized by love and a feeling of partnership. Where you were once paranoid, you are now "pro-noid": you have a sneaking suspicion that everyone in the world (consciously or not) is conspiring to help you. Your wishes and prayers are nearly always along the order of *"help me learn to love better."* You begin to live in gratitude.

Ultimately, you see all of your life as an opportunity to become better at loving. You see your relationship with your primary other as a purifying force that brings you both closer to your Higher Power; you see the world as a place to love and to demonstrate the love of your Higher Power.

In Section III, you'll find out precisely where you stand in terms of these indicators of self-responsibility, and how to make your healing journey successful by creating a road map based on the Seven Stages of Personal Healing.

EXERCISES
How Do You Join?

The Connection Indicators:
- **Attitude Toward Unfinished Business**
- **Mission in Life**
- **Quality of Relationships**
- **Quality of Relationship with Your Spiritual Resources**

1. How do you connect with yourself, with others and with your spiritual resources?

2. What incidents in your life have illustrated your willingness and ability to connect? How did these incidents reflect your level of self-responsibility?

3. How could you increase your levels of self-responsibility in these areas? What would you stand to lose by doing so?

4. What would you stand to gain?

The Seven Stages of Personal Healing

The Seven Stages
of Personal Healing

What is the most rigorous law of our being? Growth.
No smallest atom of our moral, mental or physical
structure can stand still a year. It grows—
it must grow; nothing can prevent it.
— Mark Twain

THE INFORMATION IN THIS SECTION provides you with the tools you need to take charge of your own healing.

In it, we describe the Seven Stages of Personal Healing, show you how to determine where you are now in your healing journey, explain why you should consider a healing plan and show you how to create one for yourself. The stream spirit, whom you met in Section I, returns in this section to show you how the healing journey proceeds.

FIFTEEN

An Overview of The Seven Stages

A stage has a new configuration of past and future,
a new combination of drive and defense, a new set
of capacities fit for a new setting of tasks and
opportunities, a new and wider radius of significant
encounters.

– Erik Erikson

WHEN THEIR SURVIVAL PLANS start to crumble, people who choose to answer their wake-up calls (a distinct minority) begin to follow a specific healing sequence. We noticed this sequence years ago, and began calling it The Seven Stages of Personal Healing. In this chapter, we briefly describe each of the Seven Stages and provide some metaphors for the concept that our clients and friends have found useful.

What Are the Seven Stages?

The Seven Stages of Personal Healing describe the process by which people attain high-level healing. The stages have probably existed for as long as people have searched for themselves.

The stages are not rules. They don't describe what ought to happen or what people should do. They simply describe what happens when people heal.

Each stage provides the foundation for the next. Your success with the tasks in each stage depends on your work in the preceding stages. The fastest way to heal, then, is to thoroughly complete each stage, in sequence, at the pace determined by your inner child's ability to feel emotionally safe. Anything else will leave you feeling scattered and frustrated. Learning about the stages of healing and the tools for completing each stage can help you stay focused and effective in your healing activities.

Progress through the stages occurs in a smooth, easy, natural and organic flow. You do not have to willpower your way through. Doing thorough, effective work in one stage inevitably propels you into the next.

For example, the more you loosen your inner critic's hold over you and develop a solid relationship with your feelings (Stage Three tasks), the more you will remember about your wounding. You will spontaneously recapture forgotten memories, images and body sensations and have dreams about unresolved experiences—all signs that you are moving into Stage Four: Healing.

Healing proceeds through the Seven Stages as described below.

*We become willing to find a way to live that's better for us than our survival plan. This is **Stage One: Willingness**.*

*As Our survival plan continues to deteriorate, we stabilize our lives and restructure our daily activities so we can do the work we need to do. We abstain from our principal anesthesias, move our basic physical health back on track, develop a support system that facilitates our choice to heal, and adopt daily introspection habits. This is **Stage Two: Foundation**.*

We develop the basic psychological tools and spiritual resources we need to face, and free ourselves from, our unhealed wounds. We learn to recognize and deal with our inner critic. We learn how to recognize, work with and resolve all of our feelings. We develop a relationship with the part of us that guards the feelings we hate and fear the most. This is **Stage Three: Feelings**.

Now properly equipped, we face and heal the core wounds our survival plan helped us avoid. We go into our inner forbidden territory and put to rest the issues that have haunted us for so long, prevented us from being who we are and blocked us from living the life we've wanted to live. This is **Stage Four: Healing**.

Freed from the shackles of a good chunk of these core wounds, we develop a new sense of self and spirituality based on who we really are, rather than on who our survival plan required us to be. We bask in the light of new-found self-esteem and personal power, and restructure our lives in ways that reflect who we are. We realize that our remaining unfinished business will continue to surface for a long time to come, but now we're confident that we can not only survive the pain, but benefit from facing these issues. This is **Stage Five: Rebirth**.

Having become more fully ourselves, we are now able to build and sustain relationships with others and with our spiritual resources in a far deeper and more durable way than ever before. We feel self-supporting and lovable for who we are at the very core. Because of this, we can achieve depths of intimacy that we've always wanted—or never knew we wanted. We know our relationships will expose every last wound we still carry. We are confident in our ability to heal these issues, and know that further healing will lead to even deeper relationships. This is **Stage Six: Clear-Hearted Relationships**.

Our motivation to give to others now springs from our authenticity, inner fullness and capacity to love—rather than from our unhealed wounds, neediness and self-protections. We are now able to leave the world a much better place than we found it. We can fulfill our calling in life with inner grace and compassion, without feeling attached to the outcome. This *leaves us free to contribute to the betterment of others even when feathers are ruffled in the process. This is **Stage Seven: Clear-Hearted Service**.*

Let's take a look at some of the ways people think of the Seven Stages.

Map, Business, Pyramid, House

Many of our clients think of healing as a journey that takes them from living in their wounds to living in love. If you have reached true willingness, you are ready to begin. There you are, bags packed, ticket in hand, looking forward to new horizons. As with any trip, before you start, you should probably look at a map, figure out where you are now, familiarize yourself with the territory you want to cross, and read about important landmarks.

Each stage presents you with new terrain; although we each have our unique ways of getting from Point A to Point B, we're moving over the same general territory. The Seven Stages of Personal Healing describe the territory you need to cover and provide clues to what you need to cross it. Just as hiking across a hot, flat desert requires different skills and equipment than crossing mountains or marshland, each stage requires a different kind of effort and new skills from you.

Some people see the healing process as a developing business, and their job is to move up the corporate ladder by learning new skills. Each stage is a promotion; as you advance, you continue to use the skills you have, and add more. Incorporating each new set of skills into your repertory allows you to live more fully as yourself and more fully self-responsible.

Others visualize themselves constructing a pyramid, something like Maslow's hierarchy of needs[18], to replace the old, rickety tripod of the survival plan. In Stage One, they grade the pad. Stage Two places the first layer, Stage Three the next, and so on.

The stability of each new layer of this pyramid depends on the stability of the layer below it. As you work on new layers,

[18] Abraham Maslow (1908-1970) was a psychology professor who arranged human motives in a hierarchy, with basic physical needs (such as those for food and drink) at the bottom and the need for self-fulfillment at the top. Ranked in between, from lower to higher needs, are needs for safety, love, esteem and beauty. For more information about Maslow's theories, see *Toward a Psychology of Being* (New York: Van Nostrand, 1968).

174

you might discover imperfections in a lower level that must be addressed before you can go on. If you try to go on without addressing these imperfections, the stability of your pyramid is threatened.

A variation on this analogy is to see the process as building a house. You can start with the roof timbers if you wish, but you'll make your job longer and more difficult if you do. The easiest, most efficient way to build a house is to start with the foundation. From there, you erect the framing, then the roof, the siding, and so on.

The underlying truth illustrated by all these metaphors is that people tend to heal their wounds in a particular sequence. Knowing this can help you figure out where you are. If you know where you are, you can identify the challenges that face you and equip yourself to meet them each step of the way.

In the next three chapters, we give you a tour of the Seven Stages. Later, in Section IV, you'll take a closer, more detailed look at each of the stages.

SIXTEEN

Early Healing

> A new philosophy, a new way of life, is not given for
> nothing. It has to be paid dearly for and only acquired
> with much patience and great effort.
>
> – Fyodor Dostoyevsky

EARLY HEALING IS LARGELY A MATTER of introducing yourself to a new way of living. For the first time, your mission in life is something other than avoiding pain; you focus on changing your life and then on stabilizing yourself in your new life.

Stage One: Willingness

§ § §

> THE STREAM SPIRIT *couldn't get his friends'*
> *sparkling river out of his mind. Over and over, he*
> *replayed his memories of the fish glinting below*
> *the surface, the glimpses of furry animals*
> *scurrying through the woods, the birds and*

squirrels squeaking and chattering among the branches of trees that seemed to reach the clouds. His friends had said the stream spirit's own land could look the same. Could it be true?

He gazed at the sleepberries in his hand. They were the last of the harvest. The sleepberry bushes were doing well, and there would be more fruit in a matter of weeks, but for now these were all he had. His new friends said he would have to give up the sleepberries if he were going to turn his land into a garden.

"At this point," he said aloud, "it's not much of a sacrifice; they don't work anymore, no matter how many I eat."

But he knew that it would be a sacrifice to be without anything to relieve the monotony and the pain of life in his barren desert. The stream spirit shuddered and closed his eyes in a grimace. When he opened them again, he looked around the grim landscape that surrounded him. The yearning he felt for the sleepberry-induced numbness was a twisting pain in his belly. He brought the berries to his lips. An image of the sparkling river danced in his mind, as if taunting him for the barrenness of his own lands.

In rage and despair, he stood and threw the handful of sleepberries out into the stream bed.

"It's not worth it!" he shouted. "I'll do anything—ANYTHING—to make this land look like a garden again!"

In Stage One, you finally answer the wake-up call. You become willing to go to any lengths to heal your wounds. For the first time, your intentions, your readiness and your actions line up to make healing your top priority.

Often this is a very brief stage, lasting only as long as it takes you to make a commitment to Stage Two.

Stage Two: Foundation

"Congratulations," said a voice.

Startled, the stream spirit looked around. There stood his two new friends, smiling warmly at him.

"When did you get here?" the stream spirit asked. "I didn't see you coming."

"Oh, just recently," said the first one. "Now, what was that you were saying about doing anything to pull this place back into shape?"

The three began to talk, and they talked late into the night. They talked all the next day, too. By the time his friends left, the stream spirit had a plan. His friends knew about good food he could find right there in his own lands, and they suggested he visit them regularly, so he wouldn't forget what kind of garden he was aiming for. They gave him a packet of seeds to plant, with instructions for watering and weeding. He had to get up early each morning to tend them, and to do that he had to go to bed on time each night, eat well during the day, and get some exercise.

If he followed this advice carefully, his friends said, he would be on the road to making his new garden a reality.

In Stage Two, you build a foundation for your healing by beginning to put your willingness into action. You get your life stabilized so you can pay attention to your healing work. You begin to abstain from your primary addictions or compulsions.

Stage Two healing tasks fall into four categories: Physical, Spiritual, Social, and Daily Life. Moving into middle healing depends on successfully completing these tasks. The list below briefly describes each of these categories. For more detailed information, see Section IV.

The choice to cultivate our greater possibilities is ours, not God's.... There will be no further human development unless some of us work to realize it.

— Michael Murphy

- **Physical**—Neglected physical problems can undermine all your efforts at emotional healing. If you have undiagnosed or untreated disorders—diabetes, chronic clinical depression, allergies—now is the time to get help in getting them under control, or at least mitigating their effects. Equally important to healing emotional wounds are good diet and sleep and adequate exercise.

- **Spiritual**—This category addresses your intangible needs: Play and other creative outlets, educating yourself about healing, spending time alone with yourself and developing a relationship with healing-oriented spiritual resources.

- **Social**—The people in your life can help or hinder your healing work. Tasks in this category include finding good support groups and mentors, and giving attention to your friendships and your relationships with your family.

- **Daily Life**—Logistics, such as financial concerns, chores and time management, can also promote or sabotage your healing process. Your tasks in this category include making sure you are not over-committed, eliminating melodrama from your life and relationships, balancing work with play and spending with saving, and keeping current with home maintenance and errands.

Stage Two work is extremely important to the rest of your healing work. Without a solid foundation of habits that support your healing, you won't make much progress. But with your physical, social, spiritual and daily life practices in order and oriented toward your main priority—healing—you are equipped to handle the process that follows.

SEVENTEEN

Middle Healing

Emotion is not something shameful, subordinate,
second-rate; it is a supremely valid phase of humanity
at its noblest and most mature.

— Joshua Liebman

IN THIS CHAPTER, we describe the middle stages of healing—
Stage Three: Feelings and *Stage Four: Healing*. In these stages, you
are in transition. Your life looks very different than it did while
you were in early healing, but it's clear there is much work left to
be done. You can stop healing after you've stabilized your life and
still have a life that works better than it did before. However, if
you stop here, you will not find the level of joy that awaits you if
you continue. The work you do in these middle healing stages is
critical to your ability to live peacefully and happily.

Stage Three: Feelings

§ § §

ONE DAY, WHEN THE STREAM SPIRIT *was working along the banks of his still foul-smelling reservoir, tending the little green seedlings, he lost his footing and fell in. He came up sputtering and choking, covered with slime. His friends were visiting that day, and they pulled him out.*

"You don't know how to swim yet, do you?" they asked.

The stream spirit scraped slime out of his hair. "I used to swim," he said, "but that was a long time ago. Back when the water was clean. Now I stay out of it."

"Time to get back in," the friends said, chuckling.

The stream spirit stared at them. "Not me," he said. "No way. Things are looking up, life is going to be okay, all I need to do is stick to my schedule, tend the seedlings, and stay off those sleepberries. You know, I'm just getting to where I can sleep all night again!"

*"Fine," the friends said. "You don't **have** to re-learn to swim. But it's the key to bringing this garden back to life."*

They left him alone to think about it. The stream spirit turned the idea over and over in his mind. Now that it was in his mind, he couldn't let it go. What did they mean about swimming being the key? And why was it so important? And wasn't it dangerous to immerse yourself in that stinky, murky water?

On his next visit to his friends' place, the stream spirit made an announcement.

"I've decided I want to learn to swim," he said. "After all, as long as I'm working around

*the reservoir, there's always the danger that I'm
going to fall in, and you two may not always be
there to pull me out. So I'll do it. But you two
have to teach me. Okay?"*

*The friends smiled at each other, and then at
him.*

"Of course we'll teach you," they said.

In Stage Three, you begin to recognize and accept your feelings for what they are—information about *yourself.* You begin to own your feelings, which means you no longer hand off the responsibility for how you feel to events or people. If you shielded yourself from the pain in your life by freezing out your feelings, you thaw them out in Stage Three. If you avoided your pain by allowing your feelings to overwhelm you (for example, wallowing in self-pity or terrorizing yourself with imagined fears), Stage Three is where you begin to take charge of them.

Stage Three work allows you to restore your ability to feel your feelings and grieve your losses, which is crucial for staying away from anesthesias. Without this ability, you will always find some way to shield yourself from pain, even if you give up your primary anesthesia. This is because feelings demand to be addressed one way or another. You can feel them or you can mask them with anesthesias.

It is in Stage Three that people usually learn the form *"I feel
____ when you ____ "* for expressing feelings. However, it isn't until later stages that most people can consistently use this form self-responsibly, in the spirit in which it was developed. Until then, they tend to use it to disguise criticism and blame, bludgeoning others and protesting innocence when confronted (*But
I was only telling you how I feel!*).

However, in Stage Three you begin to give yourself an attitude adjustment regarding pain, and begin to train yourself in self-responsibility. You revise your relationship with your inner critic (which guards the locked door that leads to your feelings) and learn to keep company with your feelings. All of these skills

*Many things you
perceive as nightmares
turn out to be the
process by which you
build a dream.*

– Garth Fagan

prepare you for the painful, difficult work in the Healing Stage (Four).

Because this work takes you into tender feelings and opens up childhood memories, Stage Three work is often referred to as inner child work.

The work of the Willingness Stage (One) and the Foundation Stage (Two) are critical to Stage Three work. To return to the pyramid analogy, scrimping on Willingness and Foundation, then rushing into Feelings, creates a pyramid that will topple, sending you into relapse.

The best and most beautiful things in the world cannot be seen or even touched. They must be felt with the heart.

– Helen Keller

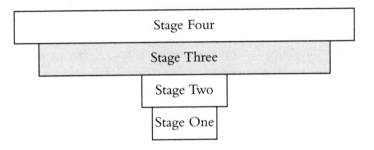

Stage Four: Healing

abyss—A metaphor for feeling your deepest pain—the pain of confronting your happy-ending fantasy and the wounds that made you develop it.

It took many long weeks of practice, but the stream spirit became a strong swimmer.

"You've done well," his friends said. "You've strengthened your muscles and learned the way water works. You don't panic anymore in the water. You can swim from one end of the reservoir to the other without getting winded."

The stream spirit, half-dozing in the sun after his morning workout, smiled. He loved hearing praise from his friends.

"So now you're ready for the most difficult part," said the friends. The stream spirit's eyes flew open.

"What do you mean, 'the most difficult part'?" he said, eyes wide. "Nothing could be more difficult than learning to swim!"

They smiled compassionately. "Yes," they said, "more difficult."

They explained that the stream spirit's land would never be the garden it was meant to be as long as the water was dammed up. Water had to be able to flow for life to come back to the land. That meant the stream spirit had to dismantle the dam.

He looked up at the huge pile of rocks and paled.

"It's too big!" he said. "I could never pull any of those rocks out! And even if I could, the flood would drown me."

His friends pointed out that he had placed the rocks there to begin with. They said his swimming skills would keep him from drowning. And in any case, they insisted, it had to come down.

The stream spirit sighed, thought about the alternatives (there weren't any that he found acceptable), and decided once again to trust his friends. After all, they had been right about everything else so far.

He climbed up to the top of the dam and looked around. A smallish rock lay at his feet. He picked it up and tossed it into the stream bed below, then noticed that a larger rock lay just below, almost hidden by a few more small ones. One by one, he tossed rocks into the stream bed. A tiny trickle of water started down the face of the dam. That was encouraging.

The larger rock below was now nearly exposed. The stream spirit, sweat running into his *eyes, dragged a long branch onto the dam and levered it under the rock. He pushed and sweated and changed position. He stopped to catch his breath and congratulated himself for learning to swim; without that conditioning, he would never have the strength to do this work. He went back to work, pushing and sweating some more. Finally, he felt the rock begin to move. His heart pounded. He threw his weight against the lever. The rock held. The stream spirit took a deep breath and gave one more monumental lunge. The rock tipped, teetered, then crashed out of its place and down to the stream bed, dislodging several more rocks along the way.*

Suddenly water filled the space where the rock had been, and then the stream spirit shared the space with the water, and then the entire reservoir seemed to push its way out through the little hole, bringing with it more rocks and branches. The stream spirit tried to ride the crest of the wave, but the force of the water rolled him over and over and over. He held his breath until he couldn't anymore. The last, panicked thought that ran through his head just before he lost consciousness was, "Why did I do this?"

When an inner situation is not made conscious, it appears outside as fate.

-Carl Jung

The Healing Stage (Four) is the watershed of the Seven Stages. This is where you confront and heal your core emotional wounds. Clustered right up against the edge of the abyss of Stage Four, with heels dug in, are those who have come through the Willingness, Foundation and Feelings Stages (One, Two and Three), but who fear and resist the deep healing work of Four. They find healing work tiresome, difficult and never-ending.

On the other side of Four's abyss are those who took the plunge. They traversed the abyss with the skills they learned in early healing and now have a completely different view of healing work. For them, healing opportunities become an invitation to joy and love. They know they can survive the worst of their wounds and the most difficult of their feelings. Gratitude gradually replaces resentment.

Most of your original wounds are locked inside you behind your happy-ending fantasy.[19] The happy-ending fantasy takes a variety of forms, from unrealistic expectations of your parents' and friends' abilities to love you in just the way you need to be loved, to the hope that this something—*this* job, *this* relationship, *this* self-help book, *this* therapy technique, *this* religion—will make you happy. Of course, this is a setup to being disappointed in love relationships, friendships, work relationships, spiritual development and even in your achievements. In the Healing Stage, you begin to dismantle your personal versions of the happy-ending fantasy to expose and heal your core wounds.

[19] Other wounds can appear in the form of personality fragmentation, of which multiple personality disorder is the most severe. This book does not address fragmentation.

Just as dismantling a dam rock by rock would be hard work, tearing down your happy-ending fantasies and feeling the pain that they hide is both painful and difficult.

The biggest boulders in your dam are the ones you created in your family of origin. Nothing that happens in your life after childhood can equal the power (both positive and negative) of those earliest relationships.

We have a friend who survived a German concentration camp in World War II. She tells us that her experience of the horrors of the camp paled in comparison to the pain she felt decades later when she faced the wounds inflicted by the "concentration camp" that was her family.

We shall not escape our dangers by recoiling from them.

— Winston Churchill

Moving out of the Healing Stage and into the Rebirth Stage (Five) does not require removing all the rocks in the dam. You just need to move enough to get a trickle of life energy flowing again. You'll deal with the most obvious stones first. For example, if one of your parents was chronically ill while you were growing up, you may deal with your relationship with that parent first, on your first trip through the abyss. Later, you may realize that your relationship with the healthy but subtly codependent parent created even deeper, more complex, painful wounds. You go back to the dam to pull out that larger, more deeply buried rock.

When you reach the end of all the light there is and you must step out into the darkness, remember that two things may happen: You either will find something to stand on or you will be taught how to fly.

— The Book of Edges

This work—grieving and healing the despair and hopelessness beneath your happy-ending fantasy—is the most painful work you will ever do on your healing journey. People who enter their abyss say it feels like walking into an endlessly deep, dark cave, or stepping off a high cliff into terrifying free-fall or cold, empty space.

Regardless of how they describe abyss work, one thing seems to hold true for everyone: After that first foray through the abyss, the quality of the healing journey begins to change. Your attitudes toward yourself and others become more forgiving, and you are more and more likely to greet life's challenges as intriguing puzzles instead of cosmic mistakes. When you encounter pain, you usually understand it as temporary. You're willing to go through it because you know that the reward is another healed wound.

You willingly return to the abyss whenever necessary to begin healing newly discovered (or recently acknowledged) core wounds. Revisiting your abyss is easier than the first time through. Your visits are shorter, the abyss seems smaller and less threatening each time, and you know what to do when you're there.

After several trips back, people don't seem to feel the urgency to move into the next stage that they did in Stages One through Four. They've reached what we think of as the happiness stages. They are no longer in constant pain. In fact, the more abyss work they do, the more they seem to enjoy the experiences that come their way, even the tougher life lessons.

Nothing you do is more liberating than abyss work. Knowing that you survived your abyss sets you on the road to freedom from your need to depend on people, beliefs, tasks or substances to feel lovable and worthwhile. As you move out of your abyss, you'll begin to appreciate the natural unfolding of the subsequent stages.

EIGHTEEN

Advanced Healing

*People often say that this or that person has not yet
found himself. But the self is not something one finds;
it is something one creates.*

— Thomas Szasz

WHILE STAGES ONE THROUGH FOUR are often grindingly dif-
ficult and painful, the stages we describe in this chapter—Five:
Rebirth, Six: Clear-Hearted Relationships and Seven: Clear-
Hearted Service—are much lighter.

This is not to say that people in advanced healing have
"arrived." Pain and suffering still happen, and there are wounds
still left to heal. But in these stages of healing, you are more able
to give and accept love, and that makes all the difference in the
work you do. One of our friends compared Stages One through
Four to clearing off and organizing a messy desk, and Five
through Seven as truly beginning to use the desk to accomplish
work with meaning.

Stage Five: Rebirth

§ § §

THE STREAM SPIRIT *awoke on the bank of the stream bed dozens of yards below the dam. He turned over and groaned. He was covered with bruises, and where there were no bruises, there were cuts or scrapes. He kept his eyes shut for a while, hoping the aches would subside.*

Gradually, a noise he didn't recognize worked its way into his awareness. He thought about the noise and tried to identify it. And then he sat straight up. **The stream!**

The noise was water flowing over the dam and down the streambed. The streambed wasn't full—in fact, it had a long way to go before you could call it full—but there was water there, gurgling along around the rocks. It covered his toes and glinted in the sun. It babbled, it chuckled, it meandered—it did all the things flowing water is supposed to do. The stream spirit giggled.

Then he gasped. **The dam!** *Aches and bruises forgotten, he jumped up and raced around a bend in the streambed. Yes, the dam was still there, but it was much smaller. Water coursed down its face, splintering the sunlight.*

The stream spirit stood there, marveling. He heard a chuckle behind him and turned to see his friends grinning at him. He leapt into their arms and knocked them both off their feet. The three of them lay there, laughing and hugging.

After celebrating the water's release, the three friends shared lunch and talked about what was to happen next. The friends explained that there was much work still to be done. The stream spirit had to clean up all the debris that was carried into the streambed by the flood, continue to pull

rocks from the dam, build sturdy levees along the
streambed to prevent flooding, stock the lake with
fish, clean and landscape the shores of the lake,
and more. The stream spirit couldn't wait to
begin. With the flowing of the water, he felt his
energy return. He knew now that the land was
his again. He already felt the life pulsing through
it.

The Rebirth Stage marks the end of procrastination and self-defeating habits, and the beginning of becoming who you really are.

Early in the Rebirth Stage, there seems to be a revolving door between it and the Healing Stage (Four). You return to the abyss on a regular basis to confront more of your happy-ending fantasy and heal the wounds it protects. It is still painful and difficult work, but your success has shown you that you will survive it. You know why you're working. You are beginning to enjoy the benefits.

Our deepest fear is that we are powerful beyond measure...We ask ourselves—who am I to be brilliant, gorgeous, talented and fabulous? Actually, who are you not to be?

— Nelson Mandela

One of the benefits—and one of the hallmarks of a Stage Five point of view—is a natural welling up of energy to deal with the backlog of unfinished business in your life. Two people in one of our groups—Amelia and Walter—found themselves spontaneously dealing with unfinished business in their lives when they reached Stage Five.

Amelia's difficulties in elementary school had convinced her that she couldn't do math. From third grade on, she passed all her math work by cheating.

Amelia attended an anger-release workshop and resolved some of the anger she had stored up over her mother's over-controlling tendencies—typical Stage Four work. As a result, she began setting boundaries with both her parents and speaking up about her needs. Several weeks later, she told the group that she had found herself in a bookstore one day browsing through adult education texts. She bought a remedial math book and started doing the exercises. Amelia's certainty that she was no good at math was rapidly dissolving into excitement over her new skills.

Walter had a similar experience. A series of traumas when he was a child left him with wounds that made him periodically back away from his girlfriend when the relationship grew uncomfortably close. A few weeks after doing a piece of abyss work related to these traumas, Walter told the group that he had finally (and spontaneously) taken care of a long-standing, deeply annoying piece of unfinished business—he cleaned off his patio. He had awakened the previous Saturday with a non-negotiable urge to get rid of many years' worth of junk he had piled up out there. It took him all weekend and produced eight large bags to be hauled away with the trash. Walter reported he felt twenty pounds lighter and much more powerful.

Another Stage Five hallmark is a change in your willingness to create authority figures. Before Stage Four, because your happy-ending fantasy is still alive and well, you tend to look for someone to tell you the answers—someone who knows the secrets of life. As you move through Stage Four, dismantling your happy-ending fantasy and mourning its loss, you begin to realize that *no one* has the answers, and (paradoxically) *everyone* has them—including you.

Erica, a sexual abuse survivor in therapy with Rebecca, came to this realization as a new relationship developed in her life. Erica had assumed that anyone who had *not* been sexually abused must be emotionally intact in ways that she was sure she was not. Anyone who did not have a history like hers, therefore, was someone she looked up to for advice and an example of wound-free living. But as she healed her wounded sexuality and changed the way she communicated with her new boyfriend about her sexual needs, she began to realize that he, too, was wounded—even though he had not been molested. This was an exciting, liberating moment for her.

"I suddenly understood that, wounded or not, I had something to offer him," Erica said. "For the first time, I feel like a grown-up relating to another grown-up, instead of a child relating to a parent."

Erica was able to apply this understanding to many parts of her life. She began to realize that the things, concepts and people she had set up as her authorities—books, experts, spiritual leaders, loved ones—did not have to be perfectly right about everything. They could contribute important wisdom on some subjects and be completely out of touch on others. It was up to Erica to decide what was true for her and what was not. And in doing so, she didn't need to choose between placing someone on a pedestal or not.

Stage Five represents the end of the arbitrary divisions and black-and-white thinking you place on the world: good vs. evil; people who have it together vs. people who don't; people you can trust vs. people you can't trust. To Stage Five eyes, people are just like you: mixtures of healed and unhealed wounds who have something to offer if you know where (and how) to look.

Because of this new attitude, you are now within reach of a full and genuine inner peace regarding your parents. They become, in your sight, just another pair of wounded people who made difficult choices, some of which wounded you.

Your feelings of self-sufficiency and self-esteem seem to deepen each day. As you clear away your shame and your need to be right, you begin to leave behind the turmoil of your earlier life and relationships. You become comfortable trusting your intuition, even when others disagree with your decisions. Gradually, you gain a whole new way of looking at your life, relationships and pain. You begin to embrace your wounds. Hard as it may be to believe from the perspective of the earlier stages, you actually become grateful for the way your wounds have shaped you. You begin to see them as sacred gifts harvested from old traumas, to help you in carrying out your life's missions.

You are now skilled at feeling, healing and grieving your losses. It is easier than ever to present an authentic self to others. This means that boundaries become a big issue. While you are able to set them now with precision, you tend to be rigid and rather unilateral in how you set them—"take it or leave it" is a common attitude. However, you are still vulnerable to blame and accusations, and can still be knocked off center by people who use them. For these reasons, you might find yourself being accused of selfishness now and then, and worrying that the accusation might be true.

However, these boundaries allow you to develop new and deeper dimensions in your relationships. You will find yourself enjoying a level of intimacy that you may have not been able to imagine before now. Possibly even harder to imagine are the deeper, more meaningful relationships that you will begin to create in Stage Six when you complete your work in Stage Five.

And Stage Five *is* a lot of work. However, it is somehow easier than anything you've done before. The stream spirit found, in the bright rush of clean, oxygen-rich water, tangible proof that he was healing. He noticed that other life was coming back, now that there was good water to drink. Every change you make now brings more joy, more love and more healing to your life.

Stage Six: Clear-Hearted Relationships

And the song, from beginning to end, I found in the heart of a friend.

— Henry Wadsworth Longfellow

The stream spirit's beautification efforts began to expand downstream. More and more of his environment bloomed. The banks of the stream, the scrub just beyond it and the forest beyond that were filled with life. He began to range farther and farther away from home, exploring more distant reaches of the land.

One day he rounded an outcrop on a slope high above his stream and paused to enjoy the view. There below him sparkled another stream. Surprised, he climbed a little higher and traced the course of the stream. About three hundred yards downstream, it joined another stream—his stream! In the distance, the stream spirit could see that the two streams made quite a powerful river.

He was stunned. Although he had always known there were other streams in other places, the stream spirit had never considered the possibility that his stream and another might actually join up. He sat and pondered this discovery until the sun neared the horizon.

The next day, the spirit returned to the confluence and walked upstream along the banks of the new stream. He admired the creative landscaping; clearly, someone had carefully thought about how to prevent erosion and encourage plant growth on the banks of the stream. "Who did this?" the stream spirit thought.

As if in answer, a stone bounced off the slope just above the bank and landed at his feet. The stream spirit looked up. He met the eyes of a stream spirit like himself, standing on a granite boulder just above his head and staring down at him with an expression on her face that mirrored, the stream spirit was certain, the astonishment on his own.

Once the two had gotten over the shock of meeting someone so similar, and then the awkwardness of introductions, they talked non-stop for the rest of the day.

Over the next several weeks, the two stream spirits hatched plans to continue exploring downstream together. As they came to know and respect each other, they decided to make the river their home together. They each brought their understanding and experience of their own streams to the new project. Within a couple of years, the river was as lovely as their individual streams. The effects of their improvements ranged far. Wildlife that hadn't been seen in the region for decades returned. Their friends and other stream spirits came often to visit.

Still, each spirit carefully tended his or her own original stream. The spirits still found ways to improve their streams, and found that doing so always benefited the river in ways they could never predict.

Your fundamental understanding of what love is—and is not—transforms as you move through this stage. When you arrive at Stage Six, you are free enough of the weight of your wounds and self-protections that you can now risk far more in your relationships with yourself, others, tasks, money, time, events and your spiritual resources. Because you feel more certain about who you are and about your ability to meet your own needs and keep yourself whole, you can relax your vigilance about your boundaries. You become more flexible about them, and strive for compassion and a sense of mutual gain.

You rapidly recognize your wounds when they're triggered and keep healing them, without blaming events or people for your discomfort (at least, not for long). Many old reactions may remain, but your inner critic lets you know when you need to take a closer look. For some people, the inner critic has become a gentle ally. Others still must deal with a harsh-voiced critic, but they respond more quickly and don't take any abuse.

You use your keeping-company ability to help others feel, grieve and heal *their* losses, even when your own needs are not being met. This is especially evident in parents who are patient and supportive with the emotional vagaries of a toddler. It takes a firm belief in your ability to meet your own needs to set them aside (without the sticky strings of codependency) so you can meet the needs of someone else.

The before-and-after table on the next page sums up the nature of Stage Six relating.

How you handle:	Pre–Stage Six	Stage Six
Endings	Relationships end unconsciously	Closure is conscious, at least within yourself
Minor hurts	Even when you know better, you tend to take things personally; another person's crabbiness, projections or blame can easily push you off-center	You don't take another person's off-center remarks or actions personally quite so often
Self-responsibility	Tend to blame the other, even when you are trying to be self-responsible	Blame and guilt make you yawn
Conflict	Tend to want to teach the other person a lesson	You are focused on cleaning up your own side of the street; whether the other person learns a lesson is up to him or her
Fear	Tend to project your fears onto the other person: *"You are too pushy and demanding."*	Fears still exist, but you are better at owning them: *"I am scared by how close we have become lately, so I want a day alone and then some time to talk about my fears."*

Your creativity at problem-solving in relationships comes into full bloom in Stage Six. You find deeper and deeper ways to be your true self while in relationship with another person. You discover a sacred element in your relationships—they are the cherished vehicles for bringing up your remaining blocks to loving.

Reaching Stage Six is fully dependent on doing thorough work in Stage Four. Back to the pyramid analogy: The more work you do in Stage Four, the higher your pyramid can reach. For example, in the pyramid on the next page, the Stage Four segment is wide enough to support one more layer—Stage Five.

Love consists in this: that two solitudes protect, and touch, and greet each other.

– Rainer Maria Rilke

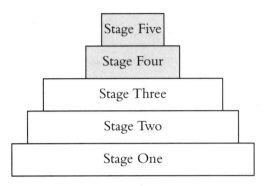

By spending more time developing the Stage Four layer, you provide the foundation for Stage Six.

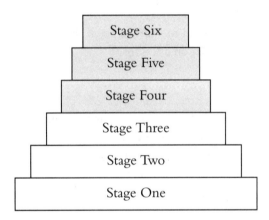

Put another way, you won't reap the benefits of Stage Six until you learn to be who you truly are, which is Stage Five work. And you won't learn who you are until you cut the emotional umbilical cord with the legacy of your wounds, which is Stage Four work.

Proof of attaining Stage Six is in your relationships. When you are truly in Stage Six, you will find another Stage Six person with whom to have a close relationship—a friend, lover, spouse or business partner. Although you may be capable of making Stage Six responses to someone whose dominant stage is Five or below, you cannot consider your dominant stage to be Six until you find at least one other person to share it with. It is only in dealing with a spiritual and emotional equal that you can reach the next deeper layer of wounds to heal, which allows you to move to Stage Seven.

Stage Seven: Clear-Hearted Service

One evening, the two stream spirits sat with their friends around a crackling fire on the wedge of land just above the confluence of the two streams. Each stream spirit had been guided by a pair of friends, so there were six altogether now.

"I've never asked you how you met," the first stream spirit said to his friends. "How did you two find each other?"

"And how did you find me?" the second stream spirit asked her friends.

The four friends looked at each other, and then as if by agreement, one of them began to speak.

"Long ago, each of us lived separately, far away from each other. We were stream spirits, just like you, and we had learned to contain and even strangle our life force, as you did. Friends found us as we found you and helped us as we helped you. Our land bloomed and thrived again, as yours does now. And we found each other as you two found each other.

"One day, our friends brought us news of stream spirits who lived in desolation the way we had once lived. Before the story was ended, we each had decided to carry our knowledge and our help to them. And that's how the four of us found the two of you. The rest of the story is your own."

The two stream spirits looked at each other in surprise.

*"There are other stream spirits who still live
the old way?" the first one said.*

*"Yes, of course," the friend answered. "There
are always others who live the old way."*

*The second stream spirit took her friend's
hand. "Let's go," she said.*

*The six friends talked long into the night. By
the time the fire burned low and the sun
lightened the eastern sky, they had made their
plans for their journey.*

Reaching Stage Seven does not mean you are fully healed. It
does mean you are healed enough to use service to others to
move forward on your healing journey, just as in Stage Six you
began to use relationships with others to heal.

While you will no doubt be of service in important ways
before reaching Stage Seven, it is in this stage that service
becomes a primary focus without taking a toll on your relationship with yourself, your spiritual development, or other people.
In this stage, you begin using your power to help others to grow
and heal. You see this as an investment in the future. Your focus
becomes your ability to extend love to others and to express
your spiritual attunement in this love. The peace prayer of
St. Francis of Assisi exemplifies the attitude of Stage Seven:

> *O divine Master*
> > *Grant that I may not so much seek to be
> > consoled as to console;*
> > *To be understood as to understand;*
> > *To be loved as to love.*

By this stage, you use everything that happens to you to
become more loving. This doesn't always occur in the moment.
But although you may be temporarily derailed by events that
trigger your unhealed wounds, you always come back to self-
responsibility. You don't let yourself off the hook. The fear that

paralyzed you before is still present, but it is less intense and you are determined not to let it stare you down.

It is important not to rush into this stage of healing. Too many Stage Seven activities before you've really gotten comfortable in Stage Five will only exacerbate whatever codependency you may have—and most of us have at least some.

Where Are You?

The Seven Stages are just another interesting theory unless you apply it to your life. Although you can get a pretty good idea of where you are in terms of the stages simply by reading descriptions of them, you'll see a far more accurate and detailed picture of your own state of healing by taking the self-assessment in the next chapter.

NINETEEN

Your Dominant Healing Stage

> For one human being to love another: that is perhaps
> the most difficult of our tasks, the ultimate test and
> proof, the work for which all other work is but
> preparation.
>
> — Rainer Maria Rilke

AT ANY GIVEN POINT in your healing journey, your work will
be concentrated primarily in one stage. This is your dominant
healing stage. Your healing self-assessment and determination of
your dominant healing stage provides the foundation for the
healing plan you will develop for yourself later in this section.

Why a Healing Self-Assessment?

Even if you believe you have a pretty good idea of what healing
stage you currently occupy, we encourage you to complete the
self-assessment in this section, for one very good reason: An
accurate assessment of your healing level will allow you to create
a personal healing plan that will promote your healing rather
than sabotage it.

It's like getting good directions when you start out on a road trip, or looking for the words YOU ARE HERE on the shopping mall directory. If you think you are at Fourth and Elm, but you're really at the corner of Walters and Meade across town, you're going to do a lot of wandering around before you figure out where you really are and get back on track.

Everyone—and we do mean *everyone*—overestimates his level of healing. Becoming a fully authentic, genuine human being is a lot more work than most people realize. A formal assessment will help you be more objective and accurate about how much healing you have done.

For example, many people who have begun their healing journey read the descriptions of the Seven Stages and conclude they are in Stage Six. This is understandable; as early as Stage Three, most people are so much more authentic that their relationships are remarkably improved. But that doesn't necessarily mean they have entered the fully self-responsible and compassionate relationships typical of Stage Six.

Others, looking at the Stage Five description, take note of the improvement in self-esteem typical of that stage. They know they feel better about themselves than they ever have before, so they figure they must be in Stage Five. Again, improved self-esteem occurs early in the healing journey and doesn't necessarily mean you've moved into Stage Five.

You may be wondering how much difference it makes whether you are in Stage Five or Stage Six. If you are interested in getting the most out of your healing work, it makes a great deal of difference. Here's why: A healing plan based on an inaccurate assessment—especially one that is unrealistically high—is worse than useless. It will encourage you to skip critical steps in the healing process, which leads to a phenomenon we call the Rubber Band Effect (described later in this section). Getting caught in a Rubber Band Effect will stall your healing, create more pain than is really necessary, and damage your faith in your own healing process. People dealing with addictive tendencies may find themselves in relapse.

An accurate understanding of your healing level, on the other hand, will help you move ahead more quickly and with a minimum of pain. (Sorry, pain seems to be a necessary part of the healing process. However, misery is, as we noted earlier, optional.

Getting a Clear Picture of Your Healing

Of the nine indicators we described in Section II, *Quality of Relationships* is the most illuminating. We are wounded in our earliest relationships, and each relationship we encounter after that reveals those unhealed wounds. In any relationship, conflict is inevitable, and conflict between two people in an important relationship is the quickest way to trigger an unhealed wound.

So we developed this self-assessment based on conflict in a hypothetical relationship. We road-tested the assessment on clients and friends, and have found it to be remarkably accurate.

There is one flaw in the assessment: It can be faked. We made every effort to disguise the responses to help our readers maintain their honesty. Even so, the more-evolved responses are sometimes easy to distinguish from the less-evolved ones. You could go through the assessment guessing at the higher-level answers and score high.

We ask that you resist this impulse. The quality of your healing plan depends on it, and the course of your healing depends on an accurate healing plan. Besides, *all* the responses are valid. The only right or best response is the one that most clearly depicts your healing stage now.

If you want help in staying honest—or just want to get some feedback—try showing your completed assessment to a trusted friend on the healing path, or a mentor. If you are especially courageous, photocopy the assessment before taking it and have a trusted mentor take it on your behalf. Then compare your answers with your mentor's. (Incidentally, whether or not you choose to share your assessment, if you don't have anyone in your life you trust enough to share it with, you can assume you are in pre-healing, Stage One or Stage Two.)

As you read through the scenarios and the possible responses, keep in mind that none of them will fit perfectly. For example, you may find one that works, except for one sentence.

Sometimes it may seem that all of them contain a little bit of truth for you; other times it may seem that none of them is even close. Don't get carried away trying to make your selections unfailingly accurate. The assessment is designed to place you in categories that will help you get a handle on your healing, not to determine whether you are a worthwhile person or are doing your healing "right" or "wrong." Our assessment can help, but ultimately you are the authority.

Some responses are written in first person *plural* instead of singular (as in "We keep each other company..."). This is deliberate, and is due both to test construction limitations and to the nature of Stage Six. It may seem unfair to base a determination of your healing level even partly on the responses of another person, but please trust us for now. Our reasoning will become clear later. We understand how challenging and scary it is to evaluate your own healing, and we do not want to help you criticize or shame yourself. But we would rather run the risk of leaving you with some uncomfortable feelings to deal with than to risk letting you think that you are more healed than you are. The long-term effects of the latter are significant. So when you come to one of those "we" responses, pass it by unless it really is true for you and your important other.

Be kind to yourself as you take the assessment. You may find yourself feeling uncomfortable, defensive or frustrated with the restrictions of some of the responses. Many people have these reactions. If this happens, try to remind yourself that this is about *you* helping *you* to heal. No one is standing in judgment of you (except perhaps yourself).

Self-Assessment Instructions

1. Write the numbers one through eight down the left side of a blank sheet of paper.

2. Read the scenario at the top of the first page of the assessment (see the box). All the questions in the self-assessment are based on this scenario.

3. Read each question and all possible responses *before* selecting one response.

As you read, you may find it helpful to remember a specific event from your recent life that resembles the one described, and refer to it and your actions in it as you review the responses.[20]

4. Choose the one response that mostly closely describes the way you would respond in the given situation and write its letter next to the appropriate question number.

Don't try to choose the "correct" response. Just be honest about your reactions. Choose the answer that is *closest* to what you believe you would do or say, even if the wording is not typical for you.

Some of the responses may be only partly true for you. Choose the one that feels the most fully true.

If you see two responses that seem to be equally true for you, choose the one that you think is the less evolved or healed of the two. Erring on the conservative side won't do you any harm, but a healing plan based on an inflated score can slow your healing process.

If a particular response seems vague, incomplete or irrelevant to you, assume that it doesn't pertain to you at this time, and ignore it.

Some responses offer multiple options, separated by a capitalized, boldface, italicized **-OR-**. If just one of these options is true for you, select the response even if the others are not.

Keep in mind that, if a particular response is right for you, it may describe something that you've never stopped to think about because it is something you do unconsciously. That's fine. If the response fits, choose it.

Don't spend hours over the responses. Most people find they arrive at the most accurate results if they take no more than thirty minutes so complete the assessment.

5. Complete question eight according to its own instructions.

6. Follow scoring instructions at the end of the assessment.

[20] Be sure to use a relationship with another adult—and preferably not a blood relation—as a reference point for the assessment. Using an incident with one of your children, a parent or even a sibling is likely to skew your score lower. Those are the most challenging relationships any of us have; conflict within them almost invariably triggers our deepest unhealed wounds.

EVALUATION
The Self-Assessment

SCENARIO:

You are having a problem with one of the most important adults in your personal life (other than a blood relation)—a relationship you deeply value. The two of you begin discussing this problem.

1. **As the discussion progresses, the tone becomes more and more heated and contentious. Soon the two of you are deadlocked in a power struggle, feeling completely frustrated in your attempts to change the course of the argument.**

   Which of the following responses best describes what you are _most likely to do today_ in this situation?

   A. I keep arguing and probably blow up at the other person because I believe he/she is causing problems in our relationship. **-OR-** I try to "make nice," smooth over our differences, or give in to make the conflict stop. **-OR-** I numb out, tune out and try to forget this conflict ever occurred.

   B. I decide that I am too triggered, or too unclear about how to reach the other person, to proceed. I probably walk away feeling disgusted and frustrated. I regain my hope for the relationship by going through the basics (for example, getting some rest and exercise, meditating, going to a support group meeting, and so on).

   C. I decide that I am too triggered, or too unclear about how to reach the other person, to proceed. I take a time-out (either physically, by leaving the room, or internally, by getting quiet for a little while) to discover what triggered me. Then, after getting centered again, I return to the other person and tell him/her how I was triggered and what I discovered about me. We discuss my emotional reactions first before returning to the issue we had originally been discussing.

D. I notice how emotional I am soon enough to do something about it before I say or do something that damages the relationship. I make a hurried exit to go off to keep company with my feelings.

E. I am tempted to respond as in A above. I want to respond differently, but I don't know how. I realize that I have been triggered, but frequently not until after I have said or done something I am likely to regret later. I want to do something to make it right and I'm not sure what that would be. I get busy trying to learn what I could do differently.

F. I'm aware of feeling that I'm caught in the middle of a replay of something very old and overwhelming. This is a familiar feeling. I know I need and want to get hold of this "something," even if I'm too angry to do that right now. I take a time out. Then I go to work to get to the bottom of whatever the "something" is.

G. We frequently both stop dead in our tracks at the first signs of escalation. We keep each other company as we compassionately take turns identifying for ourselves what we're carrying that is throwing us off course in the discussion. We tend to explore these issues at least as much together as apart, and grow closer as a result of exploring our respective issues together.

2. **Things are getting worse. You become enraged with this other person. You are so enraged that you know you can't possibly communicate your reaction in a civil manner right now.**

Which of the following responses best describes what you are _most likely to do today_ in this situation?

A. I take a break to take care of myself. This means I do things such as talk to supportive people, give myself lots of affirmations, write in my journal, try to visualize myself at peace, and so on. This allows me to feel better.

B. I never become so enraged that I can't be civil. _-OR-_ We don't hold back with each other; I vent my rage then and there, saying whatever comes to mind, even if it hurts the other person's feelings; his/her feelings are his/her responsibility. *-OR-* I use all my willpower to keep the rage under wraps, and take my revenge later. If I tell other people about what happened, they support me in my reasons for having become angry, and I feel vindicated.

C. I leave quickly, either physically or by going within. I thoroughly discharge my rage in a way that doesn't damage myself, others or property. I stop when I feel better and feel that I have resolved my emotions.

D. I try to become willing to ask my spiritual resources for help with my rage so I don't do something stupid. This works to a certain extent, but I'm still left with feelings I don't know how to resolve. *-OR-* I try to become willing to ask my spiritual resources for help with my rage so I don't do something stupid. As a result, my feelings get resolved.

E. I leave quickly. I thoroughly discharge my rage in a way that doesn't damage myself, others or property. (This may take thirty seconds or several days.) When I feel better, I stop and begin to work to get to the bottom of the unhealed wounds that set me up for this outburst. (Again, this may take a few seconds or even a few months). I like the insights I get, but I know I need to go even deeper to cleanse the wound and get it healed. I get whatever help I need to do this work.

F. I leave quickly, either physically or by going within. I thoroughly discharge my rage in a way that doesn't damage myself, others or property. (This may take thirty seconds or several days.) When I feel better, I stop and begin to work to get to the bottom of the unhealed wounds that set me up for this outburst. (Again, this may take a few seconds or even a few months). I like the insights I get, but I know I need to go even deeper to cleanse the wound and get it healed. I get whatever help I need to do this work.

And then I keep going until I reach a sense of forgiveness toward myself and the other person for having become so enraged. I may feel dismayed about how long it takes to reach this state of forgiveness (and sometimes it takes many months), but I don't give up. I apologize to the other person and share with him/her what I discovered about what was really going on inside me.

G. I leave quickly, either physically or by going within. I thoroughly discharge my rage in a way that doesn't damage myself, others or property. (This may take thirty seconds or several days.) When I feel better, I stop and begin to work to get to the bottom of the unhealed wounds that set me up for this outburst. (Again, this may take a few seconds or even a few months). I like the insights I get, but I know I need to go even deeper to cleanse the wound and get it healed. I get whatever help I need to do this work.

And then I keep going until I reach a sense of forgiveness toward myself and the other person for having become so enraged. I may feel dismayed about how long it takes to reach this state of forgiveness (and sometimes it takes many months), but I don't give up. I apologize to the other person and share with him/her what I discovered about what was really going on inside me.

Then I make a realistic plan with the other person about how I will deal with my anger in the future; our plan is respectful of each other and helpful to my healing.

3. **The two of you finally get to a point in this discussion in which you try to figure out what went wrong.**

   Which of the following responses best describes what you are *most likely to do today* in this situation?

   A. I talk with myself to get some distance on the harsh messages that rise up inside me about myself or the other person. I struggle to get past these messages to my deeper feelings, but they either remain elusive or they swamp me.

   B. I begin working to free myself of the deepest causes of my reactions. Even if it takes me months to do it, I eventually free myself. I begin to feel relieved because I have discovered hidden unhealed wounds, and I know I can heal them. I know that this unfinished business has contaminated my responses to the other person and kept me from dealing with the issue at hand. I embrace the gift of this conflict as an opportunity to heal. I feel a sense of forgiveness for myself and the other person. I feel powerful and ready to move forward, healthier for having had this experience.

C. I get stuck because I can't get to the cause of the flashback, projection, rigid belief or false hope that is at the bottom of my reactions. **-OR-** I get to the cause of my reactions, but I get stuck there because I can't free myself of it.

D. I usually don't dwell on trying to find out what went wrong in these kinds of situations. When I do, I try to figure out what the other person did wrong.

E. I hope that taking care of myself by doing something healthy (such as getting a good night's sleep, going for a run, attending a support group meeting, talking with supportive friends, or whatever else I usually do to take care of myself) will clear things up.

F. I become confused and frustrated. I don't know how to get to the bottom of what went wrong, but I really want to. I actively seek help, no matter what I have to do or where I have to go to find it.

4. A day or so after the discussion, you become clear about your part in what went wrong.

Which of the following responses best describes what you are *most likely to do today* in this situation?

A. I think carefully about how much I should tell the other person about what I discovered was the root of my reactions. I worry that he/she will leave me, shame me, or use the information against me if I tell this dark little secret I've discovered about myself.

B. I tell the other person I am sorry I didn't respond more helpfully during our discussion. I tell him/her generally what I discovered about myself. I tell him/her how my perceptions have shifted because of this discovery and how forgiving I feel toward myself and him/her. I'm aware of feeling more powerful than ever about my boundaries and my ability to care for myself.

C. When a fight is over, it's over. And if it's not, that just how relationships go. I don't usually follow up.

D. I tell the other person about the feelings I went through, but I can't say much about their source.

E. I tell the other person about the ways I discovered I was stressed, in a bad mood or physiologically out of balance, and apologize.

F. I apologize to him/her, but I'm not able to say exactly what I did wrong. But I really mean it. I don't understand why people often tell me I'm being vague. I'm telling them what I know.

G. I describe in detail the role I played in helping our discussion deteriorate. I describe the feelings I had. I describe how the blaming or shaming feelings I had led me to unexpected discoveries about myself. I describe what I did that helped release me from the wounds that blocked me from responding in a more centered, honest or loving way. We talk compassionately about each of our parts in what occurred. We both are genuinely interested in each others' discoveries. We celebrate together because we feel closer than ever.

5. **After you talk together about your roles in what occurred, the other person proposes that the two of you develop a plan to help you both deal more constructively with similar situations in the future.**

   Which of the following responses best describes what you are *most likely to do today* **in this situation?**

   A. I tell the other person what I want him/her to do for me, and I ask what I can do for him/her. If he/she doesn't cooperate, I take care of myself apart from him/her. If he/she asks me to change the way I respond to him/her, I become resentful, because it seems to me that the other person should deal with his/her own reactions without asking me to change.

   B. I think his/her proposal sounds like a great idea, and I really do want things to improve between us. However, I'm baffled by the process—I truly don't know quite what he/she is talking about. I do want to help, though, so I go along.

C. I tell the other person what I'm going to do differently. I invite him/her to tell me what he/she is going to do differently. We build a bridge between our two sets of needs. We agree to a plan that assumes we will be triggered in the same ways again someday. Our plan includes realistic steps for each of us to handle our reactions a little bit differently than last time.

D. It seems to me that I've done what I needed to do. I got my feelings out, and that should be enough to make changes happen between us.

E. I make a plan to handle future situations differently. However, my plan assumes he/she/I won't be triggered in the same way again. I don't realize how unrealistic this is until one of us is triggered again.

F. I make a plan for taking better care of myself so I can avoid replays of this situation in the future. I find a way to disengage and take time-outs before I say or do damaging things. I make a plan to get myself re-centered faster if I do lose it.

G. I don't make plans with people for dealing with similar situations in the future. **-OR-** I agree to the plan he/she proposes, even though I know I can't follow through with it, just to get him/her off my back. **-OR-** I accept the other person's plan for doing things differently next time so that I won't have to face his/her nonsense again. **-OR-** No one has ever suggested making a plan; I don't know what I would do if this happened.

6. The "next time," inevitably, arrives. The two of you get triggered again. This time, you both try to implement the plan you made. However, there seem to be flaws in the plan. Somehow, it doesn't work as you thought it would.

Which of the following responses best describes what you are *most likely to do today* **in this situation?**

A. I expected the other person's behavior would change, now that he/she knows how it makes me feel. But he/she is behaving the same way, and I feel resentful. I'm pretty good at keeping commitments to take a time-out when I'm emotionally overwhelmed. But when the other person doesn't follow through on his/her commitments, I can come pretty close to losing it. I sometimes do, because of my disappointed expectations. I feel resentful or unimportant. I don't know what to do about this; I go back and forth between wanting to chew him/her out for being undependable and making excuses for him/her. It's hard for me to refrain from this internal drama and keep my feelings company instead. But I try my best.

B. I find I can't implement our agreement because I overestimated the amount of progress I've made. **-OR-** I discover, to my surprise, that our plan doesn't prevent me from being triggered. I feel frustrated and as if I'd reached a dead end. I tell the other person about this, even though I may be embarrassed and afraid of retribution. If the other person has not kept his/her agreement, I watch for symptoms of my remaining false hope: my tendency to either take this personally or to overlook it and focus on his/her good intentions. I know my false hope sets me up for repeated frustration and resentment. I notice that I am more interested in discovering the truth about what I can and can't count on from this person than I am in feeling abandoned or in keeping hope alive that he/she can be what I want him/her to be.

C. I realize that I am better at following through on agreements I make for what I'll do *after* a conflict appears than I am on agreements to *prevent* conflicts.

D. I don't make agreements. **-OR-** I make agreements, but often forget what they are. If I forget and the other person calls me on this, I find excuses. If I keep my agreement but the other person doesn't, I lay into him/her.

E. I react similarly to response A above, except that I take his/her negligence very personally, almost as though my survival is on the line. I *know* that my reaction has at least as much to do with something deep and old within me as it has to do with the other person's lack of follow-through, but it's sometimes hard for me to *believe* it.

F. I remember the agreement we made, but discover that I can't implement it. I quietly stop trying to implement my side of the agreement, and hope the other person doesn't notice.

G. I spot the flaws in my agreement. I talk with the other person in depth about this. We modify our agreement to make it "do-able." If this doesn't work, I assume something even deeper is blocking me, so I continue to explore my core wounds until I find the missing piece and deal with it. If the other person doesn't keep his/her agreement, I talk to him/her about this. If I am not satisfied with his/her response, I face and accept what this response tells me about how close we can be regarding this issue. I revise my expectations of this person or, if necessary, change or end my relationship with him/her.

7. Despite your best plans, you continue to be triggered in the same way, over and over.

Which of the following responses best describes what you are *most likely to do today* in this situation?

A. I try to take better care of myself. I go to some support group meetings or talk with supportive friends. I pray to be released from these character defects. I hope these actions will help.

B. I take the steps necessary to deepen my exploration and release work until I get to the roots of whatever is keeping this pattern repeating in my life. I continue until I'm free of it.

C. I acknowledge that I have placed limits on the amount of intimacy or happiness I think I am entitled to. I decide to challenge these limits. I give myself credit for being in the process of becoming more open to higher levels of happiness and intimacy than ever before.

D. I tell myself and the other person, *"This is just who I am. Get over it. If you don't like it, you can always leave."*

E. I take this failure as proof that I'm so flawed that I can't handle intimacy beyond a certain, very shallow point. I plunge into grief and begin to deal with my sadness over this problem.

8. **Mark the scale below at the place on it that reflects how honest you think you were in completing the self-assessment.**

How Honest Were Your Responses?

| 0 | | 1 | | 2 | | 3 | | 4 |

My responses reflect the
way I actually do respond
most of the time

My responses reflect
how I want to be able
to respond

The closer to zero your response is, the more helpful the results of your self-assessment will be in helping you develop a healing plan that is right for you. So if you have marked the scale anywhere to the right of the number 1, please review your responses and revise them until you can rate your answers between 0 and 1.

Scoring Your Assessment

Score your response to each question using the chart below.[21]

1:___	2:___	3:___	4:___	5:___	6:___	7:___
A. 0	A. 2	A. 3	A. 4	A. 5	A. 3	A. 2
B. 2	B. 0	B. 5	B. 5	B. 1	B. 5	B. 4
C. 5	C. 3	C. 4	C. 0	C. 6	C. 2	C. 5
D. 3	D. 1	D. 0	D. 3	D. 3	D. 0	D. 0
E. 1	E. 4	E. 2	E. 2	E. 4	E. 4	E. 3
F. 4	F. 5	F. 1	F. 1	F. 2	F. 1	
G. 6	G. 6		G. 6	G. 0	G. 6	

---

[21] There are no Stage Seven responses, for a couple of reasons. First, we couldn't figure out how to distinguish, in an assessment of this type, the difference between Stage Seven service and the kinds of service people perform in earlier stages of healing. Second, we assume that people who are truly in Stage Seven would not need this book to tell them so.

Total the seven individual scores. Enter the total in the QUESTION TOTAL box below.

Now, look at the mark you made on the scale in question 8 and assign it a value based on its position on the scale. (For example, if you marked the scale halfway between 0 and 1, you would give it a value of 0.5; three-quarters of the way would be 0.75.) Enter this number in the HONESTY SCALE box below.

Subtract your HONESTY SCALE from your QUESTION TOTAL and enter the result in the YOUR SCORE box on the right. This is your score. Check the table below to see in which stage your score places you.

| QUESTION TOTAL | − | HONESTY SCALE | = | YOUR SCORE |

If your score is between...	...you are in:
0 and 5	Pre-Healing
6 and 11	Stage One
12 and 18	Stage Two
19 and 24	Stage Three
25 and 30	Stage Four
31 and 35	Stage Five
36 and 40	Stage Six

Dealing with Your Reaction to Your Score

Many people are discouraged when they see their scores. As we said at the beginning of this chapter, most of us overestimate our healing level. In the face of an overly optimistic appraisal, hard evidence to the contrary can be upsetting.

But then, that is the reason we wrote this book. If you scored lower than you thought you would, it could be because you needed a plan and didn't have one. Most people are not trained to think holistically about their healing journey. The fact is, the focus, needs and driving force of a survival plan are diametrically opposed to those of a healing plan. Unless you know that and make a plan to keep from moving in the direction your survival plan has set for you for the past twenty, thirty or forty years, you will spend a certain amount of time heading up the wrong roads. So please don't waste time berating yourself for being less healed than you would like to be. Instead, try to see this disappointment as proof that you are not getting as much as you deserve from the investment you make in your healing journey.

Interpreting Your Score

Although your score holds the key to your healing process, it is not as simple as a single number might imply.

For example, Samuel, who thought he was probably in Stage Five (Rebirth), scored 23—late Stage Three (Feelings), verging on Stage Four (Healing). When we looked at his assessment, we saw that he tended to choose Stage Three or Stage Six responses. (The score for each response is the number of the stage for which it is typical; a score of 2 means that response is typical of a person whose dominant Stage is Two.) Samuel's friends verified that he had learned a lot of Stage Six relationship skills. However, Samuel himself, once he thought about it, acknowledged that, while he had done a lot of Stage Three (Feelings) work and was pretty good at relating to people in a compassionate way, he had been avoiding facing his primary happy-ending fantasy. The object of his happy-ending fantasy was the "perfect relationship with the right woman," which he unconsciously (and sometimes, consciously) believed would bring an end to his loneliness and dissatisfaction. That his happy-ending fantasy was still intact was evident in his pattern of relationships. Over and over, Samuel chose women who looked like his lost first love and who were too immature or addicted to sustain a long-term relationship with him—or anyone else.

Samuel treated his score as a wake-up call. After his initial wave of shame subsided, he read about abyss work and developed a plan to help himself confront and heal his happy-ending fantasy and the wounds that caused him to develop it. Only when he undertook this work did he discover that his lost first love was as traumatizing as it was because of an even more painful prior abandonment by his older sister when Samuel was a child.

Samuel's story is not at all unusual. For example, Anna had been doing healing work for a few years and believed she was in touch with her feelings. She guessed that she was in early Stage Three. However, her self-assessment placed her in pre-willingness. She was disheartened until we pointed out that her recent history validated her score. Anna had ended a year-long relationship just two months before. She knew she didn't want the blame and emotional distance of her relationship with Tyrone, but she wasn't sure what she did want. She didn't really see what part she played in the breakup, and frankly didn't believe she had one. When anyone suggested to Anna that the binge eating she tended to do when upset might be linked to problems in the relationship, she shrugged it off.

"So sometimes I eat too much. Big deal," she insisted. "I'm not hurting anyone and I'm pretty happy with the rest of my life."

In short, Anna was back at the question of willingness: Was she willing to commit to abstaining from bingeing and to feeling her grief and exploring her part in the breakup?

We like to compare the human personality to Swiss cheese—it's full of holes that, in humans, represent neglected or damaged skills and abilities. Nobody thinks less of Swiss cheese for being full of holes, and we shouldn't think less of ourselves for having holes in our personalities. However, unlike Swiss cheese, human beings are held back from fulfillment and happiness by their holes. The point of an assessment like this one is not so much to find out how healed you are as it is to locate the holes in your healing so you can begin filling them.

Furthermore, this assessment examines your responses at your weakest point—the bull's eye of a target of concentric circles. At the outer edges of the target are our relationships with strangers. Closer in are acquaintances and business associates. The next ring represents friends. In the bull's eye are the closest, most important relationships.

Who Is Closest to Our Unhealed Wounds?

— Family
— Close friends, spouse, lover
— Coworkers, casual friends
— Acquaintances
— Strangers

Most of us operate at a higher level of healing at the outer edges of the target, in our relationships with friends, acquaintances and business associates. In close relationships—especially when conflict occurs—your unhealed wounds force you to behave at your lowest healing level. It is that lowest healing level that puts the ceiling on your happiness and sense of fulfillment in life.

Your assessment therefore provides a wealth of information about your wounds by uncovering your weakest points. For example:

- If you thought you were in Stage Four (Healing) or above, but your average score was lower than that, you probably have some holes to fill in early healing work.

- If you thought you were in Stage Five (Rebirth), but your average score placed you in Stage Two (Foundation) or Three (Feelings), you may be doing something we call the Two-Five Jump, which we describe later in this section.

- If your individual response scores vary widely or are clustered like Samuel's, this also indicates healing work from earlier stages that you must complete before you will move ahead.

- If you thought you were in Stage Six but scored lower, you may be settling for too little in your primary relationship, or you may not have a clear picture of what a healthy relationship looks like.

- If your score is very low—1.5 or below—ask yourself, *"What is it that happened to me in the past that I'm afraid will happen to me again?"* Examine your false hopelessness and your ideas about what horrible things will happen to you if you deliberately expose your wounds. Then use the suggestions in Chapter Twenty-Three to bolster your willingness and create a realistic picture of the benefits of healing.

A close look at your results will help you create a healing plan that fits your "holes." A close-fitting healing plan can help you raise your potential for happiness, both in your intimate relationships and in the rest of your life.

In the next chapter, you'll get a chance to evaluate your healing level in your non-dominant stages.

TWENTY

Your Secondary Healing Stages

The task we must set for ourselves is not to feel secure,
but to tolerate feeling insecurity.

— *Erich Fromm*

No one ever lives in just one stage at a time. We all have work to do in other parts of the journey—usually tasks that we neglected earlier. You'll find that the bulk of this work is concentrated in one level, which we call your secondary stage. Now that you've identified your dominant healing stage, you're ready to use the checklists in this chapter to determine what other skills or habits may need your attention.

Checklist Instructions

The following pages contain lists of traits typical of people who have mastered most of the tasks and resolved most of the issues in a given stage. We suggest you photocopy the rest of this chapter and use it to complete this self evaluation, so you can easily re-evaluate yourself in the future.

Read each item. Then:

• If it describes something about how you behave, feel or think *most of the time* today, check the **T** box for "True."

• If it doesn't describe you, check the **F** box for "False."

• If it simply doesn't apply to you, leave both boxes blank and go on to the next item.

Stage One Mastery Characteristics

T F

1. ☐ ☐ I know I could not go back to life the way it was before I became willing to heal and change.

2. ☐ ☐ If I thought I had to go back to life as it was before willingness, I would lose all hope.

3. ☐ ☐ My willingness to heal my wounds gives me hope about what my life can become or where it seems to be going.

4. ☐ ☐ Healing my wounds—so I can feel good about me and be in loving relationships, productive and of service—is the most important thing in my life.

5. ☐ ☐ I am totally committed to my recovery and my full healing.

6. ☐ ☐ I am willing to go to any lengths to live a life of integrity, peace and lovingness.

7. ☐ ☐ I am willing to go through the pain of healing because I know this is what it takes to reconnect with myself and others.

8. ☐ ☐ I hold no hope that continuing my addictions or anesthesia use will ever bring me anything I really want.

9. ☐ ☐ I can name the effects my anesthesia use has had on my life.

10. ☐ ☐ I am willing to face life without anesthesia.

11. ☐ ☐ I am willing to feel my pain.

Stage Two Mastery Characteristics

T F

1. ☐ ☐ I abstain from my addictions.

2. ☐ ☐ If I have a history of using substances to numb my feelings, I have made and implemented a plan to stop.

3. ☐ ☐ If I have a history of using people, beliefs or behaviors to numb my feelings, I have made and implemented a plan to stop.

4. ☐ ☐ If I have health problems, I have adjusted my life, my schedule, and my expectations of myself so my health problems do not interfere with my healing activities.

5. ☐ ☐ My diet doesn't create physical problems for me.

6. ☐ ☐ If I have chemical or physiological imbalances in my body, I have taken measures to stabilize them.

7. ☐ ☐ If I have physical concerns that could distract me from my healing work, I have taken measures to mitigate them.

8. ☐ ☐ I have a mentor or sponsor—someone whose healing work is at least a little ahead of mine—with whom I discuss my journey.

9. ☐ ☐ I actively gather information about healing and about my primary addictions or anesthesias.

10. ☐ ☐ I consistently allocate a substantial chunk of my time and life energy to recovery, healing, wellness or personal growth (in the form of a twelve-step program, support groups, therapy, study, or any other pursuit that supports my growth and change).

11. ☐ ☐ I have developed spiritual resources that I trust to guide me in my healing.

12. ☐ ☐ I practice staying connected with my spiritual resources on a daily basis through prayer, meditation or other spiritual practice.

13. ☐ ☐ I take daily quiet times for healing-oriented reading, writing, meditation, prayer or other spiritually nourishing pursuits.

14. ☐ ☐ I regularly spend time playing—but not at the expense of a balanced life.

15. ☐ ☐ I regularly spend time relaxing—but not at the expense of a balanced life.

16. ☐ ☐ I spend most of my "people time" with close friends who are actively doing their own recovery or healing work.

Stage Three Mastery Characteristics

T F

1. ☐ ☐ I am able to feel an entire range of feelings—all the variations of mad, sad, glad and scared.

2. ☐ ☐ I accept my feelings and know all of them are okay, no matter what they are or how awkward I feel about having them.

3. ☐ ☐ Although there are still feelings that I am ashamed of or afraid to feel, my shame or fear doesn't stop me from feeling them.

4. ☐ ☐ I can express any feeling I have without being destructive to myself, others or property.

5. ☐ ☐ I don't apologize for my feelings.

6. ☐ ☐ I don't become overwhelmed by my feelings.

7. ☐ ☐ I don't make myself wrong for having my feelings.

8. ☐ ☐ I don't avoid certain feelings by turning them into other feelings (crying instead of getting angry, getting angry instead of feeling grief, and so on).

9. ☐ ☐ I can stay with feelings that I used to run away from (by numbing out or diverting my attention to other things).

10. ☐ ☐ I can recognize that when I am defensive, it is because I have unhealed wounds.

11. ☐ ☐ I find pleasure in knowing how I feel.

12. ☐ ☐ I am getting to know myself better.

13. ☐ ☐ I have friends with whom I can share my deepest feelings.

14. ☐ ☐ There are people in my life who really know me.

15. ☐ ☐ It is easy for me to share my feelings with others.

16. ☐ ☐ I can keep myself company with all my feelings.

17. ☐ ☐ I have experienced uncomfortable feelings lifting as a result of allowing myself to really feel them.

18. ☐ ☐ I am comfortable with the feelings of others (my parents, my children, my friends and loved ones) and can allow them to express how they are feeling.

19. ☐ ☐ I am usually aware of how I am feeling.

20. ☐ ☐ I know what it means to take care of myself emotionally.

21. ☐ ☐ I can tell when others are not saying all of how they are feeling.

22. ☐ ☐ I don't cut off other people's feelings.

23. ☐ ☐ I face my feelings more often than I numb them.

24. ☐ ☐ I do not fear the spiritual force that powers the universe, whether I think of this force as God, a Higher Power or an impersonal force.

Stage Four Mastery Characteristics

T F

1. ☐ ☐ I make accurate assessments of other people's levels of healing.

2. ☐ ☐ I see and accept people's dark sides as fully as I do their sweet sides.

3. ☐ ☐ I don't idolize or villainize authority figures; I respond to them as the fallible human beings they are.

4. ☐ ☐ I am rarely disappointed by others' actions (that is, I am rarely caught off guard by my false hope).

5. ☐ ☐ I can think about my parents, childhood and family and feel peaceful.

6. ☐ ☐ I know what it was that I hoped for, but didn't get, from my family of origin.

7. ☐ ☐ I have grieved the hopelessness of my childhood; I now feel very little residue regarding how powerless I was then.

8. ☐ ☐ I have grieved the traumas, disconnections and abuses that happened to me.

9. ☐ ☐ I no longer feel impaired by what happened in my past.

10. ☐ ☐ Most of the time, I don't compare myself to others or see others as better than or less than me.

11. ☐ ☐ I no longer fantasize about a perfect love that will make me happy.

12. ☐ ☐ I no longer rely on people, places or things for my happiness.

13. ☐ ☐ I understand why I created the kinds of relationships I did before I confronted my happy-ending fantasies.

14. ☐ ☐ I rarely attract the same old situations that caused me so much pain in the past.

15. ☐ ☐ When I do attract old, painful situations, I recognize them much more rapidly than in the old days, and I respond by setting effective boundaries.

16. ☐ ☐ I have acknowledged, felt and released all the anger I had for all of the people who were my main caretakers when I was a child and teenager.

17. ☐ ☐ I am no longer stuck in either denial or anger.

18. ☐ ☐ I understand each of my parents' roles in my family's dynamics.

19. ☐ ☐ When old wounds are triggered in me, I become aware of this more quickly than ever before, and I know how to work with them.

20. ☐ ☐ I neither blame others nor shame myself when I lose my peace.

21. ☐ ☐ I feel empowered—rather than shamed—by the knowledge that I only lose my peace when an unhealed wound inside me is triggered.

22. ☐ ☐ There is no feeling I am afraid of feeling.

23. ☐ ☐ There is no memory I am afraid to remember.

24. ☐ ☐ I no longer fear being abandoned by others.

Stage Five Mastery Characteristics

T F

1. ☐ ☐ People generally know where I stand.
2. ☐ ☐ Most days, I feel good about myself.
3. ☐ ☐ I usually stick to my boundaries.
4. ☐ ☐ I can (and do) smile at myself in the mirror.
5. ☐ ☐ I genuinely like myself.
6. ☐ ☐ I am comfortable looking most people in the eye.
7. ☐ ☐ I owe no back taxes.
8. ☐ ☐ If necessary, I have cleared up my credit history.
9. ☐ ☐ I pay off my credit cards in full on a regular basis.
10. ☐ ☐ Most days, I like my job.
11. ☐ ☐ My life is moving forward.
12. ☐ ☐ My closets are as clean and organized as I need them to be.
13. ☐ ☐ I am comfortable with the clutter level—or lack of it—in my home.
14. ☐ ☐ I have resolved nearly all of my past unfinished business.
15. ☐ ☐ I don't accumulate large amounts of unfinished business in my life.
16. ☐ ☐ I can tell you my personal life mission and my top five life goals.
17. ☐ ☐ I usually don't put up with situations I don't like.
18. ☐ ☐ I'm learning to trust my intuition.
19. ☐ ☐ I reconcile my checkbook on a regular basis.
20. ☐ ☐ I have a financial plan that makes sense to me and includes strategies for getting out of debt, staying out of debt, nourishing myself in the present and preparing for my future.
21. ☐ ☐ I have very few resentments.

22. ☐ ☐ I am as physically fit as I want to be.

23. ☐ ☐ I am completely free of dependence upon anesthesias of any kind.

24. ☐ ☐ I know how to relax, re-charge and have fun—and I do so on a regular basis.

25. ☐ ☐ I get things done on time.

26. ☐ ☐ Fear rarely dictates my decisions.

27. ☐ ☐ I don't take myself too seriously.

28. ☐ ☐ I usually feel liked by others.

29. ☐ ☐ Most of the time, I feel good about my physical appearance.

30. ☐ ☐ Rather than trying to rescue or control the people in my life, I allow them to experience the consequences of their actions, both positive and negative.

31. ☐ ☐ My life is not filled with people who don't take care of themselves.

32. ☐ ☐ I understand what it means to take personal responsibility for my perceptions, interpretations and wounds.

33. ☐ ☐ I usually take responsibility for my perceptions, interpretations and wounds instead of shaming myself or feeling victimized by other people or situations.

34. ☐ ☐ I know what it means to make amends.

35. ☐ ☐ I don't hesitate to make amends when I feel they are warranted.

36. ☐ ☐ I have the job skills and training I need to move forward in the career I have embraced.

37. ☐ ☐ I am moving forward in my career.

38. ☐ ☐ My job and life purpose are aligned.

39. ☐ ☐ There is nothing in my past that haunts me.

40. ☐ ☐ Most of the time, I am on time.

41. ☐ ☐ I usually plan my time well.

42. ☐ ☐ I rarely feel controlled by time.

43. ☐ ☐ I refrain from rescuing unwilling people and feel comfortable about it.

44. ☐ ☐ I help people who are willing.

45. ☐ ☐ I recognize and am comfortable with my emotional and physical limits.

46. ☐ ☐ I'm comfortable with my weight.

47. ☐ ☐ I feel independent, without being addicted to independence.

48. ☐ ☐ I rarely need to numb out.

49. ☐ ☐ I am comfortable with my sexuality.

50. ☐ ☐ I feel a deep sense of personal competence, wholeness and self-sufficiency.

51. ☐ ☐ I know how to laugh and play by myself and with others.

52. ☐ ☐ I regularly set aside time to play by myself and with others.

53. ☐ ☐ I enjoy my own company apart from others.

54. ☐ ☐ I can usually tell others about my experiences without shame.

55. ☐ ☐ For the most part, I am unashamed about who I am, even though I still have some unhealed wounds.

Stage Six Mastery Characteristics

T F

1. ☐ ☐ My primary relationship is healthy.

2. ☐ ☐ With most people, I am comfortable asking for what I need.

3. ☐ ☐ I know how to work through conflicts, and I do so.

4. ☐ ☐ I can tell when my intention is to protect myself and my wounds.

5. ☐ ☐ I know that I always play a part in whatever occurs between myself and another person.

6. ☐ ☐ Sooner or later, I take responsibility for my part in conflicts with other people.

7. ☐ ☐ I do not try to control others.

8. ☐ ☐ I am honest about myself without shaming myself or blaming others.

9. ☐ ☐ I am comfortable being vulnerable with others.

10. ☐ ☐ Because I trust myself to care for myself, I am able to trust others.

11. ☐ ☐ Because I trust myself, I am comfortable not trusting others, even if my lack of trust is based solely on my inner feelings and intuition.

12. ☐ ☐ In my relationships, I readily bring up issues that concern me.

13. ☐ ☐ I do not let resentments accumulate.

14. ☐ ☐ I have very few undelivered communications.

15. ☐ ☐ Most of the time, I choose being happy over being right.

16. ☐ ☐ I rarely allow other people or events to steal my peace of mind.

17. ☐ ☐ I generally feel intimately connected to my spiritual resources on a moment-by-moment basis.

18. ☐ ☐ I usually follow my intuition.

19. ☐ ☐ I am not afraid to fight; I know how to fight cleanly and I know what to do to help create a mutual state of "no residue."

20. ☐ ☐ I have a solid sense of who I am.

21 ☐ ☐ My close relationships bring me and the other person closer to our spiritual resources.

22. ☐ ☐ My close relationships enhance rather than diminish my sense of who I am.

23. ☐ ☐ When I am triggered, I view it as a signal to look within myself for an unhealed wound.

24. ☐ ☐ I know how to give within my limits and without losing myself.

25. ☐ ☐ I don't ask others to give me what they cannot give.

26. ☐ ☐ I would like to be married to me.

27. ☐ ☐ I have few illusions that something outside of myself will make me happy.

28. ☐ ☐ I make assessments of others without making them bad or wrong.

29. ☐ ☐ I participate in relationships without giving myself up.

30. ☐ ☐ I can set boundaries without trying to control or blame others.

31. ☐ ☐ My solutions respect all boundaries—mine and others'.

32. ☐ ☐ I have and use a system for handling money, time, tasks and life goals with my significant other that is mutually nourishing.

33. ☐ ☐ I am comfortable with my responses to social, political, economic and ecological issues.

Stage Seven Mastery Characteristics

T F

1. ☐ ☐ I am clear about what forms of service I am most deeply drawn to and gifted in.

2. ☐ ☐ My service work emerges from a sense of taking care of myself and feeling good about me.

3. ☐ ☐ My service work is motivated by love—not self-righteousness, indignation, anger or a need to control, blame, punish or change others.

4. ☐ ☐ My service work in no way compromises my personal healing, my integrity or my relationships.

5. ☐ ☐ My service work is not a primary way of gaining self-esteem or approval from others.

6. ☐ ☐ My service work is not a prerequisite to feeling a sense of well-being.

7. ☐ ☐ However, I always feel further healed as a result of the service work I do.

8. ☐ ☐ I usually don't give beyond my limits.

9. ☐ ☐ Even though I am highly productive, I am far more concerned with role-modeling wholeness, high-level personal healing and loving connectedness than I am with doing tasks or maintaining high output.

10. ☐ ☐ I have lots of energy most of the time while still feeling inwardly serene and balanced.

11. ☐ ☐ I am rarely triggered by other people or events; when I am, I rapidly return to peace.

12. ☐ ☐ I see life situations and relationships as tools that uncover my wounds and allow me to heal myself further.

13. ☐ ☐ I feel a deeply nourishing sense of interdependence with others and with my spiritual resources.

14. ☐ ☐ I actively follow the spiritual path I've chosen; I feel more deeply nurtured by it—and more loving toward all people—as time goes by.

Determining Your Secondary Stages

When you have reviewed and marked all seven lists, go back through the lists for the stages prior to your dominant stage with a colored highlighter. Highlight each item for which you checked the **F** box.

The highlighter marks tell you which tasks you need to address outside your dominant stage. You will probably find more than one stage in which you have a large cluster of high-lighter marks. Most people have lots of marks in the stage just below their dominant stage, and perhaps a few in the stage before that.

These unfinished tasks from previous stages are as critical to your healing journey as are the tasks of your current dominant stage. We'll explain why in the next chapter.

Healing Plans and the Nature of the Journey

If we do not know what port we're steering for,
no wind is favorable.

— Seneca

Aɴɴᴇ Lᴀᴍᴏᴛᴛ, in *Bird by Bird: Some Instructions on Writing and Life,*[22] tells about having her tonsils out at age twenty-one. A week after the surgery, she requested more pain medication. The nurse told her that what she needed was not to numb the pain but to exercise her throat muscles by chewing gum. Anne was horrified. She said the nurse explained that muscles surrounding a wound will cramp around it to protect it from further violation; relaxing the muscles is a matter of using them, even though it hurts to do so. She sees an emotional parallel in this wisdom:

> *I think that something similar happens with our psychic muscles. They cramp around our wounds—the pain from our childhood, the losses and disappointment of adulthood, the humiliations suffered in both—to keep us from getting hurt in the same place again, to keep foreign substances out. So those wounds never have a chance to heal.*

[22]Pantheon, 1994.

If Anne is right (and we think she is), emotional healing is a matter of exercising seized-up psychic muscles to expose the wound beneath. When her tonsils were removed, she had a nurse to tell her that the exercise was necessary and the pain was temporary. A healing plan is like that nurse. It reminds you that your pain is not a signal that you are about to die, but that you are opening long-frozen psychic muscles.

This chapter describes some of the ways your psychic muscles will try to close up around your wounds, and how a healing plan can help you stay with the program.

The Influences

How fast will I travel? How far do I have to go? How much will it hurt?

Sooner or later, everyone wants to know the answers to these questions. No one can predict the course of his own (or anyone else's) healing journey with absolute accuracy. However, we've discovered influences and principles that can predict tendencies. There are four factors specific to how wounded you are and a couple of general rules of the road.

The Serenity Prayer Factors

We call these the "serenity prayer factors" after the serenity prayer of Alcoholics Anonymous:

> *God, grant me*
> *The serenity to accept the things I cannot change;*
> *The courage to change the things I can;*
> *And the wisdom to know the difference.*

There are two factors that you can change, and there are two you can't change, and knowing the difference makes all the difference. The two factors you can't change are:

• **Damage Already Done**—How much damage you sustained from your primary anesthesias before you began your healing, and how deeply you were wounded as a child. The deeper the wounds and the more extensive the damage, the longer the journey will take. People who survived sexual abuse or unusually cruel physical or emotional abuse usually need more time to approach their core wounds than people whose childhood abuse history was less severe. Similarly, climbing back from extensive physical or emotional damage wrought by years of substance abuse, overeating, out-of-control gambling or other anesthesia use can take a long time.

- **Amnesia Level**—How much you have forgotten of your childhood disconnection, wounds and dysfunction. Amnesia especially may be a problem for you if the disconnection was either profound and dramatic, or subtle and covert. It takes time and discipline to break through these barriers.

It should come as no surprise that the two factors you *can* affect are both aspects of willingness. They are:

- **Willingness to Re-Organize Your Life**—The priority you give to your personal healing process. If you are unwavering in your commitment to spend your life energy, time and money on your healing first, over all other activities and commitments, you are likely to proceed more quickly than if you take a more *laissez-faire*—or a less focused— approach.

- **Willingness to Do Your Healing Work in an Orderly Way**—The priority you place on addressing the themes and tasks of each step of your healing and how well you resist the urge to skip steps.

Fortunately, the nature of the healing journey is extremely generous—it will accept any amount of willingness in any form. You may only be willing enough to become willing to *consider* the *possibility* that *perhaps* you should take a look at re-organizing your life. That's enough for starters.

Two Healing Journey Principles

In addition to the four serenity factors, our clients have revealed to us the existence of a set of healing principles—rules of the road—that govern everyone's healing journey, no matter how deep or superficial the wounds. These rules are like the law of gravity and other physical principles. You can violate them, but not without suffering consequences. Two of them have special meaning and application for the nature of the healing journey itself. The first one is:

We live life at the level of our wounds, not our wishes.

This means that, no matter…

> …how much you *wish* you were healed…

> …how much positive thinking you do…

> …how many affirmations you recite in front of the bathroom mirror….

> …how well you anesthetize yourself against the pain…

> …how good you are at acting healed…

…you will always be brought back to the truth of your unhealed wounds. You can't fake healing. Your agenda for healing exists independent of what you think it ought to be. It determines the course of your healing journey, just as a the nature of physical injuries dictates the course of medical treatment. If what you need is to heal a compound fracture of the tibia, it will not help to have your teeth capped.

The other law that has serious implications for your healing is:

The healing journey proceeds in sequence.

The healing journey is not a race. However, once undertaken, it must continue steadily forward. Your pace must be slow enough to allow you to heal every wound you encounter, but not so slow that you come to a dead stop and try to set up camp in one stage. And you can't skip steps. Well, you *can* skip steps, but, just as jumping off the roof of your house carries stiff penalties for attempting to violate the law of gravity, skipping steps brings consequences.

The consequences? The Rubber Band Effect.

The Rubber Band Effect

Regardless of how long it takes or how willing you are, the journey is not accomplished in a straight line. We all hope our healing journeys through the seven stages look something like this:

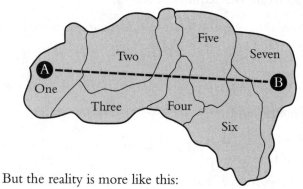

But the reality is more like this:

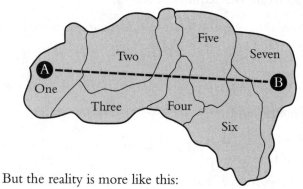

The path twists and curves because of the Rubber Band Effect.

When you try to avoid a wound (by skipping over painful stages or digging in your heels so you can stay in a current, relatively comfortable stage), you violate healing principles. This violation activates The Rubber Band Effect, whose job it is to bring you back into alignment with your healing journey. It won't let you avoid your unhealed wounds for long. If you try to move ahead too quickly, it pulls you back to the wounds you tried to ignore. If you stay in one stage after your work there is completed, it pulls you forward to confront the wounds of the next stage.

How to Activate the Rubber Band Effect

There's more than one way to avoid wounds and thus activate the Rubber Band Effect. Some of the more common triggers include:

- The Two-Five Jump
- Dabbling
- The God Sidestep
- Falling In Love
- The *"I've Arrived!"* Full Halt
- The Premature Abyss
- Life

THE TWO-FIVE JUMP

The Two-Five Jump is how most people create the Rubber Band Effect for themselves.

Derek, a recovering cocaine addict with four months clean and sober, said to us one day, "I can see where I am, and I can see so clearly where I want to be—the kind of person I want to be. But I'm not there yet, and I'm impatient."

Derek was firmly in Stage Two, and doing a good job of building his foundation. He attended Cocaine Anonymous (C.A.) meetings, talked several times a week with his sponsor and was working on the "searching and fearless moral inventory" recommended in step four of the twelve steps. His diligence had allowed him a glimpse of what was to come in Stage Five (Rebirth). The gap between what he is today and what he will be in the future is the work of Stages Three (Feeling) and Four (Healing).

However, several months ago, Derek's impatience got the better of him. His willingness lagged and he tried to skip these stages and move directly from Stage Two into Stage Five. He started to concentrate on doing daily affirmations, thinking positive, reading more self-help books and going to more meetings. Without realizing it, he was trying to detour the feeling work of Stage Three and the abyss work of Stage Four.

Fortunately, the Rubber Band Effect quickly brought him back to finish this crucial work. Derek's C.A. sponsor recognized what was happening and suggested he pay attention to the wake-up call his life was sending him. Derek got himself back on track, found a good therapist and is now learning how to feel all his feelings without judgment.

Most Two-Fivers are easy to spot. They tend to look good on the surface—sober, successful, well-organized and apparently happy—but if you look closely, you'll notice the signs of anesthesia use. Two-Fivers tend to be:

- Workaholics, or
- Religious zealots who fear and avoid feelings, or
- Chronically late or absent, or
- Living in homes that are chronically disorganized, or
- Constantly entering and leaving relationships with the "wrong" people, and claiming that their own level of growth and healing allowed them to get out in time, or
- Full of affirmations and talk of transcending the past.

No matter what forms Two-Fivers take, you'll nearly always hear something from them about the past being over and done with and no longer a consideration in today's struggles.

FALLING IN LOVE

Another way to activate the Rubber Band Effect is to do good work in Stages One through Three, dip a toe in the abyss of Stage Four, then suddenly fall in love. Julio tried to take this detour.

"This is different than the other relationships I've been in," Julio said to us about his new love. "I've changed, and I've made a wiser choice of partner. And besides, now I know how to handle an intimate relationship."

Julio quit his therapy group, confident that he had done enough work and looking forward to a happy marriage. Six months later, he sheepishly called for an appointment with David. He had come face to face once again with his happy-ending fantasies. The emotional high of the early days of his relationship had faded and his unhealed wounds had begun to run the show again.

Of course, we gladly welcomed Julio back into group. There is no shame in getting caught in a Rubber Band Effect, and no right or wrong way to travel this territory. Julio moved into his abyss, and with the help of his group, is making it through, one step at a time.

DABBLING[23]

Some people play around the edges of healing. They attend self-help group meetings, go to therapy, join spiritual movements— but never really commit to doing the difficult emotional work. We call these people dabblers.

If you are dabbling in a twelve-step program, you are probably attending meetings sporadically (or even faithfully), yet wondering why the program doesn't work, because you still feel bad or repeat old patterns. But you aren't really working the program; you haven't done what twelve-steppers call a step study; found a sponsor, buddy or mentor; and you probably haven't looked closely at your own role in your addictions.

Herb is a dabbler. He attended meetings of Adult Children of Alcoholics (A.C.A.) and Codependents Anonymous (Co.D.A.) for four years. When he shared at these meetings, he usually

[23] In twelve-step circles, this is sometimes called the A.A. Waltz. It consists of doing the first three steps (admitting to having a problem that has made your life unmanageable and needing outside help to solve it) without ever getting to the fourth step (a searching and fearless moral inventory). For more information about the parallels between the Twelve Steps of A.A. and the Seven Stages of Personal Healing, see the chart on pages 408-09.

sounded sad and distressed. Lerissa ran into him at a self-help seminar a while ago.

"Do you think the twelve steps work?" Herb asked wistfully. "I mean, is your life different since you started going to meetings?"

Lerissa said that she thought the steps were invaluable and that her life had changed immeasurably over the previous few years, through a combination of therapy and working the steps. Herb said he hadn't seen much in the way of results in his life and was wondering why. Lerissa probed a little further, and discovered that, although Herb had done some Stage Three (Feelings) work, he had never completed a key activity of the twelve-step programs—the "searching and fearless moral inventory" of the fourth step. He had met with and rejected a number of therapists and had never found a sponsor or mentor. Herb had faithfully attended meetings, and that's about as far as his work went.

As a result, he was feeling the classic symptoms of the Rubber Band Effect: he felt stuck in his journey, dissatisfied with life, and confused by the progress others around him seemed to be making.

Dabblers haven't really reached Stage One. Like Herb, they are toying with the idea of willingness, dipping a toe into healing and swishing it around, but never diving in.

Dabbling is everyone's right. In fact, most of us do it to one degree or another. It can be an important phase—like a test drive before deciding to buy a car, or auditioning a cast for a new production. However, you delude yourself if you believe you can simultaneously dabble and heal your wounds. Hanging out between healing and living out your survival plan, and whining about it, eventually will get you some pointed advice (if you're lucky): fish or cut bait.

THE GOD SIDESTEP

Early in the healing journey, many people begin to suspect that this is spiritual as well as emotional work. They are right. Spiritual work is unavoidable. Unfortunately, many people fear and avoid this work. Those of us who were raised with a vicious, demanding, rigid, angry or indifferent "God" have good reason to fear spiritual work. It brings us face-to-face with our worst fears.

The God Sidestep appears in many forms:

- **Being over-controlling.** People who need to stay on top of every detail of their lives (and often, of the lives of the people around them) usually live by an unspoken rule that *"I must take care of this, because God can't be trusted with it."*

- **Holding on to over-generalized stories about the world.** Such as *"Nice guys finish last," "People who are soft and open get trampled," "If I'm trusting, I'll get sucked in and duped,"* or *"Life will just beat you down sooner or later."*

- **Egomania or rightness addiction.** You just know that God hates you, and you refuse to reconsider this conclusion. Or you feel certain that no love or hope is available for you.

- **Being a doormat.** Some people mistake passivity for piety. They stand by when unacceptable things happen and say, *God will take care of this; it must be God's will*, instead of setting boundaries or talking about their preferences or feelings.

THE *"I've Arrived!"* FULL HALT, OR SETTING UP CAMP

Achieving abstinence from an addiction is a major accomplishment. However, in terms of healing that you can do, abstinence is just the beginning. If you try to stop the healing process there, the Rubber Band Effect will do its darndest to pull you into the next stage. It's better to just go along and do the work than to try to dig in your heels.

THE PREMATURE ABYSS

Another symptom of the Rubber Band Effect appears when you go for a Stage Four experience—one designed to take you into your abyss, such as an intensive weekend retreat—before you are ready. Under these circumstances, you either go numb or become completely overwhelmed.

Abyss work is overwhelming, even when you are ready for it.[24] You'll know whether your abyss work was premature by its results. When you're ready for it, you come out of your abyss a changed person. If you're rushing things, you'll have all of the trauma and none of the benefits.

[24] See Chapter Twenty-Six for a complete description of the feelings people encounter while doing abyss work.

This symptom can appear if you are working with a therapist who is pushing you a little too fast. For example, our friend Hugh was uncomfortable with the way his therapist was pushing him. He quit therapy feeling sheepish and confused. When he learned about the Rubber Band Effect and the importance of setting his own pace, he felt relieved and willing to give therapy another chance. Hugh returned to his therapist and explained what he needed and how he felt. His therapist was delighted to slow down and began helping Hugh build the tools he needed for the trip into his abyss.

Often the response to a premature abyss experience is less dramatic, however. Elizabeth attended a Stage Four-type weekend seminar in anger release. She got through it without becoming overwhelmed, but her life was unchanged. Later, Elizabeth said she felt as though something important happened that weekend, but she didn't know how to get back to it or put it to good use. What had happened that weekend was that Elizabeth's unconscious mind protected her from a deep experience because she wasn't ready for it; as a result, she surfed the waves of her emotions rather than diving beneath them to contact her wounds.

If this happens to you, be kind to yourself; there is nothing shameful about not being ready for an abyss experience. When you are ready, you'll do it.

LIFE

The Rubber Band Effect is *not* an indication that you have somehow failed. In fact, it is not necessarily even a mistake.

Just being alive is enough to activate the Rubber Band Effect. It can happen after an encounter with a person or situation that triggers one of your deepest unhealed wounds.

Yolanda found herself recycling into Stage Four (Healing) from Stage Five (Rebirth) after a couple of events. First, her younger sister, Marjorie, moved into a new stage of healing and began setting firm boundaries in her relationship with Yolanda. This upset the equilibrium in their relationship; Yolanda realized that she had been in the habit of criticizing Marjorie, something Marjorie no longer allowed. Yolanda reacted with anger, hurt and confusion.

Then Yolanda attended an intensive anger-release weekend workshop with David and Rebecca. Over the weekend, she uncovered the source of her reaction to Marjorie's new-found independence. Her family had gone through financial turmoil when Yolanda was just a toddler. She absorbed her father's fear and self-doubt when he criticized all the employers who rejected him. Little Yolanda's conclusions about control and criticism were firmly lodged in her unhealed wounds from this disconnection from her dad.

For months after the workshop, she worked on these wounds. In spite of feeling hopelessly defective, she used the methods she had used before to get through her abyss: journaling, anger-release sessions, talking and crying with friends. She got out her personal healing plan and used it to direct and track her efforts. In addition, she began working with an art therapist to reach these early, pre-verbal wounds.

Because these were such deep, old wounds, it took nearly a year of concentrated work for Yolanda to regain a sense of hope and healing. But she did it. As a result, not only is her relationship with Marjorie closer, but her attitudes toward other people are more tolerant. She told us recently that her relationship with her Higher Power has also deepened.

How a Healing Plan Helps

Planning your healing goals allows you to use the healing journey influences to help you move along, instead of treating them as obstacles or enemies of your progress. Specifically, a healing plan:

• Helps you deal with the Rubber Band Effect

- Keeps pain levels to a minimum
- Speeds up the healing process

The following pages describe these benefits in detail.

Dealing with the Rubber Band Effect

In early healing in particular, most people are almost constantly in the Rubber Band Effect because of their all-too-human desire to move out of pain and into happy times. As we've seen, you can't avoid the Rubber Band Effect entirely. But a healing plan can help you keep a Rubber Band Effect from producing a disaster. It can help you recognize the Rubber Band Effect when it strikes. And when you understand what you're dealing with, you can apply first aid. Most important, it can help you ensure that your Rubber Band Effect doesn't turn into a relapse.

How can you tell when you are in the grip of a Rubber Band Effect? Think of running a race with a giant rubber band looping your waist to a stake driven firmly into the ground at the starting line. Depending on how long the rubber band is, you will be able to move ahead for a while. But gradually you will reach the end of the rubber band's stretch. At that point, you can push and sweat and run in place, but you won't get anywhere.

The Rubber Band Effect feels like that. When it's got you, you will find yourself exerting tremendous effort to grow and heal. You go to meetings and therapy, read more books, do more step studies, try new communication techniques—and still the relationship doesn't work, the job situation doesn't improve, your sense of confusion and sadness doesn't disappear, or you can't stop obsessing over the behavior of an addict you love. You lose your balance; you lose your peace; you feel that you are in over your head. You watch yourself regress to a healing stage you thought you were finished with. You might feel stuck, empty, depressed, shamed, frustrated, or hopeless. You might even feel the old temptation to anesthetize yourself.

When you experience the Rubber Band Effect, your inner critic will gleefully jump on your back. *"See, I was right! You're a failure,"* it will crow. *"You can't do anything right! You're worthless!"*

There's only one corner of the universe you can be certain of improving, and that's your own self.

– Aldous Huxley

Don't take your critic's attempts to shame you too seriously. Beating yourself up for having a Rubber Band Effect won't help. Remind your critic that the appearance of the Rubber Band Effect is simply a red flag—a warning that you are getting ahead of yourself.

Remind your critic, too, that you have a choice: to respond to the Rubber Band Effect by recycling or relapsing. Choosing to recycle means looking for what you've been avoiding or neglecting, and addressing those issues. (More about recycling and relapsing in the next chapter.)

Keeping Pain Levels to a Minimum

We'd like to be able to say that we've discovered a way to do healing work that is pain-free. We can't. Pain is inevitable.

However, we have discovered that the process is more painful than it has to be when people fear what's happening to them, worry about whether they are doing it right or struggle with relapse. Having a personal healing plan can reduce or even eliminate these sources of extra pain.

Julio was pushed into his abyss when his girlfriend broke up with him. He had come close to his abyss several times before, but had always been frightened by the intensity of his feelings and backed off. This time, though, he knew what to expect. David talked with Julio about the fear, hopelessness and grief of the abyss, and reassured him that he was *supposed* to feel that way. He pointed out that Julio was doing two pieces of emotional work at once: he was grieving the loss of the relationship *and* the old, unhealed wounds this loss triggered (that's the abyss). David helped Julio work out a plan to get him through his emotional work and pointed out the glimmers of hope that Julio, in his pain, might have missed.

Months later, when Julio emerged from his abyss, he was able to support others as they entered theirs. Later on, he recognized the signs that he was returning to his abyss to work on more core wounds and to get the help and support he knew he needed.

Speeding Up the Process

Most psychotherapists agree that it takes three to seven years for most people to achieve a baseline level of healing—what we call the first four stages. But we have seen people move far more quickly through the first four stages—sometimes in as little as two years. What makes the difference?

Two ingredients: The tremendous amount of willingness they brought to their healing journey and having a healing plan. Our clients who use a Seven Stages healing plan to figure out where they are and keep them on course take an average of two to three years to get from Stage One (Willingness) through Stage Four (Healing). Furthermore, these folks seem to pay less of an emotional toll to make it through their abyss because they know something about what's coming and how to help themselves through it.

As we explained early in this chapter, how long *your* healing journey will take depends on the nature and depth of your woundedness and your willingness. We can't predict how long anyone will take to heal. But whether your journey takes, say, seven excruciating years or three merely painful years can depend on whether you have a healing plan. A healing plan functions like a TripTik from the American Automobile Association or a blueprint for a house you want to build. It helps you stay on track, reminds you to complete all the steps in sequence and helps you monitor (and bolster, when necessary) your willingness.

Jack had plenty of willingness when he started his journey, but didn't have a healing plan. We think his story is fairly typical of people who begin their journey and stick to it, even without a healing plan.

"I spent four years attending A.C.A. meetings, doing step studies and learning about my wounds," Jack said. "Then I had a series of experiences at work that made me really hit an emotional bottom. I didn't know it, but I had entered my abyss for the first time. I started group therapy, and nine or ten months later I walked out of the other end of my abyss. So it took me almost five years of steady work just to 'clear my desk,' as I thought of it."

(Incidentally, Jack was in his mid-thirties when he reached Stage Five. This is about the soonest most people reach this stage. It is unusual for someone to finish Stage Four—or even to reach true willingness—in their twenties. That's because your work in your twenties is to establish yourself in the world. You are busy getting a job, buying things, saving money and generally learning how to be an adult in an adult world. We have worked with young people who started healing early in their lives, but almost invariably these young adults were in such tremendous pain that they saw themselves in a do-or-die position. Most of us don't exhaust our supply of false hope until our thirties, forties or even seventies. But then, some people never exhaust it.)

To learn more about how to create a healing plan for yourself, turn to the next chapter. There you will find examples of healing plans from three people with differing wounds and healing needs.

TWENTY-TWO

How to Create Your Own Healing Plan

Once we accept our limits, we go beyond them.
— *Brenden Francis*

As we pointed out in Chapter Twenty, no one lives in only one healing stage at a time. At any given time, you are working in your dominant stage, on issues leftover from your previous stage and on issues that stretch you into the stages just beyond.[25]

The key to a successful healing plan is balancing this past, present and future of your healing journey. To keep things in balance, you should:

- Rid yourself of as much baggage from the past as you can by locating and completing unfinished work from previous stages.

- Focus your efforts on your current dominant stage, unless emergency conditions (such as a Rubber Band Effect) direct your attention to previous stages or unless your life presents a special challenge that requires you to obtain more advanced skills.

- Keep more advanced activities to a minimum

[25] Incidentally, issues typical of stages two or more above your own may sound like intellectual gobbledygook. Trying to work too far ahead will only activate the Rubber Band Effect, as we saw in the last chapter.

To help you achieve this balance, we have devised a two-part format consisting of a Long-Term Healing Plan and a Weekly Healing Plan. (Blank versions of these forms are included on pages 400-403 for you to photocopy.) As you fill out these forms, keep in mind that your intuition is always far more important than any theoretical sequence of courses, readings, workshops, therapy or other activity.

We borrowed traits and experiences from several of our clients to show you how three hypothetical people might create balanced healing plans for themselves using our plan format. These people are:

Laura, a 46-year-old recovering alcoholic with nine years of sobriety and membership in A.A. She is in Stage Four (Healing). She is married, has three teenage children and works full-time as a librarian. She survived both sexual and physical abuse. Her parents were rigidly religious and prided themselves on their children's obedience. Laura's father died five years ago. Her relationship with her mother has improved since Laura got sober, but still tends to be difficult. Laura got into therapy a year ago and is currently working on wounds that influence the way she relates to her husband. This is her first time through the abyss.

Brad, a 29-year-old computer systems analyst. His mother divorced his father when Brad was eight years old. He never saw his dad again. Brad began his healing journey eight years ago, when he joined a therapy group and began attending Co.D.A. meetings. By last year, he had progressed to Stage Three (Feelings). Then his girlfriend of three years broke up with him. The pain of the breakup pushed him into his abyss for the first time and forced him to confront the part of his happy-ending fantasy that said a relationship would make his life right. However, although Brad had done some good healing work over the years, he had never abstained from his primary anesthesia: relationships. Since he was a teenager, Brad moved from one relationship directly into the next and thus avoided confronting the pain of his unhealed wounds. This unfinished work in his healing foundation activated the Rubber Band Effect, and Brad was pushed backwards out of Stage Four into Stage One (Willingness). He treated the breakup as a wake-up call, reassessed his willingness, made a decision to stay out of relationships for a while and got back into therapy. He is now back in Stage Three.

Marta, 38, a nurse, married with no children. Marta's parents had a fairly healthy relationship with each other and with each of their three children. Although Marta grew up feeling loved and supported, and she feels close to most of her family, she understands that parts of her upbringing left her wounded. For example, she realized several years ago that she is profoundly affected in her life today by her older brother's constant criticism and teasing of her when they were children. She has worked on this issue with the help of her husband and supportive friends, and attended some personal growth seminars. She is in Stage Five (Rebirth).

First, let's take a look at the Long-Term Healing Plan format.

The Long-Term Healing Plan

Your Long-Term Healing Plan gives you the big picture. It presents an overview of the work you will do in the coming months to finish the healing work of your dominant stage and your previous stages, and the work you will do to stretch into upcoming stages. To complete it, follow the instructions below:

1. Read the introduction to Section IV and everything in that section pertaining to your dominant and secondary stages.

2. Assemble the following information:

   • The list of characteristics for your secondary stage.

   • A photocopy of the blank Long-Term Healing Plan located on pages 400–401.

   • This book, opened to Section IV.

3. Fill in the date and all other blanks in the top section of the Long-Term Plan form, using Section IV and your secondary assessment lists as reference material.

   For example, if your dominant healing stage is Stage Three, you would write "3" in the first blank and "Feelings" in the blank after the ":." If your secondary healing stage (that is, the stage on whose characteristics list you had the largest number of "False" checks) is Stage Two, you would fill in "2" and "Building a Foundation for Healing."

4. Turn to the chapter in Section IV that presents information about your dominant stage.

5. From that chapter, copy the goal and emotional work into the boxes on the form.

6. Fill out the boxes in the left-hand column (*"I need..."*).

   Some people prefer to start with a general list on another sheet of paper, and then categorize it into information, tools, people and professional help, before writing in the boxes.

7. Using the suggestions under *Activities* in the appropriate Section IV chapters, fill in the boxes in the right-hand column (*"To meet these needs, I will:"*).

Your first priority should be your unfinished tasks from previous stages. Those are the ones that will activate the Rubber Band Effect sooner or later.

There are exceptions to this rule. For example, if you are a parent whose dominant stage is Two, it might be appropriate to sign up for parenting classes, even though parenting skills technically are Stage Six pursuits.

As you fill out your Long-Term Healing Plan, be realistic about what you are actually willing to do. It won't help your confidence to reach for the stars if you know you are only motivated enough to reach for the treetops (or possibly just to find some trees).

Laura's Long-Term Healing Plan

Laura's hot issue is the effects of the sexual abuse she suffered as a child. She is concentrating her efforts on healing these wounds. She had ignored the potential for their impact on her life until recently. In therapy, she has learned that their impact is profound, and she decided she was ready to face their residue. As soon as she began talking to her therapist about the events (she had never spoken of them before to anyone) she was plunged into her abyss. She began to feel depressed, weepy, angry, frightened and hopeless—all feelings she had locked up inside herself since the abuse occurred. Furthermore, she was frightened by the intensity and scope of the feelings themselves.

Her therapist has supported Laura's exploration and suggested she seek more information about sexual abuse and its effects on survivors. Laura decided to obtain a list of Incest Survivor's Anonymous (I.S.A.) meetings and other groups and find one she likes. She writes these goals in the *Information about* and *Networking* boxes. In looking over her secondary evaluations, Laura realized that she needs to do some Stage Three work regarding the way she expresses her feelings to her husband, specifically on items four through nine. She tends to rage at her husband and uses her rage as a substitute for boundaries and for feeling her grief. She has several friends who are learning in a technique called Compassionate Communication (developed by Marshall Rosenberg, Ph.D.; see *Stage Three Healing Resources* in Chapter Twenty-Five for more information). They have spoken highly of the technique, and Laura decides to use it to fill the holes in her Stage Three work.

Long-Term Healing Plan

for _Laura_

Date: _Aug. 10, 1995_

My dominant stage: _4 : Healing_
Goal: _learn to recognize / expose the wounds_
Emotional Work: _traverse my abyss_

My secondary stage: _3 : Feelings_
Goal: _Make friends w/ my feelings_
Emotional Work: _meet the "wants"_

I need...	To meet my needs, I will:
Information about: surviving sexual abuse	find a support group meeting for survivors of sexual abuse; get suggestions for reading
To develop tools to: communicate better w/ my husband	attend classes in communication
To network with people who: survived sexual abuse	have coffee after ISA meetings with some of the members
Professional help to: confront and stay with my grief and rage instead of running away from them	continue in therapy

Brad's Long-Term Healing Plan

Except in regard to his relationship addiction, Brad has a fairly solid foundation for healing. When he was thrown into his abyss and back out to Stage One to deal with his willingness to heal this wound, he went through the familiar steps of assessing his willingness and re-arranging his life to support the healing. He returned to group therapy and his Codependents Anonymous (Co.D.A.) meetings, joined a professional organization for computer programmers to distract himself from romantic relationships, and went on a relationship fast—six months without dating. So he's built a good foundation on which he can begin the feelings work of Stage Three. He just needs to continue what he's doing.

Brad also discovered that he tends to replace the anesthesia of an all-consuming romantic relationship with other anesthesias—television, in particular. He also realized that he had neglected items twelve, thirteen and fourteen in the list of Stage Two characteristics—all spiritual resources and spiritual practice items. Brad said he had been avoiding "dealing with all that spiritual stuff" because he fears God. But he's ready to confront his fears now.

Long-Term Healing Plan

for _Brad_

Date: _Aug 11_

My dominant stage: __3__ : _Feelings_	My secondary stage: __2__ : _Foundation_
Goal: _make friends with my feelings_	Goal: _Re-Organize my life_
Emotional Work: _Meet the teen_	Emotional Work: _Break up with my Anesthesia_

I need...	To meet my needs, I will:
Information about: My Career Co-Dependence Spirituality	Get books on Co-Dependence, Career, spirituality
To develop tools to: Be alone Communicate with my Higher Power	Journal
To network with people who: - Have Careers - Who pay as much attention to their career as to their relationships - Trust & love their Higher Power	Go to CoDa meetings
Professional help to: Stay with my feelings — esp. loneliness and fear — when they come up	Therapy CoDA Stay away from TV

Marta's Long-Term Healing Plan

Marta's dominant stage is Five (Rebirth), but her intensifying reactions to her brother indicate she is moving back into Stage Four. Their relationship as children was hostile. Marta's parents were largely unaware of the way Doug (who is five years older than Marta) bullied and criticized his sister. She developed an ability to shut down emotionally around Doug that got her through. Now, however, Marta finds herself flying into a rage at the slightest hint of disapproval from Doug.

Marta decided she needs information about why she responds to her brother the way she does, so she plans to read up on such relationships. She realized that she has trouble setting boundaries with her brother. She used to stay silent when he criticized her, while seething inside; now she tends to get defensive and argue with him. Neither strategy feels good to her. She decided to investigate seminars in her city that teach boundary-setting skills.

Marta wants the support of people who have healed some core wounds. This is often difficult to bring about. There aren't many Stage Five people around yet, and, as Marta says, "you can't exactly place an ad in the personals that says, 'post-abyss person with compassion, spiritual interests and medium-high levels of self-responsibility seeks friendship with same.'" She decides that, at this point, she will just have to keep her eyes peeled for people who might be where she is in the healing journey. In the meantime, she will continue to share with her husband and one or two friends, who are, if nothing else, supportive.

Finally, Marta felt she could use the help of a good therapist to gain some insight into and release from her wounds.

Long-Term Healing Plan
for Marta

Date: **Aug. 14**

My dominant stage: **5 : Rebirth**
Goal: **Welcome the new me!**
Emotional Work: **Expand Comfort Zone, Forgive**

My secondary stage: **4 : Healing**
Goal: **Learn to Recognize, Expose & Heal Remaining Wounds**
Emotional Work: **Abyss**

I need...	To meet my needs, I will:
Information about: Why I react to my brother the way I do	Read books on the subject of sibling relationships Write in my journal
To develop tools to: Set boundaries with my brother	Find Seminars in boundary setting skills
To network with people who: Have been to their abyss & are now in stage 5	Work on distinguishing two-givers from those who have truly done their abyss work Attend some personal growth seminars, lectures & workshops to find some stage 5 people. Pursue friendships with the people I meet
Professional help to: Explore my issues with my brother.	Get into therapy

The Weekly Healing Plan

The purpose of the Weekly Healing Plan is to make your healing journey a daily reality. Writing down activities you plan to do during the week to help you meet your long-term healing goals will keep you on track. We recommend that you set aside a half hour at the beginning of each week to set up your weekly plan, and then transfer your planned activities onto your calendar. Many people make a ritual of this time. Frances schedules a half hour on Sunday evenings for reading and meditation, followed by a half hour to fill out her Weekly plan. Often, it takes less time than that—just ten minutes or so to write in her weekly appointments, reading and meetings.

Using your Main Healing Plan and the activities guides in Section IV, follow the steps below to fill out your Weekly Healing Plan.

1. Fill out the date blanks at the top of the form.

2. In the **Activity** box, describe *one* specific activity that will help you meet the first need on your Long-Term Plan. Use the suggestions in Section IV, or make up some activities of your own, or ask friends in recovery for ideas.

3. Fill in the **How often?** box with the number of times this week you plan to do this activity.

4. Fill in the **When?** box with the days and times you plan to do this activity. Be sure to transfer this commitment to your daily appointment book so you won't forget.

5. In the **Potential Roadblocks** box, describe resistance you may encounter from others and from yourself. Anticipating such roadblocks allows you to make a plan to deal with them, so they are less likely to sabotage your efforts.

6. Develop a strategy for dealing with the interference you anticipate, and describe it briefly under **How will I handle roadblocks?**

7. At the beginning of each week, review last week's plan. Place a check in the ✓ column for each activity you completed. Carry over to this week's plan the activities you didn't complete last week. Think about what interfered with their completion, and incorporate that into the **Potential roadblocks** box on this week's plan for that activity.

Laura's Weekly Healing Plan

Based on her long-term plan, Laura decided that her number-one priority this week is to find a support group meeting she likes. She knows it may well take more than a week to find one in which she feels comfortable, and so she is prepared to make this her number-one priority for as long as it takes. She is starting with the I.S.A. schedule. This week's activity is to choose a meeting or two that fits her schedule, and attend. Since she hasn't picked the meetings yet, she leaves the **When?** box blank. She anticipates that her family may object, if the meeting cuts into her time with them. After some thought, Laura concludes that her family is supportive enough of her efforts to heal that she could deal with this roadblock before it appears by holding a family meeting and explaining its importance to her. Her family is aware that Laura is a molestation survivor, although they don't know the details.

Laura's second activity is to get a copy of the schedule of presentations, groups and classes at her city's Center for Compassionate Communication. This is an easy one for Laura. She plans to call the center with her request tomorrow.

Her final activity is probably the most challenging: Laura wants to tell her therapist about the first time she was molested by her uncle. Laura has just begun to talk about her sexual abuse, but only in very general terms. Doing battle inside her are two powerful impulses. One, implanted over years by her uncle and the others who molested her, is to keep the secret—to never, ever tell. Her abusers convinced her that terrible things would happen to her and to the people she loved if she told, and so she never did. The other impulse, gathering its own momentum over the time she has been in therapy, is to tell everything—names, dates, places and exactly what happened. Laura wants to tell, and she believes that it is important to do so. She feels ready, although scared. She trusts her therapist and suspects she is strong enough to ride out the feelings when they come. But she's not sure. From her experience, she knows that she can probably deal with her fear by talking about it first.

Weekly Healing Plan

for _Laura_

Activity	How often?	When?	Potential roadblocks	How will I handle roadblocks?	✓
revise ISA schedule, put 1 or 2 meetings and 7e!	1-2 times	?	family demands	let family down and explain that this is important; ask for their support	
call center for compassionate communication for schedule	1	Aug 14	none	—	
go to therapy - TALK!	1	Aug 16	fear of feeling the pain and shame	talk about fear FIRST	

Brad's Weekly Healing Plan

Brad decided, based on his secondary evaluation, that the biggest, most important holes in his healing journey are the ones regarding his spiritual practice and Higher Power. When he decided to go on a relationship fast, he realized that he would need something to replace the comfort he derived from relationships. But friends' suggestions that he explore some form of prayer or meditation filled him with rage. Brad was healed enough to recognize this reaction as evidence of an unhealed wound.

As he wrote, thought and talked about his wound, Brad realized that he sees God as demanding, rigid and angry—not the kind of Higher Power he wants to turn to when he s in pain, or to entrust with his life and healing. Thanks to a suggestion by a Co.D.A. mentor, Brad suspects his fear of God is founded in his relationship with his father, a workaholic with little time for his son. Before he abandoned the family, Brad's father taught him to view God as impersonal and vengeful. As a result, he views all religions with suspicion and is unwilling to address his spiritual wounds in any form of church, temple or mosque. However, he feels a deep longing for a sense of guidance and purpose in his life. He knows that, in the absence of anything else, he will attempt to fill this need with relationships, something he doesn't want to do again. Brad decided it's time to heal the wound.

He decided to begin his search by reading books and listening to tapes—a comfortable first step for him. His plan for this week is to visit a bookstore and pick out one book each on spirituality and codependence.

Brad plans to begin keeping a journal this week. His objective is to write in his journal every day, even if it's just a couple of sentences.

He also plans to subscribe to a magazine about computer programming, to encourage interest and motivation in his career.

Brad has a long-standing, firm commitment to healing and has developed a fairly well-disciplined daily schedule that supports healing activities. Therefore, he doesn't anticipate encountering any roadblocks that are likely to sabotage his latest efforts. If he discovers any during the week, he'll add them to his plan next week, along with a ideas for dealing with them.

Weekly Healing Plan

for _Brad_

For the week of _Aug 13-20_
through _____

Activity	How often?	When?	Potential roadblocks	How will I handle roadblocks?	✓
Go To Bookstore	1	Wed	None		
Subscribe to Programming Journal	1	Wed	None		
begin a Journal	7	Once/day	None		
Go to CoDA meeting and talk to one person	1	Thu	None		
Therapy	1	Mon	None		
Keep TV Watching down to 3 hrs/week	3	m-1hr T-1hr T-1hr	None		

Marta's Weekly Healing Plan

Marta's activities for this week consist of research: she plans to visit the bookstore near the hospital where she works to check out the self-help section; to get some information about upcoming seminars; and to find out whether her health insurance covers therapy.

She can see minor roadblocks for each activity. Wednesday is the only day she has time after work to visit the bookstore, and she knows she is often too tired to bother with anything other than going straight home. She decided to prepare for her excursion by getting to bed earlier than usual the night before, and to be sure to eat a healthy lunch (which she tends to skip) on Wednesday.

Marta has no idea where to look for news about seminars. However, she remembers her friend Gail has attended a number of them and might have some leads. She also remembers that the bookstore usually posts notices of upcoming personal growth events.

Finally, Marta feels shy about asking her human resources representative questions about coverage for mental health expenses. After some thought, she decides that HR reps are used to hearing such questions and are supposed to keep them confidential. She decides to remind herself of these facts and of how much she needs and wants to get help, and to share her anxiety with her friend Gail. She also plans to confront her fears by asking the HR rep about what they do to maintain confidentiality.

Weekly Healing Plan
for __Marsa__

Activity	How often?	When?	Potential roadblocks	How will I handle roadblocks?	✓
Visit bookstore to review self-help section	Once	Wed	I might try to blow it off because I feel too tired	Go to bed an hour earlier Tues. night; be sure not to skip lunch on Wed.	
Research available seminars	Once	Thurs.	Don't really know where to look	I'll call Gail for ideas- she's into this stuff	
Find out from HR what & how much therapy my insurance covers	Once	Tues.	Embarrassment about asking - they might think I'm weird.	Remind myself that they are used to questions and that all info they receive is confidential! Take a deep breath; remind myself how much I need/want this - get a pep talk from Gail	

Re-Thinking Your Plan

Your healing plan is not a static document. It will evolve over time as you heal. Mark a date on your calendar some time between three and six months from now to re-assess your healing level, evaluate your needs and revise your healing plan.

In the meantime, be alert for signs that your needs have changed. When the Rubber Band Effect pulls your attention to neglected wounds, you will need to revise your healing plan.

In addition, as you grow and heal and your life circumstances change, your needs and expectations also change. Your healing plan should be responsive to these changes. Applying what we call the "Enough" Principle to your plan can keep it fresh and useful.

The Rubber Band Effect and the Recycle/Relapse Choice[26]

26 For more information about relapse and relapse prevention, see Terence Gorski's *Counseling for Relapse Prevention* (with Merlene Miller, Herald House-Independence Press, 1982). While his work is addressed to counselors, it contains profoundly important information for all those who wish to maintain their abstinence.

The Rubber Band Effect presents you with a choice similar to the one you were given when your survival plan faltered.

When your survival plan threatens to fall apart and you get a wake-up call, you can ignore the wake-up call (by entering a window of willingness, improving your safety plan or choosing purgatory) or surrender to healing. In the Rubber Band Effect, when you get so caught up in your woundedness that not only does your healing grind to a halt, but you feel you've actually started moving backward, you have a similar choice: relapse or recycle.

When you *recycle*, you treat these occurrences as old wounds presenting themselves to be healed. If you have already dealt with parts of these wounds before, you realize that these are deeper layers now available to you.

When you *relapse*, you return, *without awareness*, to anesthesia use and other self-destructive behaviors. This return is invariably accompanied by an *"ah, screw it"* sort of attitude. Your willingness to change these behaviors—or even to see them as problems of yours to deal with—evaporates. In effect, relapse is returning to a pre-willingness state.

The relapse-recycle phenomenon is a lot like the Disneyland experience. Disneyland is known for long lines. On a busy day, you may wait in line for hours to get on one of the popular rides like Space Mountain. Sometimes, when you're stuck in one of these lines, you feel as if you've been standing in the same spot for twenty minutes. It becomes easy to think that "the ride will never come," (as did Rebecca and David's four-year-old nephew on his first trip to the Magic Kingdom). Even so, the line slowly but surely snakes around. At any given time you are much closer than you used to be. And, eventually, the ride does come.

When you recycle, you stay in line. You stick to your work, even when you feel confused or discouraged. In relapse, on the other hand, you give in to your frustration and discouragement and leave the line. It's as if you say, *"There is no ride and I'm not waiting anymore."* Of course, you can turn a relapse into recycling as soon as you become willing again—just as you can get back in line at Disneyland. Usually, however, you have to go to the back.

Your state of self-awareness underlies the biggest difference between recycling and relapse. When you recycle, you notice what's happening and take action to get your healing journey back on track. When you relapse, you muffle your awareness and head for the anesthesias.

JANELLE'S NEAR-RELAPSE

Janelle, a 45-year-old teacher, nearly sacrificed her career to drinking and drug use. She finally responded to her wake-up call, completed a residential treatment program and followed up with therapy and twelve-step meetings. She had been in recovery for nearly eight years when she was diagnosed with breast cancer. She had surgery and began radiation treatments, which made her ill. Several members of Janelle's cancer patient support group smoked pot to relieve the nausea that came with the radiation treatments. Janelle thought long and hard about whether this might be an option for her. She discussed the issue with her sponsor, her therapist and a couple of close friends. Finally, she made a careful decision that it was worth the risk— knowing that marijuana use is illegal and in spite of some advice to the contrary.

For several weeks, Janelle kept her pot-smoking under control, and it helped alleviate the horrible vomiting the radiation caused. However, for months after the treatments ended, Janelle continued to smoke occasionally, "to calm my nerves." One evening, as she rolled a joint, she realized that the baggie of pot she had purchased just days before was now empty. She dropped the joint, called her sponsor, went to a twelve-step meeting that night, and renewed her commitment to staying clean and sober.

Janelle was teetering on the edge of relapse. Her willingness to re-examine her life and motives turned her Rubber Band into a recycling episode instead. As she talked with her therapist about her reasons for continuing her pot use after the physical need for it was gone, she discovered the pockets of unwillingness and unhealed wounds that she was being called back to heal. She revised her healing plan to reflect her new focus and changed activities.

Avoiding Relapse

When people relapse, they usually do so because they are ultimately unwilling to surrender to the healing process. They cling to the belief that they can heal themselves if they do *some* healing work—just the part they deem necessary. They have convinced themselves that they are exempt from doing the rest of it.

One study on relapse behaviors indicates a direct correlation between relapse and avoiding one particular issue in recovery. The issue was different for each person: for some, it was an old relationship; for others, it was unresolved anger or abuse issues. Regardless of the issue, everyone's relapse correlated with their refusal to face their particular version of forbidden territory.

You will relapse sooner or later if you refuse to acknowledge and deal with the issues the Rubber Band Effect brings you. This means doing what Janelle did: going all the way back to the Willingness Stage to re-evaluate your healing plan and bolster your willingness to heal.

What keeps a recycling episode from becoming a relapse is willingness, intent and follow-through.

- **Willingness**—A recycling episode will not erode your willingness to face whatever needs facing, even though your willingness may be masked for a moment or two. A person in relapse loses (or never found) willingness and usually denies that there is anything she needs to face to begin with. Someone who has once found willingness always comes back to her commitment to heal. Have faith in the commitment you made. It's not revocable.

- **Intent**—In recycling, your intent remains the same (although sometimes with a temporary vacation): to confront and heal your wounds. In relapse, the intent is to avoid something at all costs. What the "something" is varies from person to person, but it invariably includes believing that you can heal without having to do certain things— things that any truly healing-focused person knows can't be avoided.

- **Follow-through**—After a recycling episode, you go back to fill in the gaps in your healing and then pick up from where you left off. After a relapse, you generally have to start the healing process all over again from the beginning (although you may sometimes be able to return to your pre-relapse level of healing more quickly than you did the first time).

Recycling may last anywhere from a moment to weeks. In some situations, you will complete a recycling episode by taking a deep breath and releasing your need to be right about a conflict or other issue.

In other situations, you may have to do what Janelle did and spend time addressing an unhealed wound. This may involve figuring out where you got sloppy in your healing. Sometimes you need to develop a tool that you thought you could do without, such as better communication skills.

The cure may not be easy, but it's simple: Find the hole in your healing and then do what's necessary to fill it. Follow the three steps below to pull yourself through a recycling episode:

- **Ask yourself a question** recommended by Stephen Covey, author of *The Seven Habits of Highly Effective People:*[27] "What's the one thing I'm not doing right now that if I were, would make the biggest difference?"

  If the answer isn't immediately apparent, review Stage One *Emotional Work* in Section IV and identify what you've stopped doing or have avoided doing.

- **Take action** based on what you discover. This usually means revamping your healing plan. When you've taken the needed action, the recycling episode will end.

- **Seek help** from a trusted healing-oriented friend or a therapist if, after you take action, you notice that you're still recycling. You missed something.

Over time, you'll get a feel for your movement through the stages and your changing needs. You are less likely to arrive at the verge of relapse before realizing that it's time to make a course correction. Like Corrine, whose story appears below, you'll recognize the signs of a Rubber Band Effect and almost instinctively adjust your healing plan.

CORRINE'S RECYCLING

Corrine was working on Stage Five issues in a cognitive therapy group after having done a fair amount of abyss work. For several months, this was exactly what she needed. The concentration on thought patterns and concrete suggestions for behavior changes suited her, and she jumped in with enthusiasm.

Then she attended a weekend intensive and found herself confronting an old issue. She felt hopelessly stuck. She found herself saying to friends, "I thought I was done with that wound!" She didn't see how she could ever heal herself, and she began to suspect that she couldn't trust her own inner guidance; after all, she thought she had seen the last of this issue, and here it was back again. (Incidentally, this is not at all uncommon; as you live life, the Rubber Band Effect returns you to unhealed parts of core wounds, and you may find yourself wailing the same phrase. Don't let it worry you; it's part of the normal healing rhythm.)

In despair, Corrine went back through Chapter Fifteen (*An Overview of the Seven Stages*, this section) to try to figure out what she had done wrong. One sentence jumped out at her: *"Early in the Rebirth Stage (Five), there seems to be a revolving door between it and the Healing Stage (Four)."*

She realized immediately that her experience in the weekend seminar had sent her back into her abyss. Suddenly, Corrine understood that her despair and pain were symptoms of Stage Four work. She put her company-keeping skills to work to get through the fear and sadness, and spent lots of time writing in her journal.

Shortly after the workshop, Corrine began to find the cognitive work boring. She felt impatient with it and began to wonder what she was doing there. After several weeks, she left the group, did some research and joined an art therapy group.

"It was amazing," she said. "As soon as I started working in this new group, I realized that this was where I needed to be. All my self-doubts and worries about whether I was running away from my wounds by leaving the cognitive group disappeared. I realized that I *could* trust my instincts—that I could trust my healing process to guide me to what I need."

Corrine went back to Chapter Twenty-Six (*Stage Four: Healing*) in Section IV, read up on healing activities for that stage and reworked her healing plan to reflect her new-found needs.

The "Enough" Principle

Another factor that determines when you need to revise your healing plan is the "Enough" Principle. The "Enough" Principle states:

Healing is a series of approximations.

This means that you heal your emotional wounds in baby steps, not by Olympic bounds. It asks you to treat yourself as kindly as you would treat a toddler learning to walk and talk. And it means that sloppy attempts at healed behavior are just fine.

Your healing process will lead you down what may seem like a circuitous road: from a sloppy rendition of healed behavior, to a less sloppy rendition, to a marginally graceful rendition, to an almost-graceful rendition, to a more graceful rendition, and finally, to a graceful rendition of healed behavior.

If your inner critic begins carping about the speed of your progress, refer it to the Enough Principle.

How do you know when you've done enough? It depends. Your measure of "enough" changes from one day to the next, depending on what you want for yourself. For example, when you go through your abyss the first time, mere survival is enough to move you into the beginnings of Stage Five (Rebirth). But if what you really want is a Stage-Six-type relationship, making it into early Stage Five isn't enough. For that, much more is required. When you become aware of wanting more, it's time to revise your healing plan.[28]

The Enough Principle also reminds you to be reasonable about how much you expect yourself to do. Our friend Lou pointed out that, after he and his wife finish their work days, have dinner, feed and bathe their two toddlers and put them to bed, they have one hour to spend together before they fall into bed exhausted.

"That hour is precious to me," Lou says. "I have no intention of giving it up for anything."

But Lou also feels committed to his healing journey. Given the circumstances of his life, his healing journey gets less time than it might if he were single, didn't have children or were independently wealthy. As it is, his life is well-organized. He budgets thirty minutes to an hour a day for healing activities, and usually sticks to his schedule. It is enough. (It is important to note, however, that Lou is, at this writing, in late middle healing. None of his wounds is threatening to tear his life apart. If he were in early healing, it would be a good idea to make healing activities his first priority for a while, or he might not end up with a wife to spend time with.)

If you make unrealistic plans, you are setting yourself up to fail and feel discouraged. Do everything you can, and do everything you need to do. It may be that the best you can do right now is to fill out your long-term healing plan and tack it up on the wall over your desk as a reminder to write that support

[28] Incidentally, one thing is true regardless of what you want: you can't know whether you've done *enough* unless you first know how much you've done. Keep track of what you have done, and stop to congratulate yourself from time to time. Celebrate your successes.

group meeting down in your daily planner each week. That may be enough. On the other hand, you may have time and need enough to do much more. If your healing stage is One (Willingness) or Two (Foundation), you may need to do much more just to keep your life from blowing up.

All of this brings us back to our original premise: You're in charge. You get to decide. You're paying for the ticket—how far do you want to go?

Troubleshooting Your Plan

If you find yourself resisting keeping the commitments you make in your healing plan, isolate your problem in the form of a statement, like "I'm sick and tired of going to meetings!" Then check out the table on the next page for possible causes and suggested remedies.

Section IV provides descriptions of all your potential destinations. With some blank healing plan forms, the results of your self-assessments and the information in Section IV, you are now ready to take charge of your healing journey. Happy trekking!

◆

How to Troubleshoot Your Healing Plan

If you're saying:	You:	And it might help to:
"This is too much to do, it's too hard and I'm sick of it. I want a break!"	• May have bitten off more than you can chew and are over-dosing on recovery.	• Lighten up. Give yourself more fun and re-charging time. • Go back to the basics. Reinforce your Stage Two foundation.
"I'm frustrated and impatient about my progress. Why am I still doing this old stuff?"	• May have gotten ahead of yourself. Are you overesti-mating your dominant stage?	• Re-evaluate your dominant stage, and adjust your healing plan accordingly.
"I know I've got my dominant stage accurately identified, but I still feel stuck."	• May be trying to go it alone. • May not have infor-mation you need. • May be weaker in some of your previous stages than you thought. • May be in the Healing Stage (Four).	• Get extra support and/or input. • Consider further reading, a pertinent workshop or class, calling on your sup-port system (especially a mentor or sponsor) more or doing some therapy. • Re-evaluate your secondary healing plan and strengthen the weaker areas. • Get extra support and reassurance for this demanding work, if you are in the Healing Stage (Four).
"It seems as if I'm just not willing."	• May be willing but think you are unworthy.	• Have your inner critic write you a no-holds-barred letter telling you why you should be afraid, why you don't deserve to be happy, or why this healing garbage is unimportant. • Have your inner child write to you about his or her fears or sense of unworthiness. • Write letters back. • Get outside support.

A Stage-by-Stage Look at Healing Requirements

A Stage-by-Stage Look at Healing Requirements

*It is never
too late
to give up
your prejudices.*
– *Henry David Thoreau*

To COMPLETE YOUR PERSONAL HEALING PLAN, use the information in this section to research the tasks of your dominant and secondary stages. For each stage, we present goals, emotional work, self-responsibility keys, activities, pitfalls, stage-specific healing resources and healing exercises. Descriptions of these elements follow.

Goal

This is a behavior, skill or habit that you will be able to do when you have completed most of the work in the stage. Understanding and reminding yourself of the goal of your current stage can help you remain focused on your healing work.

Emotional Work

Each stage has a characteristic set of feelings that must be experienced. Your emotional work consists of greeting, accepting and feeling the feelings. Under the *Emotional Work* heading, we describe what kinds of emotional challenges you are likely to encounter in each stage. Emotional work is closely connected to activities, which often bring up feelings that you may have kept under wraps (hidden even from yourself) for most of your life.

Self-Responsibility Keys

These are the issues of self-responsibility you are likely to face in each stage. For a quick reference, check the chart on pages 410-11 called *How Self-Responsibility Grows Through the Seven Stages*. The shaded boxes show you which issues of self-responsibility are of primary importance in each healing stage.

Activities

Activities are pursuits that help you reach the goal and accomplish the emotional work of a given stage. Some activities create opportunities to do emotional work; other activities consist of the emotional work itself.

In addition to the information in this section, we've provided a chart on page 404 called *A Stage-by-Stage Guide to Healing Activities* that summarizes the best activities for each stage and the activities to avoid in each stage to prevent triggering the Rubber Band Effect. In choosing an activity, try to select the ones that are likely to give you the biggest results for the investment. For example, reading about anger release represents a minimal investment in money, time and emotional commitment, and it will give you minimal results. Attending an anger release workshop, while it represents a bigger investment, stands to provide exponentially more significant results.

Under this heading, we sometimes describe types of therapy that are especially helpful for people in a particular stage. These are not hard-and-fast recommendations. There are many kinds of therapy you can use to address issues in any given stage. But to be most efficient, you need to keep in mind which developmental task you hope to complete and stay focused on that task. Otherwise, you may find that you've made the therapy model itself more important than the issues. Don't make a religion of your therapy model or a guru of your therapist. If you find yourself saying, *"If I can just learn _____, [fill in with a technique] I will be happy or at least pain-free,"* you have created a happy-ending fantasy.

Sometimes you won't be able to find anyone in your area who practices a specific therapy model we recommend. This is not a tragedy. Work with what is available to you. If you are especially interested in one of our recommendations, ask your practitioner to investigate it.

Finally, we offer the same advice given to those who attend twelve-step meetings: take what works and leave the rest. You know what's best for you. Trust your instincts. Stay focused on your goal. Use your healing plan.

Pitfalls

Pitfalls are anything that can create the Rubber Band Effect.

One pitfall common to all of the stages is the temptation to try more advanced activities in hope of hastening the healing process. It's okay to stretch into the next stage or two, especially if the demands of your life require you to develop certain skills. For example, parenting skills, which we classify as Stage Six and Seven activities, may be critical for you to learn even if you are barely into Stage Two (Foundation).

However, if you are skipping important emotional work in your current stage to tackle more advanced tasks, you will only bring the Rubber Band Effect down on yourself.

Stage-Specific Healing Resources

This consists of a list of books, tapes, techniques and therapeutic models suitable for the healing stage.

Sometimes a resource appears in two stages. That's because some resources are helpful for one reason in one stage and another reason in another stage.

The *Miscellaneous* category contains a list of materials by authors other than ourselves that we have found helpful. It is by no means an exhaustive list. We've tried to provide a good cross-section of the material that seems to be most useful. When you find a book that really works for you, check its suggested reading list for more titles.

Willingness Works Resources lists tapes, workshops and workbooks produced by the authors. You can order materials and sign up for workshops by telephone, mail or fax. Ordering information can be found at the back of this book.

Stage-Specific Healing Exercises

We have included a sampling of exercises tailored to the needs of each stage. This list is not intended to be exhaustive, either. You'll find many more exercises in the books and tapes listed under *Healing Resources*. However, these exercises should give you a good start on identifying and resolving your issues.

It's Up to You

We have no ax to grind in terms of methods, approaches or models you choose in any stage. We do want you to make sure that you match your needs in each stage with resources that can actually help you do your work in that stage.

As a consumer of the vast array of personal healing resources available today, you owe it to yourself to proceed in the most efficient manner possible. So whatever work you choose to do, please remember: the stages, the goals and the sequence are simply our ideas. *You* choose the forms through which you will do your work; our material can show you how to get the most of the healing resources you choose.

If you are a therapist, this section can help you identify therapeutic models that can help your clients through each stage.

TWENTY-THREE

Stage One: Willingness

Help! I've fallen and I can't get up!
  — Woman in security system commercial

WILLINGNESS IS THE BEGINNING OF THE HEALING JOURNEY. Its work focuses on admitting that you need help and on forging a commitment to healing.

It's important to note that Stage One lasts only as long as it takes to get into Stage Two (Foundation). For many people, it can be extremely brief—an instant of clear thinking. Other people wander in and out of Willingness for months or years until the wake-up calls become too loud to ignore.

Goal: Get Honest

In this stage, your goal is to abandon your denial about your pain. You commit to using no more Band-Aids—the anesthesias that kept your pain away. You lose your illusions about your ability to manage your life and your addictions by yourself, and you decide not to try to get them back.

When you reach the true willingness of Stage One, you finally commit yourself to healing, even though it means you'll have to stop running from and, instead, *feel* all the pain you've been avoiding.

Emotional Work: Hit Bottom

Most people do not reach Stage One if they believe in any other options. They generally arrive in a therapist's office or a twelve-step meeting in extreme pain, waving a white flag.

But true willingness does not arrive just because your life falls apart. You must answer the wake-up call by taking your pain seriously and acknowledging the message it's sending you: *Life the way you are living it doesn't work. Get help.*

Your emotional work is simple: Allow this process to occur; allow yourself to hit bottom. This means that you respond to your pain by facing it head-on and feeling it, rather than throwing your favorite anesthesia at it.

Remember Sharif? He's the stockbroker we met in Section I who finally committed to healing over a cup of coffee with a recovering rage-aholic. He is a great example of someone who had been brought to his knees over and over by his wounds, but who ignored the natural progression to willingness. Finally, he responded. Something in his conversation with Alex got through to him in a way that none of his life's catastrophes could.

Rachel hit bottom when her intellectual shields against pain were shattered by conflicting evidence. Raised by alcoholic parents, she shielded herself from pain with critical attitudes and by figuring things out. In a quest to understand her upbringing, she read extensively about the effects of alcoholic families. She learned that children of alcoholics often grow up to become alcoholics themselves, or to marry alcoholics. Rachel thought that knowledge was her power and her shield; since she knew about the possibilities, none of them would happen to her. Her faith in knowledge began to crack when she found herself in a relationship with an alcoholic.

One day Rachel's friend Gillian called with the news that *her* new boyfriend was an alcoholic. (Pablo had hidden his drinking from Gillian for the first few weeks of their relationship. He blew his own cover when he stood Gillian up for a date and she discovered him at home, passed out on the couch.) Pablo, frightened that he was going to lose Gillian, agreed to attend A.A. meetings, and Gillian asked Rachel to go to Al-Anon with her. Rachel readily agreed.

In their town at that time, Al-Anon included under its wing meetings of Adult Children of Alcoholics (A.C.A.). When Gillian and Rachel picked a meeting from the Al-Anon schedule, they failed to notice that it was marked Al-Anon/A.C.A.

At the beginning of the meeting, someone read aloud a list of personality characteristics of A.C.A.s[29]. Rachel was astounded— all items on the list not only applied to her, they had been the topics of most of her therapy sessions over the previous several years. She said later that it felt like someone had read her journal out loud.

[29] This list, usually referred to as "the laundry list," is available at most A.C.A. meetings.

However, by the end of the meeting, she had numbed the pain of recognizing herself among this group with her favorite anesthesia. She rationalized. On the way out to the car, she remarked to Gillian, "These people aren't so special. This is just a list of garden-variety neuroses. Everyone feels this way. For example, aren't you afraid of authority figures?"

"No," said Gillian.

Rachel paused. *Well, that was just one item*, she thought. "How about saying 'no'?" she asked. "Don't you have trouble saying 'no,' and feel guilty when you do?"

"Nope," Gillian said.

Rachel read the entire list of thirteen items to Gillian, who identified with one or two of them. Rachel, of course, identified with all of them. Stunned, she realized that she was wrong—*not* everyone felt this way. Gillian, who hadn't grown up in an alcoholic family, did not feel this way. The incident brought Rachel to willingness. She began attending A.C.A. meetings immediately.

(There is a delightfully paradoxical epilogue to this story. Years later, when Rachel recounted the episode to a friend, the friend pointed out that, although Gillian seemed unwounded to Rachel, the fact that Gillian was in a relationship with an alcoholic was in itself an indication that she had unhealed wounds. Ironically, it was Gillian's own denial, expressed in her inability to identify with the A.C.A. list, that broke Rachel's denial, a fact that filled Rachel with wonder at the creativity of wake-up calls. And eventually, Gillian took a closer look at her family. She recognized in her family's patterns the same alcoholic dynamics discussed at A.C.A. meetings, even though no one in her home drank.)

Self-Responsibility Key: A New Response to Pain

Pre-healing, you viewed pain as something inflicted upon you by forces outside yourself. It was to be avoided at all costs. But once you become willing to heal, your perspective on pain and your relationship to it begins a dramatic shift.

Response to Pain: For the first time, you respond to the pain in your life as if it were telling you something important, instead of muffling it with anesthesia. This represents your first gesture toward willingness.

Level of Investment in Victimhood: In Stage One, you demonstrate your willingness to consider the possibility that you might be able to live without your anesthesias and beyond the control of your wounds.

Activities: Re-orientation

Stage One is a period of changing direction. Whatever change you want to see in your life, Stage One is the time you give up on the old direction and choose the new one.

Stage One activities include anything that will help you leave behind the old ways and commit to the new ones. For people with addictions, this means getting de-toxed and beginning abstinence. These activities:

- Challenge your notions of what is "normal"

- Help you appraise your willingness

- Help you embrace healing.

Challenging Your Notions of Normal

Behavior considered normal and acceptable for people living out of their wounds doesn't cut it for people who want to heal. In Stage One, you begin to identify old, unhealthy ideas and replace them with new ones. Some activities that help begin this lifelong process are:

- **Reading introductory recovery books**. Browse the recovery and self-help sections of your favorite bookstore, or consult the suggested reading list at the end of this chapter.

- **Attending self-help meetings that focus on your primary anesthesias and listening with an open mind and heart.** Recovering people have formed groups to help themselves deal with a variety of anesthesias and other problems.[30] Some groups are listed in the white or yellow pages of your phone book. Check with your therapist, pastor, physician or local treatment or mental health center for others. Self-help groups can be found through such organizations as:
  - Overeaters Anonymous
  - Alcoholics Anonymous
  - Exceptional Cancer Patients
  - Adult Children of Alcoholics
  - Codependents Anonymous
  - Incest Survivors Anonymous
  - Recovery, Inc.
  - Debtors Anonymous
  - Empty Cradle
  - Al-Anon

[30] One study estimated that there are over two hundred self-help groups based on the twelve steps of Alcoholics Anonymous alone.

- Nar-Anon
- Cocaine Anonymous
- Sex and Love Addicts Anonymous
- Emotions Anonymous
- Artists Recovering Through the Twelve Steps

- **Attending workshops that deal with recovery on an introductory level.** Check with your therapist or members of your self-help group for recommendations. Also, check at independent, alternative or new age bookstores for newsletters, flyers and newspapers that might carry ads for workshops.

- **Talking with friends whom you consider to be on a healing path.**

Appraising Your Willingness

[31] Review Chapters Nine and Ten if you are unsure of the differences between true willingness and a window of willingness.

Are you hanging out in a window of willingness?[31] Or are you truly ready to stop looking for better numbing agents and get on with the healing journey? To help you figure out where your willingness begins and ends—and to help boost your willingness—try the following activities:

- **Speak up at self-help meetings**. Get used to sharing your foibles and shortcomings.

- **Go to therapy.** However, *stay out of depth therapy* at this point in your healing. This means that therapy should be restricted to crisis intervention and getting help developing your personal healing plan. Beware of therapists who insist on working on a deep emotional level from the start—this is guaranteed to produce the Rubber Band Effect in short order.

- If you are blocked, emotionally overwhelmed or controlled by an addiction, **consider signing up for an in-patient or out-patient treatment program**. Sometimes people need extra help at the beginning to make progress.

Embracing Personal Healing

Find ways to make your commitment to yourself real. You can make it real by making it tangible—by speaking or writing your commitment with others as witnesses. We call this *proclaiming*.

Proclaiming is an important tool in recovery—one you'll use throughout your healing. In proclaiming your intentions to trusted friends and mentors, you make yourself accountable for your healing. If you clarify your commitment and declare it out loud, you can't bargain your way out of it as you can if you keep it just between yourself and your Higher Power. Proclaiming also allows you to be vulnerable to others, which is a critical step in healing. You take yourself out of isolation and put yourself in position to be called on the carpet if you don't keep your commitments. Few experiences are more powerful.

One proclamation method is a cause-effect inventory, in which you compare your fears of changing with the consequences of not changing. Turn to the end of this chapter for instructions on creating one.

You can take your proclamation a step further by making a ceremony of it. Sharie Liden, Ph.D., a San Diego psychotherapist, "married" herself at the beach to commemorate her commitment to her healing. She dressed in white and gold—colors that symbolized for her the merging of opposites within herself—and went to the beach at sunset with a trusted friend. Standing in the surf, she recited a vow to move out of survival and into healing and to never knowingly abandon herself to her anesthesias again. She tossed her bouquet to the ocean and signed a "wedding contract" she had created for the occasion.

You can do something of your own design to mark your willingness to heal. At the end of this chapter is an example of a contract you can make with yourself.

Stage One Pitfalls: Diversions from the Pain

In Stage One, the temptation to escape your pain instead of staying with it is still quite strong. Even though you are no longer using your primary anesthesia, you may find yourself inventing other, more subtle ways of numbing yourself.

Use the troubleshooting chart below to keep yourself on track. However, if you find yourself confronting over and over any of the problems described in the chart, you're probably not ready to start your healing journey in earnest. If that's the case, be kind to yourself. Admit that you're not ready, take care of yourself as best you can, and watch for signs that willingness has arrived.

If you suspect you are doing this:	Try doing this instead:
Mistaking a window of willingness for true willingness.	• Bolster your willingness by reminding yourself that you *can* change and that you *can* heal your core wounds. • Do a cause-effect inventory. • Talk to your sponsor or mentor.
Developing willpower skills.	• Explore your fears of what would happen if you relinquished control. • Explore your ideas of the character of your Higher Power; consider the possibility that they are inaccurate. • Talk to your sponsor or mentor.
Focusing on using a new anesthesia rather than on abstaining from your original, primary anesthesia.	• Identify what it is you fear about focusing on your primary anesthesia. • Get honest with yourself: There will be no progress without sobriety. • Talk to your sponsor or mentor.
Getting into depth therapy.	• Be kind to yourself when you find yourself shutting down or feeling

blocked; it's a signal that you need
to slow down.
- Switch the focus of your therapy, or
switch therapists.
- Talk to your sponsor or mentor.

Stage One Healing Resources

Miscellaneous

Bradshaw on the Family. John Bradshaw.
Health Communications, 1988.

Care of the Soul. Thomas Moore. Harper Perennial, 1994.

Codependent No More. Melody Beattie. Hazelden, 1987.

Repeat After Me. Claudia Black.
M.A.C. Printing and Publications, 1985.

The Road Less Traveled. M. Scott Peck. Phoenix Press, 1985.

Wake-Up Calls. Eric Allenbaugh, Ph.D. Bard Productions, 1992

When Society Becomes an Addict. Anne Wilson Schaef.
Harper & Row, 1987.

*When You Can You Will: Why You Can't Always Do What You
Want to Do…and What to Do About It.* Lynne Bernfield, M.A.,
M.F.C.T. Berkeley Books, New York, 1993.

Willingness Works Resources

Answering Your Wake-Up Calls (tape)

The Power of Willingness (tape)

Sensible Self-Help: The Tape

Sensible Self-Help: The Workshop

A Therapist's Guide to the Seven Stages of Personal Healing (tape)

↳

Stage One Healing Exercises

Cause-and-Effect Inventory

1. Draw two lines down the middle of a sheet of paper, separating the paper into three columns.

2. At the top of the first column, write "Anesthesias and Self-Protections." In this column, list everything you use to shield yourself from whatever causes you pain—your own feelings, other people's feelings or the effects of your behaviors on yourself or others. (Check the definition of anesthesia from the Glossary if you need a reminder.) Your anesthesias might include television-watching, smoking, drinking, shopping, compulsive exercising or overeating.

   Self-protections (also known as defense mechanisms) can also be used as anesthesias. For example, you might react by becoming angry and defensive any time someone objects to your fast and aggressive driving style. Other self-protections include rationalization (*"I had no choice but to overeat on Christmas day because of all the food that's around and because of the stress my family puts on me,"*), projection (finding and judging in others' behavior the very thing that you do), rebelliousness, vengeance, blame, numbness, becoming overwhelmed by your emotions, trying to control the behavior of others, acting helpless.

3. In the second column, list the effects each item has on your authenticity in your relationship with yourself, with others, with your career, with your Higher Power.

4. In the third column, write down how you use these anesthesias and self-protections to deal with the uncomfortable or unexpected.

Make a Contract with Yourself

Photocopy the contract on the next page or create one like it. Then have a ceremony with supportive friends to sign it and celebrate.

◆ CONTRACT ◆

SURVIVAL LIVING IS NO LONGER OKAY FOR ME. Trying to live this way has become an uncontrollable habit and has caused my life to become unbearable to me.

NOTHING SHORT OF A FULL COMMITMENT to reducing my pain tolerances, learning to work with my feelings and tackling my core wounds will allow me to live as a healed person.

I AM WILLING to do whatever it takes to accomplish this healing.

THERE IS NOTHING MORE IMPORTANT to me than my own personal healing.

I AM PREPARED to revise my time, energy and financial allocations to reflect this commitment.

I MAKE THIS COMMITMENT on this _____ day of _____, 19_____.

Signed,

_____
Your signature

Before a Loving Witness,

_____
Signature of your witness

TWENTY-FOUR

Stage Two: Foundation

Suit up and show up.
— Advice given to newcomers
to twelve-step programs

In Stage Two, you put your willingness into action, and your life begins to look different. Everything starts to change: your circle of friends, your daily schedule, perhaps even your appearance. These changes support you in the emotional healing work you will do later on.

Goal: Re-Organize Your Life

Your goal in this stage is to get your life in order so that it supports rather than sabotages your healing. This means building a foundation of new behaviors, habits, relationships and knowledge that is solid and complete enough to support you through your entire healing process. To build this foundation, you abstain from your primary addiction and participate in activities from each of the four categories described in this chapter.

Emotional Work:
Break up with Your Anesthesias

In Stage Two, you "break up" with your anesthesia-driven lifestyle and diversions. This work is just as difficult as breaking up with a lover. It will likely leave a gaping hole in your life, because you are breaking up with the life you built around your anesthesias—the friends you practiced it with, the familiar places in which you practiced, the good feelings and sense of safety it created for you.

For peace of mind, we need to resign as general manager of the universe.

— Larry Eisenberg

Self-Responsibility Key: Hiring a New Manager

In Stage Two, you begin the process of removing your ego from the throne of your life and finding a replacement. This is spiritual work.

Quality of Relationship with Your Spiritual Resources: The biggest change you make in your self-responsibility in Stage Two is in your choice of—and relationship with—your Higher Power. In Stage Two, becoming familiar with your new spiritual frame of reference becomes your way of life. As you do the work of Stage Two, you evaluate every activity, every person, every encounter in terms of its ability to help you keep to this new path you've chosen.

Activities: Enhance Your Healing

Never underestimate the power of Foundation activities. The solid grounding that a complete Stage Two provides will ensure that the work you do in Stages Three through Seven will stick. If you give short shrift to this foundation, the Rubber Band Effect will continue to bring you back to its stabilizing influence.

How you spend your time can enhance your healing work or distract you from it. If you are to stay on track in your healing journey, you must evaluate and adjust your activities so they enhance, rather than divert you from, your healing work.

We divide Stage Two activities into four main categories: Physical, Spiritual, Social, and Daily Life. Within each main category are four sub-categories, as illustrated in the table below. As you evaluate your activities and habits in each area, ask yourself:

- Does this habit or activity support my healing work, or does it distract me from healing?
- If I think it enhances my healing, can I specifically list how it does so?
- If it isn't a distraction now, will it become one if I stop monitoring it?

Another important concept for Foundation-building is *daily renewal*. Each of the four categories of activities requires attention on a daily basis. How much you do each day depends on your own needs. During times of stress, you may need to spend a minimum of thirty minutes in meditation each morning, while in quieter times you feel just fine with a five-minute session. If you have never stuck to an exercise schedule, you will probably need to start out with a short, easy workout. If you're used to running eight miles a day, then that may be your minimum. Whatever your needs are, be sure to attend to them every day.

The very fact that we desire a change is a sure sign that, in time, we can change—especially if we intelligently and responsibly choose to act in ways that honor this new direction.

– Marsha Sinetar

Daily Renewal

Physical	Spiritual	Social	Daily Life
Sleep	Higher Power	Friends	Crisis Containment
Food	Inner Work	Mentors	Money
Exercise	Learning	Support Groups	Home
Biochemistry	Play	Family	Time

Physical

A healthy, well-cared-for body is essential to the pursuit of emotional healing. Removing physical barriers that impair your ability to focus on emotional healing is not itself healing work. However, it frees you from distractions that can keep you from doing the healing work.

Use the support group you'll develop in this stage to help you stay physically balanced. And seek help from health care professionals for anything you can't reasonably handle on your own. Nancy, a manic-depressive who was becoming stabilized through medication, asked her support group to let her know when they thought she was heading into an episode. She explained what to look for and the role of her medication in controlling her illness. With the group's help, she was able to get extra help from her physician before the next episode took hold and forced her into the hospital.

Physical activities are divided into four main categories: sleep, food, exercise, and biochemistry.

SLEEP

Enhancement: You are get as much sleep as you need, and your sleep is peaceful; you wake up feeling rested and refreshed.

Distraction: You do not get enough sleep; you nap a lot or often feel fatigued, irritable or overwhelmed; or you sleep too much, using sleep as a drug to avoid feelings and stressful situations. You may simply need to get to bed earlier or you may have a sleep disorder or other physical problem that needs medical attention.

FOOD

Enhancement: Your eating patterns meet the requirements of your physiology; you do not regularly overeat or undereat; you understand your body's needs and make sure you meet them each day.

Distraction: You overeat or undereat, consume too much sugar and fat or not enough fresh fruits and vegetables, or ignore food allergies or carbohydrate addiction. Most diets can use some improvement. If you are really into food as a distraction, you probably use it to avoid feelings you don't want to face.

EXERCISE

Enhancement: You have good stamina and muscle tone and don't carry a lot of pent-up energy.

Distraction: You are nearly always achy, are easily exhausted, or have pent-up energy that makes it impossible to get quiet. Compulsive exercising can be a distraction, too.

Clear the way for pain-free exercise, if necessary, by taking care of sports injuries or broken or poorly fitting prosthetic devices.

BIOCHEMISTRY

Enhancement: A balanced biochemistry—no unaddressed illnesses or chemical conditions.

Distraction: Untreated imbalances or illnesses; chemical use or abuse. Either will alter or numb your feelings and block your efforts to heal.

If you know (or even suspect) that you suffer from a chemical imbalance or other physical problem (such as clinical depression, bipolar [manic-depressive] illness, low blood sugar, diabetes, epilepsy or hypertension), see your physician. Also, identify and abstain from using other chemicals (including your primary anesthesia) that cloud your ability to think clearly.

Man may be captain of his soul, but he's also victim to his blood sugar.
– Rachael F. and Richard F. Heller

Spiritual

Spiritual activities are some of the most important parts of the foundation you build in Stage Two. They are a constant that will serve you for the rest of your life, no matter where you are in your healing.

There are four types of spiritual activities: Higher Power work, inner work, learning and play.

HIGHER POWER WORK

Enhancement: You set time aside each day for prayer, meditation or inspirational reading; you expose yourself to new ideas about spirituality and challenge your own ideas about the Higher Power behind your spiritual resources; you meet regularly with people who nurture and support your search for a loving Higher Power.

Distraction: You avoid doing any spiritual work at all; or your activities—spiritual group attendance, meditation, prayer, inspirational reading—begin to edge out all other activities; or you use religion and religious or spiritual practices to avoid feelings and to avoid doing healing work.

Stage Two Higher Power work consists of three steps:

- **Admit that you used your anesthesias** as your Higher Power or spiritual resource

- **Admit that you need a better Higher Power** or set of spiritual resources

- **Begin the search** for a better Higher Power or set of spiritual resources

Remember, humans always make decisions within some frame of reference—alcohol, religion, gambling, food, control or anything else that seems to help make sense of the world. In Stage Two, you create a vacuum by jettisoning your old frame of reference. It is important to consciously fill that vacuum with a new Higher Power or set of spiritual resources before you find yourself unconsciously filling it with a new anesthesia or set of rules.

The exercises described at the end of this chapter can help you identify a Higher Power that can see you through your healing journey. Then, develop and maintain this new relationship by:

- Practicing some form of **prayer, meditation or visualization**. Set aside time each day for these activities.

- Attending **gatherings** that provide you with spiritual sustenance. This may include study groups, meditation groups or religious services. Schedule weekly time for such gatherings and place your highest priority on these commitments.

INNER WORK

"Inner work" is what we call any activity that helps you get to know yourself better—your emotions, values, dreams, fears and hopes, how you interpret the events of your life, and so on.

Enhancement: Your inner work increases awareness and understanding of emotions and your emotional processes and other internal workings. Inner work that enhances your healing can include daily journaling and exercises (like the ones in this book) and emotional release. For emotional release, find activities that allow you to express feelings you may be holding in: Go to sad movies to release tears, go to children's movies to release playfulness and joy, beat a tennis racket on the bed to release rage.

Distraction: You obsess about your internal state to the point that you become almost totally self-involved; you don't know how to do inner work or don't make it a priority.

LEARNING

Enhancement: You set aside regular time to read, listen to tapes, attend lectures or watch videos that provide information about healing and recovery, especially regarding your anesthesia, your family's dysfunction and your physical conditions. See the Stage Two reading list for ideas. Get specific recommendations from people committed to their own healing. Build reading time into your schedule, and place your highest priority on this commitment.

Distraction: You are stalled by indecision about where to start; you regularly allow yourself to be diverted from learning activities; you substitute learning activities for emotional work and intimate contact with others.

PLAY

In our achievement-driven culture, we tend to discount aimless, "frivolous" activity. If it isn't a chore, doesn't earn us money, improve our psyches, result in a product, keep us healthy or fulfill an obligation, it isn't appropriate to spend time on it. We think play is a deeply spiritual activity, essential to spiritual and emotional growth. In play, we recharge our batteries. We literally re-create ourselves.

Enhancement: Your play time helps you maintain (or regain) perspective and a sense of humor about yourself.

To be considered truly playful, an activity must be focused on the joy of the activity itself, rather than on what it will bring you. Sometimes it takes a while to get the hang of playing. Brainstorm with friends about play ideas. Here are some to start you off:[32]

- painting (especially finger-painting)
- rollerblading
- the zoo
- playing with pets
- board games
- camping
- browsing thrift stores
- tether ball
- fairs
- amusement parks
- picnicking
- slumber parties
- cloud-watching
- hiking
- dancing
- the beach
- drawing
- playing softball
- doing crafts
- flying kites

[32] Try not to let your expectations get too far out of line here. Play requires a sense of emotional safety, deep vulnerability and spontaneity, and therefore does not come into full bloom for most of us until Stage Five.

Distraction: You don't play because you don't know how or think it is a waste of time; you become self-indulgent about play time, regularly allowing it to take precedence over other activities.

Daily Life

One of the first places healing work becomes apparent is in daily life.

MONEY

Enhancement: To the greatest extent possible, you don't allow your work to interfere with your recovery; you have enough money to pay your bills; you pay bills on time; your level of debt

It's all right to have a good time. That's one of the most important messages of enlightenment.

– Thaddeus Golas

is manageable; you feel reasonably comfortable with your financial situation and have a plan for improving it over time.

Distraction: You work so much that you have trouble fitting in other, non-work activities; more than thirty percent of your monthly income goes to pay off debt; you regularly pay bills late; you stay in a damaging or abusive job.

HOME

Enhancement: You do chores and run errands on a regular basis, so you have little or no backlog.

Attending to your life's basic needs in a systematic way removes another barrier to healing: organizational chaos. We have seen entire weeks get lost in chores—washing the car, cleaning house, cooking, running errands. Suddenly it's Monday again, and we haven't gone to a meeting or meditated one minute for a week. Get the little stuff down to a routine so you don't have to think about it.

- Make a bare-minimum list of the practical activities you must do to prevent your life from falling apart while you're working on healing (laundry, grocery shopping, cooking, cleaning). The list should be fairly short.

- Eliminate all other activities until your new habits are firmly rooted. Get help if you're not sure how to simplify.

Distraction: Your home is too chaotic to be nourishing; the errands and chores you ignore are making you feel crazy and scattered.

TIME

We all operate under the same limitations when it comes to time. Nobody has more than twenty-four hours in a day or seven days in a week. But some people seem to cruise through with time to spare, while others feel constantly pressured and short of time.

Your attitude toward and use of your time enhances your healing when you keep from over-committing and are generally efficient and well-organized.

Enhancement: You use a time-management system that works for you; you are clear about your daily and weekly priorities and usually give them the time and energy they deserve; you sometimes say "no" to new commitments.

To get balanced, try some of the activities described below.

• Read Stephen Covey's *The Seven Habits of Highly Effective People* to learn to be more efficient and deliberate about how you spend your life's energy.

• Check out time planning systems, and start using one that suits you.

• Take a time-management class.

• Make no new commitments for a specific period of time— six weeks, three months, a year. This will keep your list of incompletes down and help you concentrate on personal healing activities.

Distraction: You are overcome by chaos and clutter; you constantly commit to more than you can do; you tend to use busy-ness to protect yourself from painful feelings.

CRISIS CONTAINMENT

Enhancement: Your life shows a distinct absence of melodrama and emergencies.

Distraction: You go from one crisis to the next; you use crises to avoid healing work, allowing them to direct your life rather than making decisions that will resolve them or at least put them on hold.

Sometimes hitting bottom is the result of a crisis. If you use pills, perhaps a car accident wakes you up. Chronically depressed people might be scared into getting help when they find themselves making suicide plans. An overspender might hit bottom when her car is repossessed. A codependent might hit bottom when he finds himself feeling suicidal after his marriage breaks up.

The problem with a crisis-provoked bottom is that it can fool you into thinking that recovery is about resolving crises.

Certainly crisis resolution is an improvement over the total chaos that brought many of us to surrender in the first place. However, moving into true healing requires that we set up our lives so preventable crises simply don't occur anymore. That means anticipating the situations that create crises and making plans so either they do not occur or they don't derail us when they do.

For example, Iris always got into screaming fights with her boyfriend when he criticized her, which was often. The fights left her depressed and angry, and she responded to these feelings by overeating. In examining her overeating crises, she first concluded that she simply shouldn't "let him get to me" when he started arguing with her.

Then she realized that, given her needs both to keep his approval and prove that he was wrong about her faults, she had no choice but to get hooked into the argument. She struggled with feeling ashamed that she could not control her reactions, but gradually understood that the important thing at this point in her healing was to stay out of crisis-provoking situations. She decided to leave the house each time her boyfriend picked a fight and to call friends in Overeaters Anonymous, her main self-help group. She also started attending Co.D.A. meetings to get advice and support for dealing with his criticism and her reactions to it.

Follow the steps below to get your crisis containment program going:

- **Identify crisis-provoking situations** so you can avoid or develop plans to contain them

- **Identify your primary anesthesias** and abstain from them

- **Participate** in appropriate self-help programs.

Social

No one heals alone. Very frequent contact—several times a week, if not daily—with support groups, mentors and healing-oriented friends is a must. Ask your therapist and your healing-oriented friends for recommendations for support groups that might fit your needs. Make a point of spending less time with the people in your life who are still in survival (pre-healing) mode, or who are moving in and out of willingness. Begin or continue therapy.

Schedule time with your support system, and place your highest priority on these commitments.

FRIENDS

Enhancement: Your friends share your healing journey and support your efforts to heal.

Distraction: Your friends don't understand or are openly hostile to your efforts, or continue to use anesthesias themselves.

As you heal, your circle of friends is bound to change. Try not to give yourself a hard time about this. You might feel more drawn to some people than to others. You might not feel as close to certain people as you used to—might even be bored by them. If so, you will certainly feel sad about that and might even feel guilty. Remind yourself that healing involves letting go of patterns and people, and allow yourself to grieve.

MENTORS

Enhancement: You have at least one person in your life to whom you look for guidance and wisdom who is a step or two ahead of you in the healing journey.

Distraction: You don't seek or trust anyone's advice; you tend to find abusive mentors; you tend to place your mentors on a pedestal and then discard them in anger and disappointment when they turn out to be only human.

It may not be easy to find someone to be your mentor. Keep looking. Many healing people find that they outgrow their early mentors. And keep in mind that you don't necessarily have to have a personal relationship with your mentor. Many of our clients think of authors such as John Bradshaw or Pia Mellody or Sharon Wegscheider-Cruse as their mentors. They become thoroughly familiar with their mentor's attitudes and philosophies through their books, tapes, lectures and seminars, and then think about their lives in those terms: *"What would Sharon say about my conflict with my boss this morning?"*

Other people listen carefully to certain members of their self-help meetings and find help and sustenance in their observations.

SUPPORT GROUPS

Enhancement: Your support group provides enough structure (regular meeting times, set format, help for beginners) to help you feel comfortable and to learn the ropes; your support group is composed of people who share your healing journey; your support group encourages your independence and celebrates your successes.

Distraction: Your support group frequently supplies you with true-but-not-useful platitudes when you're hurting (*"Just turn it over!"*); your support group attendance takes up so much time you don't have time for other healing-related activities; you don't attend any support group meetings; you are afraid to take any action in your life without getting feedback from your support group first; your support group is critical, negative or controlling.

FAMILY

Enhancement: You know how much time you can spend with your family without reverting to old, destructive behaviors such as anesthesia use, whether this means thirty minutes a year or several hours a week; you stick to these limits.

Distraction: You don't limit your contact with a family that is abusive or constantly engages you in conflicts; your family's needs or demands dictate that you spend minimal time or no time in healing activities.

Stage Two Pitfalls: Too Much Talk, Too Little Action

The temptation in Stage Two is to either move ahead quickly, without first getting firmly rooted in your foundation work, or to stop in your tracks, thinking you've arrived at a destination called "healing."

Stage Two Pitfall #1: Depth Therapy

Stay out of deep psychotherapy work. Your needs in Stage Two are centered on organizing your life to support the work to come. Delving too deeply into your feelings at this point can lead to what we call premature insight or premature forgiveness—knowledge that leads to a full-speed retreat back into anesthesia use, or at least into hiding out emotionally. If you do get into therapy at this stage, be sure to choose a therapist who won't push you too fast. If you get scared in therapy or feel that things are going too fast for your comfort, let your therapist know how you feel. If he or she continues to push, find a new therapist.

Stage Two Pitfall #2: Mistaking Abstinence for Healing

If you're a recovering addict or alcoholic, it's easy to think that, now that you are sober, you're healed. While Stage Two work is absolutely essential to healing, abstinence and foundation-building activities are just preparation for the work, not the healing work itself. Give your attention and effort to Stage Two, but don't resist when your instincts begin to pull you into Stage Three.

Stage Two Pitfall #3: Mistaking New Levels of Happiness for Healing

In twelve-step circles, a phenomenon known as the pink cloud occurs just after someone achieves sobriety (of whatever type he or she needs) and gets a first taste of life without the pain caused by anesthesia use. The pink cloud is the way we fall in love with healing, and is a necessary—and fun—part of the road. However, don't make the mistake of trying to stay there. After a little while, the excitement and exhilaration of your new life are bound to fade a little. That just means that you are moving into the next stage. Let it happen.

Some people never cross the bridge from Stage Two to Stage Three (Feelings). Since they've stopped their anesthesia use, they often describe their lives as "improved." But it's not emotional or spiritual thriving and won't be satisfying for those who want more from life.

Stage Two Pitfall #4: Premature Insight

Understanding your life is not the same as healing your life. Some people stop when they get insight, and use the insight to stay where they are. Examples of the effects of premature insight are: *"I'm so bored in my marriage; that's why I drink and use;"* and *"I know my parents abused me, but they did the best they could, and anyway, that's in the past."*

Stage Two Pitfall #5: The Two-Five Jump

If you've avoided feeling your feelings most of your life, they can look pretty scary when you get up close to them. For this reason, many people move right up to Stage Three (Feelings), get a glimpse of the intensity it brings, and try to bypass it and Stage Four (Healing) to get to the "goodies" waiting for them in Stage Five. That's the Two-Five Jump.

For a detailed discussion of the Two-Five Jump and its consequences, turn back to Chapter Twenty-One. In the meantime, try not to avoid the Feelings Stage. Stay in close touch with your support network and your mentor, therapist or sponsor. Listen when people tell you that it's okay to feel whatever it is you are feeling.

Stage Two Healing Resources

In Stage Two, taking action about your wounds is more important than reading about them. (Reading is important, too, of course, but if you have a tendency to escape through books or to think you are solving your problems by learning a lot about them, reading can be a trap.) However, you may need specialized information about your wounds, addictions and physiological imbalances before you can take action. Because information on physiological and emotional concerns changes daily, we hesitate to provide titles. Instead, we recommend browsing the self-help, health and diet and psychology sections of your library or a bookstore. By reading and trial-and-error, you'll discover your own imbalances and remedies. If you know you have a physical or psychological condition, consider ordering a literature search from The Health Resource, Inc. (564 Locust Street, Conway, AR 72032, 501/329-5272). Their reports provide the most recent information on health-related topics culled from hundreds of mainstream and alternative journals.

With that caveat, we offer the titles below as good general references.

Miscellaneous Books and Tapes

Browse the self-help section for books about your specific bio-chemical imbalances (such as clinical depression, bipolar illness, and so on) and about your favorite anesthesias.

Sounds True catalog provides hundreds of self-help tapes by mail. For their catalog, call 800/333-9185.

Helpful to practically anyone in early healing: books and tapes about stress management, exercise and nutrition. Specific titles follow.

The Alternative Twelve Steps: A Secular Guide to Recovery. Martha Cleveland and Arlys G. Health Communications, Inc., 1992. (Especially helpful for atheists and agnostics.)

Anxiety, Phobias and Panic: Taking Charge and Conquering Fear. Reneau Z. Peurifoy, M.A., M.F.C.C. LifeSkills, 1992.

Any daily meditation book. (Most bookstores carry a whole section—usually in or near the self-help section—devoted to quiet time books. They are so issue-specific, the titles of these books sometimes read like talk-show listings. Browse your local bookstore for one that fits your needs.)

Breaking Free From Compulsive Eating. Geneen Roth. Signet, 1984.

The Carbohydrate Addict's Diet and *Healthy for Life.* Dr. Rachael F. Heller and Dr. Richard F. Heller. Dutton, 1991 and 1995. (Wonderful books for those who suspect they have an eating disorder. These landmark works offer a dietary "cure" for the carbohydrate craving that drives the problems of so many people in Overeaters Anonymous and weight management programs.)

Care of the Soul. Thomas Moore. Harper Perennial, 1994.

How to Identify Addictive Behavior. Dr. Robert Lefever. PROMIS Publishing Ltd. of London. 1988. (Currently out of print; look for it in the library or used bookstores.)

How to Live Between Office Visits. Bernie Siegel, M.D. HarperCollins, 1993

Inner Simplicity. Elaine St. James. Hyperion, 1995.

Leaving the Enchanted Forest: The Path from Relationship Addiction to Intimacy. Stephanie Covington and Liana Beckett. Harper & Row, 1988.

Letters from Women Who Love Too Much. Robin Norwood. Pocket Books, 1988.

Life Design: Living Your Life by Choice Instead of Chance. Peggy Vaughan and James Vaughan, Ph.D. Center for Life-Design, 7843 Girard Ave., Suite C, La Jolla, CA 92037. 619/454-0136. (This is one of the best Stage Two resources we've seen. The Center offers a weekend seminar in its planning techniques, but will send the book if you can't get to California.)

Love, Medicine and Miracles. Bernie S. Siegel, M.D. Harper & Row, 1986.

Minding the Body, Mending the Mind. Joan Borysenko, Ph.D. Sound Ideas, 1988.

Peace from Nervous Suffering. Dr. Claire Weekes, M.B., D.Sc., M.R.A.P. Signet, 1990.

Peace, Love and Healing. Bernie Siegel, M.D. HarperPerennial, 1990.

The Recovery Resource Book. Barbara Yoder. Simon & Schuster, 1990. (Currently out of print, and therefore somewhat out of date. However, it's still a great reference. Look for it in libraries and used bookstores.)

The Road Less Traveled. M. Scott Peck. Phoenix Press, 1985. (A classic; you can read this book over and over and still find fresh insight and hope each time.)

Simplify Your Life. Elaine St. James. Hyperion, 1994.

Streamlining Your Life: A Five-Point Plan for Uncomplicated Living. Stephanie Culp. Writer's Digest Books, 1991.

The Twelve Steps: A Way Out. Anonymous. Recovery Publications. 1987. (One of the first step-study guides for adult children of alcoholics, this workbook also provides excellent help for people who grew up in non-alcoholic, but dysfunctional, families.)

Women Who Love Too Much. Robin Norwood. J.P. Tarcher, 1985.

*You Mean I Don't **Have** to Feel this Way?* Colette Dowling. Macmillan, 1991.

Willingness Works Resources

Finding Your Inner Purpose (tape)

How to Journal (tape)

Self-Responsibility: Healing's Secret Ingredient (tape)

Stage Two Healing Exercises

Identify and Rehabilitate Your Higher Power

At the heart of your spiritual resources is the core frame of reference through which you interpret events and make choices. We refer to this core frame of reference as a Higher Power.

1. Identify your pre-healing Higher Power—your addictions, neediness, controlling behaviors, or whatever served as the power behind your spiritual resources. Refer to the definition of Higher Power in the glossary if you need a reminder. To help you zero in on your personal definition, ask yourself:
   - Who (or what) helps me?
   - How does it help me?
   - What do I have to do to get its help?
   - How do I feel toward this helping thing on a good day? On a bad day?

   Some clients and friends have identified their pre-healing Higher Power as: alcohol, religious institutions, a need for approval, rules, food, having enough money, fitting in, being seen as smart and attractive, and knowing all the answers.

2. List the qualities of a nurturing Higher Power. If you have discovered that the power behind your spiritual resources is angry, punishing, ruthless and demanding, you may be hard-pressed to imagine one that is caring and loving. Look around you. Whom do you know who displays these gentler qualities? Perhaps there is someone who has been kind to you when you were in pain—a therapist, a mentor or sponsor, a teacher, a close friend. Use this person as a reference to create a word picture of a loving power.

Anne Lamott, in *Bird by Bird*, suggests a light-hearted approach to an exercise such as this. For example, if you picture your Higher Power as a

> *...high school principal in a gray suit who never remembered your name but is always leafing unhappily through your files...maybe you need to blend in the influence of someone who is ever so slightly more amused by you, someone less anal. David Byrne is good, for instance. Gracie Allen is good. Mister Rogers will work.*[33]

You may also find some helpful ideas in *The Alternative Twelve Steps: A Secular Guide to Recovery* by Martha Cleveland and Arlys G.

Define and Revise Your Life Mission

The power of your spiritual resources provides a framework from which you can more easily make choices in life. Allying yourself with this set of spiritual resources means accepting the mission it lays out for you.

1. Write a Mission Statement that describes your purpose in life as if you were living in accord with the priorities and guidelines of your current spiritual resources.

2. Now write a Mission Statement that describes your purpose in life if you were already living in accord with spiritual resources that are loving and nurturing.

Identify and Evaluate Your Support Network

The people you spend your time with have an enormous influence on your healing journey. Therefore, it is a good idea to spend more of your time with healthy, supportive people and less (or none at all) with those who sabotage your work. This exercise can help you to figure out which relationships tend to enhance your healing and which may be distracting you.

Please note! This exercise is NOT intended to help you criticize or judge the people in your life or to provide the basis for a lecture to them on how to improve themselves. Its purpose is to allow you to concentrate more fully on your own healing

---

[33] Pantheon, 1994.

journey. We do NOT recommend sharing the results of this exercise with others, except perhaps your sponsor, therapist or mentor.

1. Draw columns on a piece of paper similar to the example below.

2. In the left-hand column, list the people in your social circle—your friends, relatives, neighbors, co-workers, and so on.

3. In the next column, write a word or two to describe your relationship with each person (for example, sister, best friend, next-door neighbor).

4. Assign each person a number from one to five to indicate what you believe to be his or her ability to keep company with feelings (his or others'). (Your scale could be something like the following, or whatever else works for you: 1=nonexistent, 2=keeps company some of the time, 3=keeps company about half the time, 4=keeps company most of the time, 5=can be counted on to keep company virtually all the time.) Write this number in the **KC** column.

5. Assign each person a number from one to five (using a scale similar to the one above or one of your own invention) that reflects your assessment of his or her level of self-responsibility. Write this number in the **SR** column.

6. In the last column, write a word or two describing how big a role anesthesias play in each person's life.

Name	Relationship	KC	SR	Anesthesia
Sylvia	sister	2	3	keeps busy all the time
Al	friend	4	3	in healing process—doesn't use anesthesia

Use this information to help you decide whom to spend time with and how much time to spend.

Evaluate Your Activities

Evaluate your activities for their enhancement/distraction potential, using a photocopy of the chart on the next page.

Activity Evaluation Form

	Activities that Enhance My Healing	Activities that Distract Me from My Healing
Physical		
Sleep		
Food		
Exercise		
Biochemistry		
Spiritual		
Higher Power		
Inner Work		
Learning		
Play		
Daily Life		
Money		
Home		
Time		
Crisis Containment		
Social		
Friends		
Mentors		
Support Groups		
Family		

TWENTY-FIVE

Stage Three: Feelings

I can't recall any case of pain which didn't, on the whole, enrich life.

— *Malcolm Muggeridge*

I<small>N</small> S<small>TAGE</small> T<small>HREE</small>, you switch from the largely external focus of Stage Two to an internal focus: your emotions.

Goal: Make Friends with Your Feelings

Whatever your survival strategy in childhood was, your relationship with your feelings undoubtedly suffered. You may have learned to pretend you didn't have feelings, twisted them into a shape that was acceptable to your caregivers, or learned to live in a state of crisis.

In Stage Three, you learn to keep your feelings company (which was what you needed your caregivers to do) instead of shutting down or becoming overwhelmed by them. Your Stage Three work will convince you that your feelings are friendly pieces of information, not the frightening, unpredictable beasts you may have thought they were.

Emotional Work: Meet the "Inners"

If you're like most people at the beginning of Stage Three, you have put your inner critic in charge and banished your inner child to the closet. (Some people let the inner child out for tantrums from time to time.) In Stage Three, you re-negotiate your relationships with the "inners." You begin the long process of transforming your inner critic into an ally, and you invite your inner child, who holds your feelings and your wounds, to come out, be healed and live. This work requires you to learn to be a parent to yourself in ways that your caregivers could not.

Self-Responsibility Key: Owning Your Feelings

In Stage Three, you begin to entertain the idea that your feelings belong to *you*. This allows you to reclaim your abandoned ability to feel, grieve and heal your losses.

Ability to Feel, Grieve and Heal: You learn to recognize and identify feelings that you previously ignored. You begin to understand what it means to "stay with" your feelings, and you learn how to do that, at least part of the time.

Activities: Learn the Tools

Stage Three activities acquaint you with the concept of self-responsibility. You develop and learn how to use the tools that foster self-responsibility: company-keeping and inner critic negotiation skills. There are a number of activities that promote your abilities with these tools, including:

- **Reading** any good book on parenting (see the list at end of this chapter), or taking parenting workshops or classes. Even if you are not a parent in the biological sense, you are learning to love and care for the part of yourself that is your inner child. The principles of good parenting are the same.

- Signing up for **workshops** or classes that specifically address inner child and inner critic issues, feelings and grieving, relationships, boundaries and forgiveness. Marriage Encounter, Couples Encounter, and Compassionate Communication seminars are all good sources for this stage.

- Starting or continuing **therapy**. You can now move more deeply into your feelings, but be sure to listen to any twinges that say, *"Slow down."* Your deepest work is still ahead of you. Useful forms of therapy in Stage Three include (but are not limited to): person-centered therapy, transactional analysis, cognitive therapy, focusing and voice dialogue therapies.

Stage Three Pitfalls: Avoidance of Feeling Work

If your survival plan revolved around not having feelings—and most survival plans do—your impulse will be to shy away from doing feeling work. The impulse can be so strong that you can even convince yourself you are doing good healing work when you are actually avoiding feelings. Since Stage Three is all about feelings, most of the pitfalls you'll encounter have to do with developing ways to avoid them. Pitfalls #1 through #4 deal with the ways you might try to avoid feelings entirely.

On the other end of the continuum are people who "over-feel." These are folks who are often overwhelmed by their feelings. When they have strong feelings about something, they are immobilized by the emotions. Some of them even use their feelings *about their feelings* as a drug against the real issues they are avoiding. For example, they might be overcome by anxiety over a confrontation, stay focused on their fear, and never move through it into action. Or they may begin to luxuriate in tears and sorrow, reveling in the attention they get for their pain. Like a dehydrated traveler who stumbles on an oasis, they may be tempted to submerge themselves in feelings and never get on with their journey. For these folks, the danger of Stage Three is getting stuck there. Pitfalls #5 through #7 address their tactics.

Stage Three Pitfall #1: The Two-Five Jump

The Two-Five Jump, listed as a pitfall for Stage Two, is still a danger for people venturing into Stage Three. For a detailed discussion of the Two-Five Jump and its consequences, turn back to Chapter Twenty-One. In the meantime, try not to avoid the challenging work of Stage Three. Stay in close touch with your support network and your mentor, therapist or sponsor. Listen when people tell you that it's okay to feel whatever it is you are feeling.

Stage Three Pitfall #2: Spirituality as Drug

Anything can be used as an anesthesia. In Stage Three, as you discover that your Higher Power is not actually out to get you, you may find a spiritual practice that fills you with joy. That's wonderful. You may be tempted to turn to that practice when you are distressed. That's okay. You may start using your spiritual practice to keep the so-called bad feelings away. That's anesthesia use. Your spiritual practice should do things like support your healing, recharge your energy and renew your faith in a trustworthy Higher Power. Don't let it divert you from your healing work.

Stage Three Pitfall #3: Relapse

Inevitably, as you explore feelings you haven't allowed yourself to feel, you will uncover unhealed wounds. It is tempting to return to your anesthesias at this point to relieve the pain. If you do slip, make your amends, re-establish your abstinence and get back onto the healing path. Best of all, stay in close touch with your support system so that you can lean on them to get through the pain.

We can deceive ourselves into thinking we are developing spiritually, when instead we are strengthening our egocentricity through spiritual techniques.

— *Chogyam Trungpa Rinpoche*

Insights and discharges of emotion are not enough.

— *Fritz Perls*

Stage Three Pitfall #4: Believing that Insight Heals

It doesn't. Although understanding your processes and your wounds is a great starting point, it is only that—a starting point. Insight allows you to talk about your wounds. Feeling the pain of your unhealed wounds allows you to heal them.

Stage Three Pitfall #5: Putting Down Roots

Stage Three contains a pitfall similar to one in Stage Two: Believing you're "all better" because you're out of crisis. By Stage Three, your life often is in pretty good order compared to the way it was pre-healing. It's tempting to heave a sigh of relief, sink down into your new-found comfort, and plant roots. Don't. Life wants more, and eventually will Rubber-Band you forward into the next stage. Resistance creates pain.

Stage Three Pitfall #6: Depth Therapy

Stage Three is still too soon for depth therapy. You will explore your feelings extensively in this stage, but not your deepest wounds. Stage Three is the time for becoming comfortable with your emotions, working through any fear or shame you have about them, learning how to recognize them and express them self-responsibly, and learning to manage them so they don't over-whelm you. It is a time for building the trust that at least some people will stay with you through your feelings process.

Stage Three Pitfall #7: The Spoiled Inner Child

Sometimes a person on the healing journey is so happy to see his inner child emerge—and feels so guilty about having kept him under wraps for so long—that he lets the kid run wild. This spoiled inner child can be a real pain. Typically, he will insist on getting his way, throw tantrums when he doesn't, never take responsibility for his part in conflict, and generally act like a four-year-old having a bad day.

Just because you've finally let your inner child out of the closet doesn't mean you should never impose discipline on him or her. The idea in Stage Three is to establish a healthy relationship with your inners, and in the case of your inner child, this means being a good parent. Good parents don't allow their children to hurt themselves or others or damage property. They give their children room to express their feelings, keep company with them while they do, model self-responsible behavior and set limits. That's what you need to do with your inner child. It can be tricky, but it's not impossible.

A variation of developing a spoiled inner child is wallowing. To complete Stage Three work, you need to learn the difference between misery and pain, and how wallowing in misery (also called "looping") actually helps you *avoid* feeling the pain. Remember the description of the disconnection that occurs when caregivers spoil a child (Chapter Two)? Wallowing is similar. When you wallow, you tend to whine, or to ask yourself unanswerable questions: *"Why does this keep happening to me?"*, *"Why can't I find a good boyfriend?"*, *"Why do I have such bad luck?"* or *"Why is everything so hard?"* The questions keep you thinking instead of feeling, and that keeps you floating several steps above the wound, rather than plunging completely into the pain. When you are truly feeling the feelings, if you have words at all, they tend to be descriptions: *"It feels like a big, sharp rock sitting just below my heart," "The pain is like a bitter cold, gray fog wrapped around my body"* or simply, *"It hurts."*

Stage Three Healing Resources

Any book with an emphasis on feelings, inner child, inner dialogues or loving yourself is a good bet for Stage Three issues. Browse the self-help section of your bookstore, and see what seems to jump off the shelf at you. Often your intuition is the best guide.

Parenting

One of the best parenting resources we've ever found is *Redirecting Children's Behavior*, a fifteen-hour course based on the work of Dr. Rudolf Driekurs, a physician who believes an autocratic parenting style is obsolete. For more information about his theories, read his book *Children: The Challenge* (E.P. Dutton, 1987). The course—and some shorter workshops—is sponsored by the International Network for Children & Families. Call 800/257-9002 for information about offerings in your area.

Feelings

Focusing, a technique for communicating with your body about your emotions, was developed by Eugene Gendlin, Ph.D. It is one of the most useful tools available for learning how to recognize and learn from feelings. For the names of focusing trainers in your area, contact the Focusing Institute.

> The Focusing Institute
> 29 S. LaSalle, Suite 1195
> Chicago, IL 60603
> 312/629-0500

The Grief Recovery Institute provides seminars and counseling about the grieving process.

> Grief Recovery Institute
> 8306 Wilshire Blvd. Suite 21-A
> Beverly Hills, CA 90211
> 213/650-1234

Interactive Guided Imagery (I.G.I.) is a wonderful tool to use within the framework of just about any therapy model. For the name of someone trained in I.G.I., contact the Academy for Guided Imagery.

> Academy for Guided Imagery
> P.O. Box 2070
> Mill Valley, CA 92592
> 415/389-9324

Miscellaneous

Creating Mandalas. Susanne Fincher. Shambhala, 1991.

Creative Visualization. Shakti Gawain.
Whatever Publishing, 1995.

Embracing Your Inner Critic. Hal and Sidra Stone.
HarperSanFrancisco, 1993.

The Feeling Good Handbook. David D. Burns, M.D.
Penguin Books. 1989.

Focusing. Eugene Gendlin. Bantam, 1981. (A tape is also available through Audio Renaissance Tapes; most bookstores carry it.)

The Healing Woman. For female survivors of childhood sexual abuse, this newsletter provides hope, inspiration and a sense of community. For subscription information, contact the newsletter at: P.O. Box 3038, Moss Beach, CA 94038 (phone: 415/728-0339).

Healing Your Aloneness: Finding Love and Wholeness through Your Inner Child. Ericka J. Chopich and Margaret Paul.
HarperSanFrancisco, 1990.

Home Coming: Reclaiming and Championing Your Inner Child. John Bradshaw. Bantam, 1990.

I Got Tired of Pretending. Bob Earll. Stem Publications, 1988.

Inner Bonding: Becoming a Loving Adult to Your Inner Child. Margaret Paul, Ph.D. HarperSanFrancisco, 1992.

The Joy of Visualization. Valerie Wells. Chronicle Books, 1990

Learned Optimism. Martin E. P. Seligman, Ph.D.
Alfred A. Knopf, 1991.

Raising a Thinking Child. Myrna Shure, Ph.D.
Henry Holt & Co., 1994.

Recovery of Your Inner Child. Lucia Capacchione, Ph.D.
Simon & Schuster, 1991.

Self-Esteem. Matthew McKay, Ph.D., and Patrick Fanning. New Harbinger, 1992.

Self-Esteem: A Family Affair. Jean Illsley Clarke. Harper & Row, 1978.

Taming Your Gremlin. Richard Carson. Perennial Library, 1986.

Why Men Can't Feel. John Lee. (Out of print. If you can find it, grab it; one of the best guides around to the male psyche.)

Your Erroneous Zones. Dr. Wayne W. Dyer. Avon, 1976.

Willingness Works Resources

Feelings: An Owner's Guide (tape and workbook)

From Inner Critic to Inner Helper (tape and workbook)

Getting Done With Your Anger (tape and workbook)

How Do I Know When I'm Triggered? (tape)

How to Journal (tape)

Integrating Your Many Parts (tape)

Self-Responsibility: Healing's Secret Ingredient (tape)

What Do I Do When I'm Triggered? (tape)

ॐ

EXERCISES
Stage Three Healing Exercises

Get to Know Your Inner Critic

1. What do you know about your inner critic? If you haven't done the inner critic exercises presented at the end of Chapter Five, do them now.

2. How do you intervene when your inner critic is active? What works best for you? What have you tried that *doesn't* work well to keep your critic in line?

3. Pretend to be your inner critic. In that role, write letters to yourself. Answer them in the role of your inner child and then as your adult self.

Identify the Ways You Disconnect

We all learn from our caregivers how to respond to our own feelings. Because our caregivers inevitably disconnected with us at some point, we all disconnect from ourselves at certain points.[34]

1. What feelings do you respond to by disconnecting?

2. What forms of disconnection do you use (abandonment, attack, spoiling, or stealing the attention)? Do you use different forms at different times or for different feelings?

Learn to Recognize Your Internal Guidance

We all have inner voices—hunches that tell us what is *really* going on while our logical mind is busy lecturing us. An important part of Feelings Stage work is getting to know these two voices and learning to tell them apart. (Other ways

---

[34]Review Chapter One if you need to brush up on your understanding of disconnections.

to think of these opposing inner voices are: higher self/wounded self; inner guide/critic; healed inner adult/frightened, damaged inner child; left brain/right brain; conscious/unconscious; inner critic/inner child; ego/intuition.)

1. How do you tell the difference between a message from your intuition and a message from your pattern-bound ego? What clues does your body give you about which voice is talking?

2. How do you honor a message from your intuition? How do you honor a message from your ego?

3. Everyone has a cast of inner selves. You might have a business manager who takes care of balancing the checkbook, keeping the house in good repair and paying the bills; a court jester who knows how to have fun and make people laugh; a professor who knows a lot and makes informed, technical decisions; and many others. Make a visual representation of your community of self, using clay, paint, crayons or whatever medium you prefer.

TWENTY-SIX

Stage Four: Healing

> *What I want to know is, what's going to take*
> *the place of my chocolate-chip cookies?*
>
> — *Carolyn, an overeater facing*
> *Stage Four work*

STAGE FOUR IS the dark night of the soul.

This is the stage in which you confront and embrace what Carl Jung called your shadow self: the aspects of yourself that you relegated to the deepest, most hidden closets of your unconscious. This is the stage in which you do the most painful—and most productive—emotional work of your healing journey.

Fortunately, this most painful work pays off big time. Stage Four work leads to more love, empowerment and peace than you had ever thought possible.

Goal: Learn to Recognize, Expose and Heal Your Wounds

In Stage Four, you learn a skill that will serve you for the rest of your journey: You learn to recognize and dismantle your happy-ending fantasies and heal the core wounds they hide (unresolved traumas, feelings and disconnections you identified in Section I). This ability powers the rest of your journey and changes the way you think about and handle your life.

You won't finish with your happy-ending fantasy or your wounds on your first trip through the abyss. In fact, you probably won't finish in this lifetime. But you *will* learn how to do the work so you can return again and again to continue the process.

Come to the edge.
No, we will fall.

Come to the edge.
No, we will fall.

They came to the edge.
He pushed them, and
they flew.

— Guillaume
Apollinaire

Emotional Work: Traverse Your Abyss

Finding your way to the other side of your abyss is the most difficult emotional work you will do. In your abyss, you confront your scariest wounds head on. Your emotional work is to hang in there and feel the feelings you fear the most.

Keep in mind that what you fear most has already happened to you. In Stage Four, you return to those experiences for a visit. If you're sufficiently prepared, nothing will happen to you by visiting your abyss that you haven't already survived. Without this preparation, though, going back to these experiences could (best case) get you stuck or (worst case) re-traumatize you.

The Tools You Need for Abyss Work

In Stage Four, you will use all the tools you've developed in Stages One through Three. Like an experienced mountain climber descending the face of a sheer cliff with pitons, carabiners and ropes, you will use your training and equipment to negotiate your emotional abyss. These tools consist of:

- **Stage One (Willingness) tools:** Commitment to abstinence and healing; commitment to dismantling survival plan; relinquishment of willpower as a tool.

- **Stage Two (Foundation) tools:** New lifestyle and support network that enhances your healing work.

- **Stage Three (Feelings) tools:** Ability to challenge and release yourself from your rules and your inner critic; company-keeping skills; restored ability to feel, grieve and heal.

The Nature of Abyss Work

It is in the abyss that you finally come face to face with your savior and enemy, false hope. When you see your false hope for what it is, you will:

- Acknowledge, think about and feel the painful, hidden truths about your life—the people in it, what happened to you and how these things *really* felt

- Grieve for, complete unfinished anger about, and feel all the unfelt pain for:
    - the loss of relationships that never were
    - the loss of relationships that were, and then ended
    - the disconnections you suffered while growing up
    - the ways you were abused
    - the choices you didn't make, the paths you didn't take

- Fully acknowledge your shame, control issues and false prerequisites for being lovable

- Question your core assumptions about your own unworthiness, shame and unlovability—and your need to be less-than-genuine

- Identify who taught you your limiting beliefs (whether it was deliberate or not) and release yourself from them

- Confront and heal whatever self-defeating and love-diminishing notions of spirituality you may still carry

- Identify and disengage from your rightness issues and your need to make projects of people

Freedom is what you do with what's been done to you.

— Jean-Paul Sartre

Everyone's Scared—and With Good Reason

When Lerissa was doing abyss work for the first time, she used to say to her therapist (as though she thought she should be excused from doing the work), "But I'm *scared!*" Her therapist would nod and say, "Yes, Lerissa. We're all scared."

Lerissa's therapist was right: just about everyone fears Stage Four work. Because of the fear, most people stop their journey at this point. The problem is, the fear doesn't go away until *after* you do the work.

We believe that you can mitigate the fear a little, though, by knowing that it is going to be frightening. It is in this spirit that we offer the following list. As you descend into your abyss and confront your wounds, it may seem to you that:

- You're going crazy (when you're simply—and understand-ably—anxious)

- You're having a nervous breakdown (when you're actually experiencing a healing breakthrough)

- You're experiencing unbearable pain (because this is the pain that once *was* unbearable for you as a child and adolescent)

- You've slipped on a banana peel, and now your only choice is to lean into the fall (true).

Q & A about Abyss Work

Some of the most common questions about abyss work are listed below, with our responses.

How do I know which incidents and issues to work on?

Some will surface directly and spontaneously: you'll know 'em when you see 'em. Others will come up indirectly, through day-dreams, night dreams or body sensations; you may be tempted to disregard these incidents or prematurely label their meaning. Still other issues will come up for you when you have been emotion-ally triggered. If you recognize and take responsibility for your reaction and treat it as a clue pointing to other unhealed wounds, you will have your healing agenda.

How will I know when I'm moving out of Stage Four?

When you spontaneously notice that more and more of your life is taking on Stage Five qualities, you will know you are on your way out of Stage Four. The good news of Stage Four work is that you don't have to finish all of it before you begin to reap substantial harvests from your work. Each chunk of Stage Four work you do will give you a liberating sojourn into Stage Five (Rebirth) before you return to deal with yet another of your Stage Four issues. It's essential to take and enjoy these breaks, and use them to celebrate your progress.

How will I know when I'm done with Stage Four?

Since being completely done with your core wounds would be synonymous with enlightenment, you'll probably not be totally done for a long time—if at all in this life. Fortunately, as we mentioned before, you can still reap tremendous benefits on the way toward that lofty goal.

However, you can gauge how much of your core wounds you have healed by asking yourself three questions:

- How much good can I allow into my life without sabotaging it or denying it?

- How deeply fulfilling, residue-free and durable are my closest relationships?

- How well can I serve without giving-to-get, compromising my well-being, or jeopardizing my precious relationships?

As long as you still have work to do in these areas, you still have core wounds to heal.

How can I move quickly through this darkest part of my healing process without skipping anything?

In addition to using the resources and exercises provided at the end of this chapter, go back to Section I. Review the chapters on wounding, the happy-ending fantasy and rules (Chapters Two through Five), and complete the exercises again. Review your earlier responses and write about the differences you see now from your more-healed perspective. Stick to your healing plan. Stay in close touch with your mentors and close healing friends. Keep a journal. Take action on anything that remotely resembles a wake-up call. And, in the end, you can always count on the Rubber Band Effect to bring you back to whatever you might be skipping.

Fran's Kitchen Remodeling Analogy

Fran Cutright, Ph.D., a San Diego therapist with a mental database full of illustrative analogies, has walked many clients through their abyss. She relates an analogy for them that puts the pain and confusion in perspective:

"Therapy is like deciding to remodel your kitchen," she explains. "One day, you look up from a decorating magazine you are thumbing through and compare the pictures there to your cramped, dark little kitchen. You decide that you are finally going to have the kitchen you've always wanted. You call the contractor and the interior designer, choose colors and materials, set the date for the work to begin and fall asleep that night with a smile on your face, dreaming of the meals you'll cook one day soon.

"Six weeks later, ankle deep in sawdust, you wonder what you could have been thinking when you took this project on. The remodeling has put the entire house in chaos. The refrigerator is in the hallway, the stove is on the back porch, there *is* no sink, and the flooring has been ripped up so that the sub-floor is exposed. You can't find anything, and even if you could it wouldn't do you any good because you can't cook or eat in the kitchen.

"Then another week goes by, and you get the counter tile in, and then the new garden window, and one day a set of cabinets. And you begin to see how your new kitchen will look one day, if only you have patience."

It's that sawdust phase, when the house is in chaos, that you face in the abyss. Your emotional work in getting through your abyss consists of hanging in there, not backing away from the pain, and simply surviving the journey to the bottom of your abyss and back up again—a journey you could not survive as a child. Later, when you return to this stage to do more work on your happy-ending fantasy and underlying core wounds, you'll know what to expect. The emotional work becomes a little easier each time you return.

Self-Responsibility Key: A New Perception of Pain

Back in Stage One, you changed your response to pain by beginning to stop running from it and to consider the possibility that victimhood wasn't the only way to live. In Stage Four, your perception of the function of pain in your life changes even more. You learn to welcome the first glimmers of pain as harbingers of coming growth. You begin to shed the victim role, because you don't need it anymore. Now you have the tools to heal what you used to have to protect yourself against.

Response to Pain: Your levels of pain peak early in Stage Four as you enter your abyss for the first time. Surviving this intense hurt gives you confidence and changes your response to pain for all time. From now on, you recognize pain as an indicator of an unhealed wound and respond by directing your healing efforts to the wound.

Level of Investment in Victimhood: By the end of Stage Four, you replace blame with a clear-eyed acknowledgment of the truth of the events that wounded you and your feelings about them, minus the cry for vengeance. In embracing your wounds, you accept responsibility for healing them. You no longer expect others—not even the people who wounded you to begin with—to do that work. This puts you squarely in charge of your own happiness and fulfillment, a position that is antithetical to being a victim, and necessary for moving into the Rebirth Stage (Five).

Activities: Intense Therapy and Lots of Support

Confronting and healing your happy-ending fantasy and the core wounds it hides is extremely demanding work. To make it through, you'll need to call on all your foundation skills: using your support network; journaling, spiritual practice and alone time; good eating, exercise and sleep habits; and a daily routine for handling chores and errands that keeps them from taking over. To return to Fran's analogy: If you were remodeling your kitchen, you would not expect yourself to cook five-course meals. You would probably rely on friends to feed you at least part of the time, and you might stock up on no-preparation finger foods. If you were used to spending time in your kitchen, you would reschedule that time to spend in other rooms in the house.

The activities you choose during this period, as well as the attitude you take toward yourself and your special needs, can make the difference between a painful Stage Four and a *very* painful, protracted Stage Four.

One of the most confusing aspects of Stage Four is the revolving door between it and Stage Five. People working through Stage Four issues often find themselves suddenly feeling good, wondering why and worrying whether they have turned their backs on their abyss.

That's not necessarily so. When you have finished with a wound, you get a little vacation in Five. Enjoy it. You'll be back in your abyss soon enough. To keep yourself un-confused when this occurs, read everything about the Rebirth Stage now so you'll recognize the signs. Then you can change your activities to meet your rapidly changing needs.

Writing

One technique we've used extensively in our own healing journeys and with our clients is letter-writing. Writing a no-holds-barred letter to a former or current abuser or to your inner critic is a powerful way to loosen old, frozen feelings and heal old wounds. You write these letters with the understanding that they *will not be sent*, unless you have fully explored the consequences with your therapist or a mentor. The purpose is to *release* your feelings, not to communicate them. Later, you can decide whether and how you wish to communicate feelings you've uncovered. See the *Exercises* section of this chapter for ideas.

Prayer and Meditation

Prayer and meditation become more important than ever before in Stage Four work. Use your daily quiet times to:

- **Reaffirm your willingness** to face and release your old pain

- **Seek insight** into the ways you resist love and happiness, and the willingness to let go of your resistance

- **Visualize letting go** of old traumas and embracing new and healthier ways of living.

Work with Others

Working with others becomes both easier and more important in Stage Four: easier, because you are now able to recognize and express your feelings, and more important, because you need companionship to get through your abyss.

THERAPY

This is the time to begin depth therapy. By now, you've learned the company-keeping skills to help see yourself through the abyss. Be sure to choose a therapist who focuses on emotional release and healing.

Often people find that their Stage Four work centers on events that wounded them very early in life, before they had learned to talk. This material often is not reachable by traditional talk therapy methods, but is accessible through non-verbal models like art therapy. Therapy models that work well for many people in Stage Four include (but are not limited to):

- Art therapy

- Body therapies (see the list under *Body Work* below)

- Eye Movement Desensitization and Reprocessing (E.M.D.R.)

- Family sculpture

- Focused Expressive Psychotherapy (F.E.P.; a form of anger release and completion)

- Gestalt therapy

- Interactive Guided Imagery (I.G.I.)

- Psychodrama

- Sand tray

The *Healing Resources* section at the end of this chapter provides leads for finding more information about these therapies.

Whatever your therapist's theories, he or she should be prepared to work with you on family-of-origin issues, your survival plan and happy-ending fantasy, childhood trauma, grief, loss, shame and control issues. Group therapy can be especially helpful, either in weekly sessions or multiple-day workshops. But in our experience, group work alone usually is not enough. Be prepared to augment your group meetings with individual sessions, at least from time to time (and especially when you first begin group).

Less helpful at this stage of healing are therapy models that don't concentrate so much on experiencing emotions, such as: cognitive therapy, behavior modification, formal Freudian psychoanalysis, rational-emotive therapy and reality therapy. Although these models can be extremely helpful in the Foundation and Rebirth Stages (Two and Five), they can derail the focus on deep wounds that you need to maintain to do your abyss work.

SELF-HELP GROUPS

Therapy is not the only way to work on Stage Four issues. Self-help support group meetings that focus on honest and self-responsible sharing of feelings can be extremely valuable. As you do this work, concentrate on *feeling* your old pain instead of just thinking or talking about it. Share these feelings and the memories they bring with trusted others in your groups and among your friends.

If you have been attending self-help meetings all along, this is a good time to re-evaluate them. Do they support healthy interaction, independence and growth? Or do they encourage members to stay stuck in blame or grief? You may need to find new, healthier meetings if your current ones tend to encourage people to remain non-self-responsible.

BODY WORK

Many of our clients in Stage Four find body work helps dislodge frozen feelings and lost memories, and also provides comfort and nurturing. If you're interested, check out such practices as:

- Acupuncture
- Alexander Technique
- Breathwork
- Dance therapy
- Feldenkrais Method
- Phoenix Rising Yoga Therapy
- Rebirthing
- Reichian therapy
- Reiki
- Rolfing
- Tai chi
- Therapeutic massage

Ask recovering friends and your therapist for recommendations. Also, check out bulletin boards at your local health food store, yoga center or meditation center, and look for local newspapers published by members of the healing or recovery community.

During your search for a good bodywork practitioner, be sure to practice setting boundaries. As you meet practitioners, be aware of your feelings about them and your responses to their approach. If you're uncomfortable, say so. If your practitioner discusses the issue and you're still not satisfied (or if your practitioner refuses to discuss the issue or blames you) find a different practitioner.

Stage Four Pitfalls: Avoidance of Feeling Work

Does that heading sound familiar? If it does, it's because we called Stage Three Pitfalls the same thing—Avoidance of Feeling Work. Pitfalls in Stage Four have the same character as those in Stage Three, because the work in Four is so similar to that in Three, only more intense. The temptation here is to avoid the difficult, painful feelings.

Stage Four Pitfall #1: Unwillingness to Forgive

> *forgiveness*—Demonstrating, through your feelings and behaviors, that you are no longer hurt or impaired in the present by the unacceptable things that you or others did in the past.

There has been much debate among psychotherapists, psychologists and self-help book authors about whether forgiveness is a necessary prerequisite to healing. Some believe it is unnecessary (at least in certain circumstances); others believe it is essential.

We understand that some people suffered tremendous harm at the hands of their abusers. We do not mean to suggest that there should be no penalty for causing harm to others. But we also believe that the only alternative to forgiveness is victimhood.

In Section II, we defined *victim* as *someone who believes his happiness or peace of mind lies in the hands of another.* If you maintain that you will not sleep well at night until the person who harmed you is brought to justice, you keep yourself in victimhood. You retain your role as your abuser's victim. It is only in releasing this role that you can truly heal. In forgiveness, you lose your attachment to the person who harmed you. You accept the pain of your wounds as your own and create your own healing and happiness without requiring an act of contrition from your abuser.

Forgiveness is separate and distinct from holding people accountable for—or requiring them to take the consequences of—unacceptable behavior. For example, we believe it is possible to believe that a serial killer should die for his crimes and, at the same time, forgive him. But we don't think it is possible to celebrate the execution of a killer, to stake your own peace of mind on his death, and at the same time be anything other than a victim. In the same vein, you may forgive the vandal caught spray-painting your back fence, but you may also require him to re-paint the fence and do community service.

Forgiveness does not mean that you must befriend your abuser. In fact, you might forgive the person who abused you *and* choose never to see him or her again. You may forgive the former lover who confesses that he or she used you, cheated on you and stole from you, but that does not necessarily mean you take this person back into your life.

Forgiveness also does not preclude seeking justice for your abuser. We salute the courage of survivors of sexual abuse who take their tormentors to court to prevent them from inflicting the same terror on other children.

Forgiveness is the mark of a truly healed wound. When you heal and release all your stored-up feelings about a trauma or disconnection, you are ready to forgive. When you accept that nothing outside yourself will save you—not even justice for the people who harmed you—you are finally liberated from the tyranny of your happy-ending fantasy. When that happens, you no longer need to depend upon other people or events to live a complete, fulfilling life.

However, because forgiveness is *both* a result and a choice, you can resist it. In this case, an irresistible force (your healed wounds) meets an immovable object (your unwillingness to forgive).

Stage Four Pitfall #2: Premature Forgiveness

After this discussion of the fundamental relationship of forgiveness to healing, it might seem that we would encourage you to forgive as many as possible, as soon as possible. Not so. It is possible to forgive too soon.

Forgiveness is equal parts a natural manifestation of healing and a decision to let go of the need for retribution or vengeance. It is motivated by a desire to be free to grow into who you really are.

Premature forgiveness is solely an act of the will. It is usually motivated by a desire to avoid pain (providing yet more proof that anything can be an anesthesia). When you decide to forgive before you have really healed—before you have felt enough of the pain of your wounds to know what it is you are forgiving—you are indulging in premature forgiveness. True forgiveness is not an option until the wounds are healed.

How can you tell whether your forgiveness is premature? Check the results.

Sometimes people try to let go of a person or situation that they are still fuming about. If they are participating in a twelve-step recovery program, they may be encouraged to release resentment by "turning it over" to their Higher Power. If the wound behind the resentment is still unhealed, the result is an ineffective head game; they end up burying their feelings instead of releasing them. And we know what happens to buried feelings. Premature forgivers find their anger or resentment returning again and again, in spite of their repeated efforts to let it go.

In this situation, "turning it over" is a poor substitute for what is really needed. The solution is to stop avoiding the angry feelings. Do some anger release work. *Then* focus on letting go. Surrender is ever so much easier when the feelings are healed.

Stage Four Pitfall #3: Rightness Addiction

> *rightness*—A frozen belief that a particular perception or interpretation is the "truth" or "reality;" being closed to evidence that does not support such a belief; the thinking equivalent (or, sometimes, the result) of a frozen feeling.

> *rightness addiction*—An unswerving conviction, sometimes approaching delusional intensity, that your fundamental beliefs about yourself and the world are correct and unchangeable.

When you feel tense, fearful, angry, defensive or in pain; react in some way that is unacceptable to you; or feel as though you are trapped and without alternatives; you are not simply responding to "the facts" or "the situation." More likely, you are listening to your own inner critic and reacting to its interpretations. We call these interpretations *core rightness beliefs.*

Similarly, when you find yourself feeling critical of someone or yourself, criticizing what someone said or did to you, or disliking how you feel around someone, you are most likely dealing with a rightness issue. If these feelings come up over and over in the same situations or with the same people, chances are you are dealing with rightness addiction.

Indulging in this addiction can keep you stuck in victimhood forever. There are plenty of situations to be right about—and probably just as many times you will need to give up the right to be right if your healing is to progress. Try the Rightness Inventory exercise at the end of this chapter. (A time-saving, one-minute Rightness Inventory is a question presented in *A Course in Miracles*: Would you rather be right or happy?)

People are disturbed not by events but by their interpretations of these events.

– Epictetus

Stage Four Pitfall #4: Avoiding Your Abyss

Standing at the edge of your abyss, peering into the murky depths and wondering where and if you will land if you jump, you may have second thoughts. *"Isn't there an easier way to do this?"* you may wonder. Or you may think you took a wrong turn somewhere; what else could explain the bleakness of this landscape? Or you may go ahead and jump, and *then* decide this was a bad idea and head back to the security of Stage Three (Feelings), or even Stage Two (Foundation). Or you may try to go around the abyss to Stage Five (Rebirth).

Any of these measures will activate the Rubber Band Effect, which means more pain in the long run. The best thing to do is to trudge through your abyss. It will hurt, but ultimately it requires less of your life energy to feel the feelings than it does to avoid them. Get support and keep going.

Stage Four Pitfall #5: Therapist Issues

All people are wounded. Therapists are people. Therefore, all therapists are wounded. Even when they are working actively on their own unhealed wounds, wounds remain. As a result, sooner or later they are likely to be triggered in the course of a session.

In light of these facts, it is unrealistic (and, in fact, an indication of an unaddressed aspect of your survival plan) to assume that:

- You will never be disappointed in your therapist
- Your therapist will never do anything that hurts you
- Your therapist "has it all together."

However, because you are also wounded, don't be surprised when you make these assumptions to one extent or another. (Even therapists do it with their own therapists.) When you realize that your therapist is capable of making mistakes, it will hurt.

No one is ever competent enough, nor is any technique ever effective enough. It is only the continuing growth of the practitioner that can guarantee competence and effectiveness.

— Thomas Hanna

At this point, a therapist who can own his or her mistakes or shortcomings is invaluable in helping you heal some of your deepest wounds. A therapist who can't do this can actually block your progress.

TRANSFERENCE

One of the phenomena that make therapy work is called *transference*, in which you project onto your therapist some of your unhealed wounds. Transference doesn't happen just in therapy. We all do it all the time, seeing in other people all the people who hurt us, terrorized us, failed us or ignored us. But in therapy, transference is heightened by issues with authority figures, the difference in power, money and the vulnerability of talking to a relative stranger about your pain. If you experience feelings with your therapist that you also experience in your relationships outside of therapy, take heart; this is a sign of transference. It signals the possibility of healing. Exploring these patterns with your therapist can bear a tremendous amount of fruit. If you are unsure about whether what's happening in your therapy is okay or not, bring it up with your therapist. (But please don't expect your therapist to see you *gratis* during these discussions. Working through these issues is as much a part of your therapy as the outside issues that you bring to each session.)

For example, if you were wounded by a parent's lack of attention, you will almost certainly find evidence sooner or later that your therapist doesn't care about you. If you do, you are likely to handle your anger and hurt however you usually do. The best thing a therapist can do under these circumstances is accept your feelings and allow you to express them.

But a therapist with his own unhealed "father wounds" who is struggling with feeling inadequate as a parent himself might instead become defensive and irritated. When that happens, you and your therapist re-create the worst of your relationship with your father. However, even that is not necessarily a terrible event. If your therapist eventually acknowledges his own wounds and his counter-transference to you, you and he can turn the incident into a profoundly rich opportunity for healing. If not, your healing work is likely to be blocked.

Sometimes people move from one therapist to another when transference surfaces, assuming that the feelings mean something is wrong with the therapeutic relationship. If you experience the same negative incidents over and over with multiple therapists, it is time to take an honest look at your part in these patterns. Ask your therapist to help you explore them. Also, teach your therapist how to support you in ways that feel like support to you. If your concerns linger even after you do this, seek an independent consultation, just as you would if you wanted a second medical opinion.

The Unhealed, Unwilling Therapist

One sign of a therapist with unhealed wounds that are dangerous to your healing journey is the one who repeats your family's original crazy-making behavior. Charley's therapist gave out homework assignments to several people in his group (such as abstaining from sweets or from calling a former lover). Then, when they didn't complete their assignments, he ridiculed them and made them sit in designated chairs, away from the rest of the group.

This is an example of a valuable therapeutic technique that is worthwhile *only when all parties agree to it ahead of time, and the purpose or goal has been made clear.* For instance, you and your therapist might agree to deliberately recreate the feelings of an abusive, critical home. If you are provided with the opportunity and the help to process and express your feelings, this type of experience can help you heal deep wounds. But without an explicit contract and follow-up, it becomes just one more wounding experience.

Group Therapy

Group therapy, in particular, can be trying. This is not the place to hold back and be polite (although it will take a while to sort things out when wounds are triggered). You can expect to replay your emotional patterns in group. The mark of good group therapy is not that bad stuff doesn't happen, but that it gets worked through to a good outcome. That's the purpose of group—not to behave in such an exemplary way that your wounds never show. (Remember, this applies to other group members, too. You'll see them acting out of their wounds, just as they get to see you doing the same thing.)

Melinda had an experience in group therapy that stands as an ideal of the way therapy works at its best. She announced in group one week that she had decided, after much thought and after many months of intensive emotional work, that it was okay to be without a relationship. This was a huge step forward for Melinda, who had always struggled with feeling lost, empty and unworthy when she was between lovers.

She was dismayed and hurt when the co-facilitator, a new therapist named Boyce, appended to Melinda's announcement, "...for now!" Boyce had his own issues about making decisions and then sticking to them long after they were useful simply because he had made a commitment to them at one point. Melinda was triggered by Boyce's response; it was important to her that her announcement was celebrated, not qualified. She reacted with anger, which in turn triggered Boyce. He became defensive and began lecturing Melinda. The two were at logger-heads for weeks. Finally, Boyce's work with his own therapist outside of group revealed the root of his wounds in his dealings with Melinda. In group one evening, he apologized and explained to Melinda that he had allowed his own issues to get in the way. He told the group that Melinda's reaction to him reminded him of his angry mother, and that he reacted to her as he did to his mother. Boyce's willingness to acknowledge his wounds and his humanity allowed Melinda to quit fighting with him, look at her resentments and anger and think about the wounds that Boyce's statements had triggered in her. His mistake became her gift.

Human Fallibility or Red Flag?

In short, don't assume that your therapist's wounds are getting in the way of your healing just because:

- His communication is sometimes sloppy
- You feel angry or frustrated with him
- You feel slighted by him
- Your group gets emotionally hot
- You become uncomfortable with the amount of conflict in your group
- He becomes defensive.

Do, however, consider it a red flag if your therapist:

- Scolds you (or another group member) for being disruptive when you react emotionally to painful events

- Allows truly disruptive behavior to occur (physical or verbal attacks, vengeful anger or blatant, aggressive unwillingness)

- Never takes responsibility for sloppy therapy, sloppy communication or his own unhealed wounds

- Is unresponsive when you raise concerns about the way he handled an incident

- Deliberately re-creates an abusive environment without prior agreement and understanding from everyone who will be present

- Stifles all conflict

- Blurs the boundaries of the therapist–client relationship by proposing or participating in dual relationships. This means employing or dating clients, socializing with or going into business with clients. And of course, sexual behavior with a client is always inappropriate.

Stage Four Pitfall #6: Frightened Friends

When Leah first ventured into her abyss, she turned to her self-help groups for solace. Unfortunately, most of the people there had not yet done their abyss work and were frightened by Leah's descriptions of what was happening in her therapy group. They shook their heads, told her it sounded abusive to them and advised her to quit.

After several individual sessions with her therapist, Leah decided her group situation was not abusive. She stuck it out, and today says she is glad she did. She said she realized that the pain she felt during those difficult months was the pain of her deepest wounds, not the pain of abuse. By hanging in there, she was able to heal core wounds that had held her back all her life.

When you enter your abyss for the first time, less-healed (but well-meaning) friends may be frightened by your experiences and the intense pain. Be prepared for this, and discuss it with your therapist. In the end, it is up to you to decide whether any given situation is abusive. But don't automatically assume you are being abused simply because you are in pain, and don't take action solely on the advice of any one group of friends.

Stage Four Pitfall #7: Cross Addictions

Anesthesias are subtle, conniving things. Just when you figure you've got one licked, another one can pop up and start hammering your survival plan back together. Sometimes, when someone gives up a dramatic addiction, like overeating or sex addiction, he or she will unconsciously pick up another one. This will usually be a quieter one, often an apparently innocent pastime like shopping or exercise. Review Chapter Six to see how easy it can be to be broadsided by anesthesia use.

Stage Four Pitfall #8: Insufficient Incentive

Crossing the abyss is not for the faint of heart. It is difficult, painful work. Sometimes the only thing that can keep you going is the knowledge that what lies ahead is worth it. But if you are not clear about what lies ahead, you may find it impossible to stay the course.

The remedy: Stay in touch with the joy that lies ahead. For example, you can:

- Read everything about Stage Five (Rebirth) that you can find.

- Call friends who have made it through the abyss and ask for pep talks.

- Keep the list on the next page handy. In fact, we suggest you photocopy the list, tape it to your bathroom mirror and read it out loud every morning.

◆

A Partial List of the Benefits of Making It Through Stage Four and Your Personal Abyss

1. More self-esteem

2. More inner peace

3. More happiness

4. Much more time spent in healthy relationships where there is lots of love and connection and not much fighting or disconnection

5. Much less depression

6. Much less anxiety

7. More optimism

8. Much, much more creativity

9. A sense that you can handle any challenge

10. More satisfaction and fulfillment in your career (which may very well change after Stage Four)

11. Integrity

12. Outside life matches inside life

13. Less people-pleasing

14. More of what you like, less of what you don't like

15. Less time repeating, more time creating

16. Life feels fun. It looks newer, fresher, more exciting and different.

Stage Four Healing Resources

Therapy models

There are many forms of therapy that can help you heal core wounds. This list represents a sampling.

ART THERAPY

A terrific way to connect with deep feelings that can't be reached through talk therapy. Look for someone who has been accredited by the American Art Therapy Association.

SAND TRAY THERAPY

This is an excellent form of art therapy practiced by many Jungian therapists (although some non-Jungians also use it). In sand tray, you select figures and objects from a large assortment and arrange them in a large, open box filled with sand to represent your inner and outer life. David compares sand tray to "having waking dreams."

GESTALT THERAPY

Known as the "empty chair therapy," in which you talk to a chair occupied by your imagined versions of people, parts of yourself, dreams, places, events. Great for getting into (and releasing) many old, frozen feelings. Look for someone with a certificate in gestalt therapy.

PSYCHODRAMA

In this form of therapy, you recreate traumatic situations from your past, with facilitators and group members playing parts you assign them. Look for someone with a certificate in psychodrama.

FAMILY SCULPTURE

Virginia Satir developed this form of psychodrama. Sharon Wegscheider-Cruse, Ph.D., a proponent of family sculpture, uses it extensively in her own treatment program, called OnSite. OnSite is located at Sierra Tucson in Arizona (800/624-9001).

We have used the following therapy models with great success in our practice. Check with local providers and self-help or new-age publications for therapists trained in their use.

FOCUSED EXPRESSIVE PSYCHOTHERAPY

Developed by Roger J. Daldrup, Ph.D., Focused Expressive Psychotherapy (F.E.P.) is the only anger release technique of its kind. Most other methods don't distinguish between expressions of anger that amplify the emotion and those that allow people to release the feeling. (Simple venting of anger tends to make people *more*, not less, angry.) F.E.P. helps participants find a form for their anger that allows them to take full responsibility for it, and thus fully release it.

The world around you may be shit, but your anger about it is your own.

— Brian Woolsey

Unfortunately, there is no formal network of trained F.E.P. therapists. Check around your community, though; you may find someone who knows this priceless technique. *Freedom from Anger* (Pocket Books, 1990), which Roger wrote with Dodie Gust, is aimed at consumers. It is out of print, but you may find it in libraries or bookstores. (Roger tells us he hopes to re-release this title sometime before the end of 1996.) *Focused Expressive Psychotherapy* (Guilford, 1988), which he wrote with Larry E. Beutler, David Engle, and Leslie S. Greenberg, is a detailed technical manual written for psychotherapists. If your therapist is open to the idea, ask him or her to read it.

Willingness Works offers weekend workshops using F.E.P. for people in Stage Four and beyond. Call or write for information.

INTERACTIVE GUIDED IMAGERY

Interactive Guided Imagery (I.G.I.) is one of the best guided imagery models around. For information, contact:

Academy for Guided Imagery
P.O. Box 2070
Mill Valley, CA 92592
415/389-9324

EYE MOVEMENT DESENSITIZATION AND REPROGRAMMING
This technique can help to gently break through even the toughest walls to get to old wounds and heal unresolved trauma.

> E.M.D.R. Network
> P.O. Box 51010
> Pacific Grove, CA 93950-6010
> 408/372-3900

Miscellaneous

Banished Knowledge. Alice Miller. Doubleday, 1988.

Bird by Bird: Some Instructions on Writing and Life. Anne Lamott. Pantheon, 1995.

Breaking Down the Wall of Silence. Alice Miller. Penguin, 1991.

Choicemaking. Sharon Wegscheider-Cruse. Health Communications, 1985.

The Courage to Heal. Laura Davis and Ellen Bass. Harper Perennial, 1992.

The Drama of the Gifted Child. Alice Miller. Basic Books, Inc., 1981.

The Fantasy Bond. Robert Firestone, Ph.D. Firestone's work is available from the Glendon Association, 4141 State Street, Suite E4, Santa Barbara, CA 93105. Phone: 310/552-0431.

For Your Own Good. Alice Miller. Farrar Straus Giroux, 1983.

Genograms. Emily Marlin. Contemporary Books, 1989.

The Grief Recovery Handbook. John James. Perennial Library, 1989.

The Grief Recovery Institute offers excellent help in confronting, feeling and releasing deep sorrow. Contact them at: Grief Recovery Institute, 8306 Wilshire Blvd. Suite 21-A, Beverly Hills, CA 90211 (phone: 213/650-1234).

Making Sense of Suffering. J. Conrad Stettbacher. Dutton, 1991.

The Miracle of Recovery. Sharon Wegscheider-Cruse.
Health Communications, 1989.

Overcoming Regret: Lessons from the Roads Not Taken.
Carole Klein and Richard Gotti, Ph.D. Bantam, 1992.

Repeat After Me. Claudia Black, Ph.D., M.S.W.
M.A.C. Printing and Publications, 1985.

Repressed Memories: Can You Trust Them? Arlys Norcross
McDonald, Ph.D. Revelle Publishing, due out in Fall 1995.

*The Right to Innocence: Healing the Trauma of Childhood Sexual
Abuse.* Beverly Engel, M.F.C.C. Jeremy P. Tarcher, Inc., 1989.

Secret Survivors: Uncovering Incest and Its Aftereffects in Women.
E. Sue Blume. John Wiley and Sons, 1990.

Thou Shalt Not Be Aware. Alice Miller. Penguin, 1984.

The Untouched Key. Alice Miller. Doubleday, 1988.

Willingness Works Resources

Fantasy Bond: The Core Wound in Search of Healing
(tape and workbook)

*The Fantasy Bond Revisited: The Secret Source of Relationship
Sabotage* (tape)

From Victimization to Empowerment (tape)

Getting Done With Your Anger (tape, workbook, and workshop)[35]

Healing the Abandonment Wound (tape)

How to Stop Repeating the Same Patterns Over and Over Again (tape)

If I'm Right, Why Am I Unhappy? (tape)

Integrating Your Many Parts (tape)

Know Your Narcissists (tape)

Stop Sucking My Energy! (tape)

Why Do You Bug Me So Much?: Owning Your Projections (tape)

[35] As F.E.P. therapists, David and Rebecca provide weekend Anger Completion Workshops on a regular basis for those in Stage Four and beyond. Call or write for more information.

Stage Four Healing Exercises

Write Letters

Not only is the pen mightier than the sword, it is often mightier than the unhealed wound. Writing letters is a powerful way to name your wounds and release your pain.

However, please *do not send* the letters you write, unless you have thoroughly discussed the potential consequences with your therapist or a trusted mentor. Writing a letter is an emotional purge, and purging *onto someone else* is always inappropriate.[36] To purge your anger onto someone else is a way of abusing others as you have been abused; in doing this, you make yourself into a perpetrator. However, having someone there as a willing witness to your purging is helpful and appropriate.

Communicating your feelings and wishes to others is best accomplished afterwards, using different techniques.

1. Write discharge letters to your primary caregivers and others you blame for your wounds. These letters can be formal (*"Dear Mr. Gielgud: It is with deepest joy we inform you that your services are no longer required…"*), or more spontaneous (*"Joe, you asshole: You can take your slimy games and stick them where the sun don't shine, because…"*). Whatever form you use, be sure to name every last feeling you had toward each person, and tell them why you are firing them, what they did that harmed you, and what you are going to do differently now that they are gone.

2. Write "Dear John" letters to people, events, places and things that have brought you pain. In these letters, explain what made them painful and tell

---

[36] For more information about the costs of venting anger onto others, read *Anger Kills*, by Redford B. Williams (Times Books, 1993).

them how and why you are leaving them behind, and for what or whom you are leaving them. Also, acknowledge to yourself that nothing is all good or all bad by describing the gifts that you received from this person, event, place or thing.

3. Write "Dear John" letters to parts of your survival programming—beliefs about yourself, the world, your Higher Power and other people—that you are ready to release. For example, you may have concluded that all members of the opposite sex in general are lying, untrustworthy users. While this belief allowed you to feel emotionally safe, it also put a serious crimp in your ability to build a close, intimate relationship. You will need to release that belief at some point for your healing to proceed. Try writing to the belief as if it were a person, to thank it for protecting you and to suggest that it can move on now. Once again, don't forget to describe the benefits that you received from this belief.

Inventory Your Traumas

1. List all the painful memories you can think of. As you write, you will probably remember others. Write them all down, in as much detail as you can remember.

2. Identify your worst fears about what's going to happen today if you continue to confront your wounds. Then compare these fears to the trauma list you made for #1. Notice the parallels. What you fear most *will* occur, already *has* occurred. That's why you fear it.

3. Write a letter (or a series of letters) giving back the trauma and what you learned from it to the person you received it from.

4. Read your lists and your letters aloud to a trusted friend who can keep you company while you have your feelings. Create a ritual to release the traumas. You may wish to burn the papers, bury them, or tear them into small bits and take them to the landfill or a compost heap. Be creative. Celebrate the release.

Write Dialogues

Play the parts of your inner critic and your inner child, and stage conversations between them. You can do this aloud, with a chair or stuffed animal representing one character and you playing the part of the other, or by doing a visualization and then writing down what each character says, as if you were creating a play. For a topic, choose whatever issue or wound is currently an issue for you. For example, you might have them talk about their attitudes toward the opposite sex, their fear of failure (or success) or their expectations of your friends.

Review Your Survival Plan

Stage Four is a good time to review your survival plan in detail. (As it falls apart, it's easier to see the pieces.) If you haven't already completed the exercises at the end of Chapters Four, Five and Six, do so now. Then complete the exercises described below.

1. Review the elements of your survival plan as they apply to specific areas of your life: relationships, work, spirituality, money, play and so on.

2. One theory of human behavior and motivation says that we all are driven by a search for love, validation and safety. How does your survival plan bring you love? Validation? Safety? How does your survival plan block your access to love, validation and safety? (You may find, if you turned to false hopelessness instead of false hope, that your survival plan doesn't aim for love or validation at all, but solely for safety.)

Do a Rightness Inventory

Your core rightness beliefs affect how you see everything that happens. David and Rebecca and two of their friends were on a Saturday outing when their car broke down. While they waited for the tow truck, they commiserated and joked about how a crisis like this would have, in the past, reinforced their pictures of themselves as victims.[37] One by one, they listed their core rightness beliefs:

- *"We are being punished for trying to have fun."*

- *"You work and work to make something nice happen, and what do you get? Nothing!"*

- *"Everything's just a BIG mess all the time anyway."*

- *"If I were more loving and more spiritual, this kind of thing wouldn't happen."*

Discovering your core rightness beliefs for the first time, however, rarely feels like a laughing matter. To uncover your core rightness beliefs, follow the steps below.

1. Complete these sentences:

    According to my inner critic, bad things happen to me because...

    According to my inner critic, I fail because...

    According to my inner critic, I am rejected because...

    According to my inner critic, life is _____ because...

    According to my inner critic, if I try hard...

    According to my inner critic, when good things happen...

    According to my inner critic, I am here on this planet...

    According to my inner critic, love evades me because...

2. Notice the similarities among the statements you wrote. Are there recurring themes in the sentences? Recurring themes might include: the influence of bad luck/good luck; the role of punishment and reward in life; the futility of working hard; the chaos and indifference of the universe; how your "inadequacy" (spiritual, sexual, financial, logistical) influences your life.

    List the recurring themes that appear in your sentences. Find the one theme that ties together most (or all, if possible) of your sentences.

---

[37] There is nothing like an emergency or a major disappointment to put the spotlight on your core rightness beliefs.

3. Condense the recurring themes into a single "affirmation" (probably a negative one). This might be *It's futile to try to accomplish anything, because I am cursed by bad luck*, *All good things are followed by bad things*, or *If you never care very much about anything, you will keep yourself safe from hurt.*

4. Re-write your negative affirmation into a positive affirmation. For example, *If you never care very much about anything, you will keep yourself safe from hurt* might become *Caring about things or people makes me more alive by giving me more access to all my feelings—the pleasant and the not-so-pleasant; I can feel all my feelings.*

5. Write a statement of willingness to let these old beliefs go. Create a special ritual to release them and to open up to a new, more nourishing belief to take its place.

List Your Disconnection Experiences

Return to the exercises at the end of Chapters One and Two in Section I. Complete them again. Compare today's responses to the responses you made the first time you completed these exercises. What has changed? What new feelings have come up for you?

It is not enough to understand what happened and have your feelings about the disconnections in your life. To heal, you must find a way to complete your grieving and anger. Refer to the *Healing Resources* section of this chapter for ideas.

TWENTY-SEVEN

Stage Five: Rebirth

...every rule in the book can be broken, except one—
be who you are, and become all you were meant to
be...

– Sidney J. Harris

IN STAGE FIVE, YOU BURST INTO BLOOM. Your work in this stage revolves around becoming accustomed to your new self. Like the stream spirit after the flood, you will re-landscape your life. This new sense of yourself will allow you to make forays back into Stage Four whenever necessary to heal more core wounds.

Goal: Welcome the New You

Doing abyss work brings you a new sense of self-esteem. Most people are surprised to discover that liking themselves is not particularly comfortable at first. That's the objective of Stage Five work: to learn to *like* liking yourself. In Stage Five, you consolidate the emotional gains you made in Stages One through Four and reorganize your life around your new-found self.

Emotional Work:
Expand Your Comfort Zone, Forgive

Stage Five is a busy time. By this point, you've acquired all the emotional tools you need; your task now is to learn to use them comfortably in more and more areas of your life. As you become adept with your tools (keeping company with your feelings, re-negotiating your relationship with your inner critic and moving more easily in and out of your abyss) you gradually become comfortable with everything life hands you. You are more and more authentic with yourself. You finish remaining unfinished business. You develop boundaries and begin to enjoy being self-responsible.

It's a funny thing about life; if you refuse to accept anything but the best, you very often get it.

— Somerset Maugham

You become willing to let go of old grievances and resentments. You complete your unfinished emotional business with the people whom you identified in Stage Four as having wronged you. You forgive yourself, others, situations and the world for the harm they may have done you, or for simply not meeting your expectations. In doing so, you release yourself from the need for vengeance.

Self-Responsibility Key: Full Acceptance

It is in Stage Five that you finally begin to accept full responsibility for your life, and to actually take pleasure in noticing where you can increase your levels of self-responsibility. This means you work on five fronts at once—more than in any other stage: Boundary-Setting Skills, Foundation of Self-Esteem, Unfinished Business, Mission, and Quality of Relationship with Your Spiritual Resources.

Boundary-Setting Skills: You set your boundaries more and more precisely. You no longer need to substitute the rules of your survival plan for your true boundaries. You often know what your boundaries are *before* they are violated, which is a welcome change for you. Early in Stage Five, you tend to set boundaries abrasively, without compassion: *"This is how I am, this* *is how I feel, too bad it doesn't fit with what you need, but I'm sure you'll adjust.*" Later in Stage Five, you begin to mellow. Because you are more certain of where you stand and of your ability to prevent people from walking all over you, you can spare some compassion for their pain. However, your boundaries still tend to be unilateral. It is only in Stage Six that you fully master the art of setting mutual boundaries.

Foundation of Self-Esteem: You begin to feel good about your ability to be who you truly are in more and more situations. You learn to notice when you hide your true self from others, and work to correct these slips. You begin to rejoice in the knowledge that being who you are is the best thing for you and for the people around you. You no longer fear the consequences of being authentic.

Unfinished Business: You begin dealing with your backlog of logistical incompletes, such as old debts, unsatisfying career choices, interrupted education, neglected paperwork and financial planning, and so on.

Mission in Life: As your foundation of self-esteem switches to your expression of your authentic self, your mission becomes focused on self-expression, too. It becomes natural to notice when you have compromised your authenticity, and you find ways to get better at being real with yourself and others.

Quality of Relationship with Your Spiritual Resources: You relax in the arms of a Higher Power whose intentions you are learning to trust. You begin to see all of life's situations—the painful as well as the joyful—as opportunities to increase your self-knowledge, authenticity, joy and ability to love.

Activities: Apply Self-Responsibility

Moving into Stage Five is like seeing the sun come out after a long period of stormy weather. It is a time of optimism; a brighter life is beginning. It is a time to clean out the cobwebs and remnants of your survival plan. It is a time to taste self-esteem deeper than you ever thought possible. It is a time to bask in the light of your successes.

At the same time, you may not be able to sit still because you know there is so much to do. You are free of much of your survival plan, and you astonish yourself with the amount of life energy that is available to you as a result. You spontaneously find yourself using it to be creative and to respond to situations differently than you ever have before.

Any activity that provides you with an opportunity to apply self-responsibility is a good one for Stage Five. Places to find these opportunities include: group therapy, seminars in self-esteem, personal empowerment and life skills; and career counseling.

Finding other Stage Five people to talk with is one self-responsibility challenge nearly all people in Stage Five face. There are not yet many Stage Fivers around (although we suspect the numbers are growing), and this can sometimes make this part of the journey rather lonely and frustrating. You may be tempted to slide back into old attitudes and behaviors to ease the pain. For example, you may try to rush your Stage Three and Four friends into the next stage, or you may criticize them for not understanding or for feeling threatened by your interests and outlook. Your own healing momentum is not likely to let you do this for long. Usually, you will be propelled back into Stage Four to heal the wounds that keep you expecting others to take responsibility for your needs for companionship. As you heal, you take responsibility for finding Stage Five friends. And you learn that the way to find other Stage Fivers is to simply send them a signal by offering your vulnerability.

Writing

By this stage, your writing activities (other than your journal) should probably take the form of goal-setting and finding your dream. Try books by Joyce Chapman, M.A. (especially *Live Your Dream*), Steven Covey and Barbara Sher, Ph.D., for ideas.

Work with Others

Your ability to work creatively and authentically with others reaches new peaks. Take advantage of this blossoming ability by:

- Participating in group therapy

- Taking on leadership roles in your self-help support groups, at work or in your other organizations

- Focusing on developing personal integrity and life skills such as forgiveness, boundaries and communication, relationships, personal empowerment, self-esteem, motivation, money management and financial planning and time planning

- Making amends and/or offering self-disclosures and boundaries (as you find necessary and helpful) to those with whom you still have unfinished business

- Describing and role-modeling your success to others.

Miracles...rest not so much upon faces or voices or healing power coming to us from afar, but upon our perceptions being made finer, so that for a moment our eyes can see and our ears can hear what is there about us always.

— Willa Cather

Stage Five Pitfalls: Resisting Full Self-Responsibility

Although Stage Five is probably the least scary stage that you will have visited so far, it does have its challenges. The task most people have difficulty with is accepting their new attributes: their strength, their level of healing, their talents and abilities. To accept these positive qualities means to take full self-responsibility for them—and for the less pleasant material, too.

Stage Five Pitfall #1: Unwillingness to Forgive

Holding resentments against those who harmed you is a way of maintaining a belief that they are responsible for your misery. When you forgive them, you release them from this responsibility and take it on yourself. The temptation is to hang on to the security blanket of blame. It still provides some warmth and comfort, but it's old, moldy, smelly, and tattered, and you'll trip over it again and again until you get rid of it.

See the discussion of *Stage Four Pitfall #1: Unwillingness to Forgive* in Chapter Twenty-Six for more information about this topic.

Stage Five Pitfall #2: Ignoring the Risks

Stage Five, with its issues of autonomy and boundaries, can threaten a relationship. You need to know this as you begin Stage Five. Not taking into account the ways you risk your primary relationships as you explore your independence can activate the Rubber Band Effect when you are surprised by your partner's reactions.

Stage Five Pitfall #3: The Dependent Therapist

Your therapist's job is to help you become independent of him or her. If he or she discourages you from leaving therapy or suggests that you are not ready to be on your own, you may be working with a therapist who is more interested in your dependence on him or her than in your healing.

When a therapist discourages you from leaving, always talk with him or her until you understand why. You don't have to agree, but it is in your own best interests to listen. Then, if you still disagree, decide whether to trust your intuition or defer to your therapist's recommendations. After all, you are the consumer; it's *your* therapy.

If you find yourself repeating this scene (wanting to leave therapy against your therapist's recommendation) with more than one or two therapists, however, stop and examine the pattern. It is likely that you are finding reasons to leave therapy just as you're about to confront an especially frightening or forbidden wound. You have every right not to look at things before you're ready (and the Rubber Band Effect won't let you completely forget any wound), but chronic avoidance won't get you the healing you seek.

Stage Five Pitfall #4: The Two-Five Jump

Are you trying to be in Stage Five by detouring around Stages
Three and Four? If so, you have cut yourself a difficult path.
Sooner or later the Rubber Band Effect will snap you back to
Stages Three and Four to finish the work there that you left
undone. It's easier to do the work in sequence. Take the self-
assessment again and concentrate on being ruthlessly honest.

Stage Five Pitfall #5: Fear of Feeling Too Good

Sometimes, people arrive in Stage Five looking over their shoul-
ders. They are waiting for the other shoe to drop—for the
monsters to crawl out from under the bed and reclaim them.
One of the most joyful tasks of Stage Five is giving up your fear
of feeling good.

The problem here is your old programming. Even though
you no longer really believe in it, your programming about not
deserving to feel good is still around, like bits of a shell you have
hatched out of that are still underfoot. The solution is to clean
house; get rid of the shell fragments. Figure out who taught you
(on purpose or not) that you don't deserve to feel good. Then
give the message back. Create a ritual to symbolically return the
message, or visualize thanking the person who gave it to you and
returning it. Repeat as necessary.

*It takes courage to grow
up and become who you
really are.*

— e.e. cummings

Stage Five Healing Resources

Miscellaneous

Are You the One for Me? Barbara DeAngelis, Ph.D. Dell, 1992.

The Artist's Way: A Spiritual Path to Higher Creativity.
Julia Cameron. Jeremy P. Tarcher/Perigee, 1992.
(If you've ever said, "Oh, I'm not really a creative person," this workbook is for you.)

Come Here, Go Away: Stop Running from the Love You Want.
Dr. Ralph Earle and Susan Meltsner. Pocket Books, 1991.

Creating a Beautiful Home. Alexandra Stoddard. Avon, 1992.

Get Out of Debt, Stay Out of Debt & Live Prosperously.
Jerrold Mundis. Bantam, 1988.

Good Bye to Guilt: Releasing Fear Through Forgiveness.
Gerald G. Jampolsky, M.D., with Patricia Hopkins and
William N. Thetford, Ph.D. Bantam, 1985.

I Could Do Anything If I Only Knew What It Was.
Barbara Sher with Barbara Smith. Delacorte Press, 1994.

Keeping the Love You Find. Harville Hendrix, Ph.D.
Pocket Books, 1992.

Learned Optimism. Martin Seligman, Ph.D.
Alfred A. Knopf, 1991.

Live Your Dream. Joyce Chapman, M.A. Newcastle, 1990.

Making Peace With Your Parents. Harold H. Bloomfield, M.D.,
with Leonard Felder, Ph.D. Random House, 1983.

Men Are From Mars, Women Are From Venus. John Gray, Ph.D.
HarperCollins, 1992.

Overcoming Regret: Lessons from the Roads Not Taken.
Carole Klein and Richard Gotti, Ph.D. Bantam, 1992. (Out of print; check used bookstores and libraries.)

Sidetracked Home Executives. Pam Brace and Peggy Jones.
Binford and Mort, 1979.

The Seven Habits of Highly Effective People. Stephen Covey.
Simon & Schuster, 1989.

*What Are Your Goals: Powerful Questions to Discover What You
Want Out of Life.* Gary R. Blair. Wharton Publishing, 1993.

What Color is Your Parachute? Richard Bolles.
Ten Speed Press, 1985.

What Really Matters: Searching for Wisdom in America.
Tony Schwartz. Bantam, 1995.

Why People Don't Heal. (tape) Caroline Myss.
Sounds True Productions (800/333-9185).

*Wishcraft: How to Get What You **Really** Want.* Barbara Sher with
Annie Gottlieb. Ballantine, 1979.

You'll See It When You Believe It. Dr. Wayne W. Dyer. Avon, 1989.

*Your Money or Your Life: Transforming Your Relationship with
Money and Achieving Financial Independence.* Joe Domingues
and Vicki Robin. Viking, 1992.

Willingness Works Resources

Acceptance Makes You Powerful (tape)

Boundaries: Your Key to Empowerment (tape)

Finding Your Inner Purpose (tape)

Forgiveness: An End to Wounds (tape)

Getting it Done: Ending Procrastination (tape)

How to Stay Responsible Around Irresponsible People (tape)

Reaching Your Goals by Stretching Your Comfort Zone (tape)

How to Benefit from Everything that Happens (tape)

The Power of Self-Responsibility (tape)

✍

Stage Five Healing Exercises

Stage Five is a time for taking stock. As your life settles into a new set of patterns, you probably will find that much has changed—your values, your goals, your dreams and aspirations. During Stage Five, most people find renewed energy for taking a closer look at these issues. The exercises described below are designed to help you discover and organize the changes in your life.

Revise Your Mission Statement

Now is the time to revise your personal mission statement—or write one if you haven't yet done so. If you wrote one back in Stages One, Two, Three or Four, much has changed since then; you may find that your mission statement no longer fits who you are. If you haven't written one yet, doing so may help you sort out needs and desires that you've only recently become aware of.

Writing a mission statement helps you clarify what is most important to you. To get started on a mission statement, make up names for one to three roles you play in each of the following categories:

- **Self-Nurturance** (Examples from some of our workshop participants include Time Manager, Exerciser, Spiritual Path Monitor, Money Manager, Personal Enrichment Coordinator)

- **Life Maintenance** (For example, Chores Monitor, Errands Supervisor, Incompletes Finisher, Relief Creator)

- **Relationships** (Spouse, Parent, Sibling, Partner, Friend, Support System Member)

- **Career/Productivity/Service** (For example, Career Re-Evaluator/Researcher, Student, Boss, Employee, Volunteer, Typist, Engineer)

From this information, develop a statement that summarizes the driving force in your life. (For more detailed information on mission statements, check this chapter's reading list.)

List Your Goals

Use your mission statement to develop specific life goals. Break them down into do-able segments, and assign deadlines to each one. Keep track of your progress in completing them.

There are many good systems you can use to help you set and make your goals. Some of the better ones include: MasterMind; Franklin Systems; Steven Covey's system; *What Color Is Your Parachute?* (particularly its appendix about developing a mission statement), and *Finding Your Mission in Life*, both by Richard Bolles; *Wishcraft* and other titles by Barbara Sher; *The Celestine Prophecy: An Experiential Guide* by James Redfield and Carol Adrienne; and Personal Resource Systems.

List Your Incompletes

List remaining task and relationship incompletes, including resentments you're still holding, and develop a plan to complete them one at a time. Give yourself deadlines and specific tasks, and check them off as you complete them.

List Your Self-Victimization Patterns

Itemize the ways you still subtly victimize or sabotage yourself and be on the lookout for these patterns so you can nip them in the bud. To find these patterns, look for relationships or issues in which you feel stuck, or situations that keep turning up over and over in your life. For example, you and your significant other may have the same argument every few months, without ever resolving the underlying issues. That's an indication of an unhealed wound that keeps you in the victim role.

When you have identified a pattern, ask yourself:

• What within me makes me repeat this theme? What do I hope to achieve?

- Who does this person remind me of? What incidents like this one have occurred in my life before? What incidents have occurred with family members that resemble this one?

- If I hate something about someone else, chances are I have the same trait (although perhaps expressed in a slightly different form). How do I manifest the trait that I'm reacting to in this other person? How and why have I distanced myself from this trait? How can I begin to reclaim this trait for myself?

Inventory Your Self

Identify your gifts, talents and skills. Then identify your deficits or handicaps. Include activities for improving your deficits and handicaps in your healing plan.

Release Your Rightness

In Stage Four, you began working with rightness issues. Unfortunately, this does not necessarily mean that you are done with them. A rightness attack can still grab you—even in Stage Five (and beyond). However, by now you are much better equipped to deal with it. When you have an attack of rightness, try identifying your beliefs and releasing them by following the steps below.

1. Clearly state what you are right about. For example: *I am right that Jeff shouldn't be so critical of other people.*

2. Complete the checklists on the next page:

How does my rightness *help* me? Being right about this makes me feel:	**How does my rightness *hurt* me? Being right about this makes me feel:**
☐ Inwardly loving, happy, peaceful and at ease	☐ Inwardly unloving, agitated, anxious, depressed, or unhappy
☐ Connected with, and nurturing toward, my inner child	☐ Disconnected from, or violating toward, my inner child
☐ Aware of and able to honor my boundaries	☐ Confused about, unaware of, or in violation of my boundaries, or willing to set them in a controlling or damaging way
☐ Connected with, and supported by, my Higher Power or spiritual resources	☐ Disconnected from, or unsupported by, my Higher Power or spiritual resources
☐ Loving toward, connected with, and effectively working with others	☐ Resentful, angry, disconnected from, or caught in a power struggle with others
☐ Willing to take effective steps toward resolving the problem	☐ Impaired in my ability to take effective steps toward resolving the problem
☐ Other:	☐ Other:

3. Based on the results of your inventory, decide whether you are willing to pay the price for being right. Is the price low enough that you are content to remain right and pay for it? Is it high enough that you are now motivated to challenge it? If you are ready to challenge it, go on to step four.

4. From whom did you learn the beliefs you identified in #1? (Your teachers may or may not have meant for you to learn these; for the sake of this exercise, this is irrelevant.)

5. Have your therapist coach you in doing emotional release work that will help you give these beliefs back to your teachers (internally, that is).

6. Identify what you want to believe instead and open your willingness to embrace each new belief.

7. Tell other people about how you carry these old beliefs until you notice yourself becoming bored with them and more interested in embracing the new ones.

Practice steps four through seven each time these rightness beliefs surface.

TWENTY-EIGHT

Stage Six: Clear-Hearted Relationships

Relationship is surely the mirror
in which you discover yourself.

— Krishnamurti

IN STAGE SIX, YOUR RELATIONSHIPS BLOOM. Stage Six marks the end of feeling alone, unique or special, and the beginning of an ability to share the journey with others on a much deeper level than ever before.

Goal: Deep Joining

Your goal in Stage Six is learn to join with others more deeply than ever before in a way that grows from your own authenticity. Before this stage, it was not possible for you to join with others on a particularly profound level; you either protected your wounds and stayed out of this level of intimacy, or you tried and lost yourself, like a fledgling attempting to fly with wet, weak wings. In healing your core wounds, you released what you had been protecting. You strengthened and dried your wings. From this foundation, you entered Stage Six.

Emotional Work: Blending

You learn to blend yourself with another person; in the process, not only do you *not* lose yourself, you become more powerfully who you were always meant to be. Some of our clients think of this blending as the meeting of two tributary rivers.

Self-Responsibility Key: Vulnerability

By Stage Six, your self-responsibility is so much a part of your nature that you want and need to risk being vulnerable. Because you've learned you will survive it, you accept conflict as a gift. (After all, once you've survived your abyss and faced your darkest secrets and fears, there's not much to fear in facing other fears. You still may not like it, but you're much less afraid of it.) You begin to allow conflict to move you closer to your remaining unhealed wounds, closer to your partner, and closer to your spiritual resources. You can sustain this level of vulnerability only when you have done enough healing work in Stages One through Five that you no longer feel the need to spend your life energy protecting old unhealed wounds.

Boundary-Setting Skills: In Stage Five, you became clear about your boundaries. Now you are ready to ease up on them a little. While you are still strong and firm about your boundaries, your priorities shift. Your emphasis is on union with the other person. Since you feel certain of your ability to create your own emotional safety and take care of yourself, you can be flexible about your boundaries. Defensiveness begins to disappear. You start to make boundary-setting a mutual activity, with both of you getting what you need and still maintaining boundaries.

Quality of Relationships: Your relationships begin to be marked by a full and open trust in your ability to work things through. You abandon your false hope that conflict will blow over. You attain a sense of playfulness and abandon in your relationships that comes about only through a deep sense of trust in yourself and your spiritual resources. Through your Stage Four abyss work, you have greatly resolved your fear of abandonment and trust issues. This leaves you free to love deeply without being blocked from deep commitment by fear. Sarcasm and biting humor have no place in Stage Six relationships. Instead, you find it easy to be tender with people.

You view your relationships as a pathway to your spiritual growth. When you are triggered, you assume that your reaction is providing a glimpse into your own unfinished business and unhealed wounds; you are less likely to become caught up in trying to clean up the other person's side of the street.

You no longer tolerate unfinished business or emotional residue buildup; you initiate plans to avoid creating them. You actively push your own limits on how much sustained closeness you can tolerate before backing off. Power struggles tend to be a thing of the past. You no longer need to make people into projects, and you no longer need the other person to change before you can be okay.

When you are truly in Stage Six, you will find another Stage Six person with whom to have a close relationship. This is the true mark of someone in the Clear-Hearted Relationships stage. In earlier stages, you might be able to make Stage Six-type *responses* to others. But you cannot consider your dominant stage to be this one until you create a Stage Six relationship with a Stage Six adult. This might not be a romantic union; you can have a Clear-Hearted Relationship with a friend or business partner as well as with a lover or spouse. In Stage Six, you are now able to need each other without having to suck each other's life energy. It is at this point that you are ready to deal with your spiritual and emotional equal.

Your willingness and ability to be in a relationship with your spiritual and emotional equal is critical to your growth and movement into Stage Seven.

Activities: Develop Relationship Skills

In Stage Six, you focus your attention on developing the ability to be in healthy and nurturing relationships in all aspects of your life.

Therapy, pursuing your chosen spiritual path (and, in doing so, confronting and eliminating any remaining fear of connecting with your spiritual resources), actively participating in healthy relationships—all are appropriate and rewarding activities for Stage Six. You develop conflict resolution skills and the ability to notice and eliminate the emotional residue of unresolved conflict that clogs most relationships.

In Stage Six, you begin to use everyday life as an activity to develop your relationship skills. You see your vulnerability as the key to creating community with any person—lovers, friends, family, co-workers, strangers on the bus. You express your self-responsibility by taking opportunities to create what *A Course In Miracles* calls *holy instants*.[38]

These moments can happen anywhere, but creating one requires being vulnerable. David tells a story about taking this risk at a party given by the parents of a friend who had just earned his Ph.D. David and Rebecca knew practically no one other than their friend; they both felt awkward and tongue-tied. Furthermore, the hosts had spared no expense in celebrating their son's achievement, and David and Rebecca felt intimidated by the opulence. They were edging their way to the door when they ran into an old acquaintance and his wife. David explained that they were on their way out.

"Why are you leaving?" the friend asked.

David evaded the question with a vague answer, then chatted for a few more minutes. The friend asked again why David and Rebecca were leaving. Again David evaded the question. The conversation continued, as good-bye conversations tend to do, and then the friend (who was nothing if not persistent) asked again why they were leaving. David said that, at that point, something clicked inside.

"I realized that I had never admitted to myself that I am shy, and feel uncomfortable at big social gatherings," he said. "I had

[38] "In the holy instant, free of the past, you see that love is in you, and you have no need to look without and snatch love guiltily from where you thought it was." (*A Course In Miracles*, Foundation for Inner Peace, 1992; Chapter 15 V, 9:7) "In the holy instant there is no conflict of needs, for there is only one." (Ibid., Chapter 15 V, 11:4) "In the holy instant it is understood that the past is gone, and with its passing the drive for vengeance has been uprooted and has disappeared. The stillness and the peace of *now* enfold you in perfect gentleness. Everything is gone except for the truth." (Ibid., Chapter 16 VII, 6:4,5,6)

always maintained that, having grown up in a very social Jewish circle in New York, I ought to be able to *schmooze* with the best of them. In that moment, I decided to give up the pretense."

He took a deep breath and admitted the truth. The acquaintance and his wife—impeccably dressed, apparently in their element—smiled, sighed and nearly sagged in their relief. "We thought we were the only ones," he said.

It was a small connection—a moment—but it was a typical Stage Six connection, made only because one person risked being vulnerable.

Keep in mind that this kind of vulnerability is only advisable when you are healed enough to offer it without expectation of an in-kind response. The man could have said, "No kidding? I love these parties! The secret is just to relax and enjoy yourself." If David still had significant shame issues or fears of abandonment or disapproval, a response like this would have triggered him and caused him great pain. While this pain is not necessarily a bad thing (since it can motivate you to heal the wounds that cause it), it is always a good idea not to rush yourself into behaving as if you were more healed than you are.

Stage Six Pitfalls: Insufficient Abyss Work

Currently, it seems there are so few people living in Stage Six that it is difficult to find traveling companions, let alone guides. As a result, it can be easy to find your self-confidence being eroded by well-meaning (or not-so-well-meaning) "helpers." One way to stay out of these Stage Six pitfalls is to make sure you do a thorough job in Stage Four.

Stage Six Pitfall #1: Your Own Insufficient Abyss Work

Stage Six is dependent on the emotional healing you do in your abyss. If you aren't finished with old relationships—romantic or otherwise—you won't be able to tell the difference between repeating an old pattern and breaking into a new way of being in a relationship. To move fully into Stage Six, you must bring every old relationship to emotional completion. (One of the principles of healing is *Whatever isn't healed in our personalities eventually shows up as a problem in our relationships.*)

If your abyss work is insufficient, you are also more likely to overestimate your therapist's level of healing, which makes you vulnerable to the second pitfall.

Stage Six Pitfall #2:
Your Therapist's Insufficient Abyss Work

Stage Six relationships are pure theory until you are there; it is difficult to explain or understand them from the point of view of someone in Stage Four or even Five. In earlier stages, even an intellectual understanding is difficult. (Which is probably one reason why completely unrealistic romantic novels and movies are so popular. Unhealed, you are likely to find these fantasies compelling. But by Stage Six, you have healed sufficiently to begin to find these fantasies unattractive and unbelievable.) At this point, you need a coach—someone who has played the game, understands the moves and recognizes mistakes. Working on these deeper relationship issues with a therapist or a workshop leader who is not yet in Stage Six can, therefore, get you off track.

Even well-meaning pre-Stage Six therapists can leave you questioning your reality. Those who have critical unhealed wounds in relationship areas can even become jealous of your Stage Six relationships. In this case, they will tend to "pathologize" what is not pathological. For example, such a therapist may respond to your statement that *"my boyfriend adores me"* by questioning your boyfriend's independence, even when all the evidence points to a healthy inter-dependence. Describing a Stage Six relationship as "very close" might produce a judgment that you are actually "enmeshed."

Stage Six Healing Resources

Miscellaneous

The Bridge Across Forever. Richard Bach.
William Morrow & Co., 1984

Conscious Loving. Gay and Kathlyn Hendricks. Bantam, 1990.

The Dance of Anger. Harriet Goldhor Lerner. Harper & Row, 1985.

The Dance of Intimacy. Harriet Goldhor Lerner.
Perennial Library, 1990.

Do I Have to Give up Me to be Loved by You?
Jordan and Margaret Paul. CompCare Publishing, 1983.
(Book and workbook)

Getting the Love You Want. Harville Hendrix, Ph.D.
Perennial Library, 1990.

One Question That Will Save Your Marriage.
Harry P. Dunne, Jr., Ph.D. Perigee, 1991.

Soul Mates. Thomas Moore. HarperCollins, 1994.

We Can Work It Out. Clifford Notarius, Ph.D., and
Howard Markman, Ph.D. Putnam, 1993.

Why Marriages Succeed or Fail. John Gottman, Ph.D.
Simon & Schuster, 1994.

Willingness Works Resources

Breaking Free of Power Struggles (tape)

Sorry It Happened, But What's the Plan? (tape)

Stop Sucking My Energy! (tape)

Using Relationships as a Spiritual Path (tape)

What a Healthy Relationship Looks Like (tape)

What Do I Do When I'm Triggered? (tape)

Why Do You Bug Me So Much?: Owning Your Projections (tape)

Stage Six Healing Exercises

The best healing exercises for Stage Six tend not to be the pencil-and-paper variety. By this time, life itself—and especially relationships—provides your primary lessons.

However, in Stage Six, you still find it immensely valuable to continue your journaling and attending support group meetings—in short, doing all the things you started doing in Stage Two (Foundation) which by now have become a way of life.

You are now pretty good at observing your own patterns and recognizing your choice points—those moments when you see clearly your options for exercising your self-responsibility and stretching your ability to connect with others. You carry much less guilt about your boundaries, so you find little to be defensive about when you sense your boundaries being challenged. Your exercises will consist of:

- Practicing being vulnerable

- Practicing setting boundaries in more compassionate ways, especially with people who don't respect yours[39]

- Making plans to deal with old patterns before you are triggered

- Using everything in your relationships that makes you unhappy as a reason to look within and heal whatever wound you find.

---

[39] This is extremely challenging work, and can't be rushed. When you are truly in Stage Six, you can respond to another's obnoxious behavior the way you would respond to an acting-out three-year-old on a day when you feel especially patient. But if you're not yet in Stage Six, your efforts in this direction will consist of trying to use willpower—much the way customer service representatives are trained not to react to obnoxious, angry customers. It's not the same thing. Chances are, the willpower solution will simply improve your ability to stuff your feelings.

TWENTY-NINE

Stage Seven: Clear-Hearted Service

…No one will ever frighten or control me, no one will
stop me from living to the full and loving to the full,
loving everyone I know and everyone I don't know,
fighting for justice without seeing anyone as an enemy.
                                    – David Dellinger

IN STAGE SEVEN, YOU DEVELOP THE ABILITY to give of the self you have uncovered, with no strings attached. You give with no emotional investment in the outcome of your giving.

At this stage, life becomes profoundly simple. The categories we have used throughout this section—goal, emotional work, and so on—tend, in Stage Seven, to merge. A single concern infuses them all: How can I lovingly extend my self to this person, this situation, this activity?

Goal: Create a Service Role

Stage Seven gives you the opportunity to perfect your ability to remain whole while helping those who are not whole. A service role provides you with the framework. Consider the following examples:

- **Trailblazer**—Generates new and wonderful ideas, techniques, possibilities; leads others into uncharted territory

- **Midwife**—A coach or facilitator who helps others "birth" themselves

- **Mentor**—Sets examples for others to emulate

- **Role Model**—Like a mentor, but in an everyday context; does not place self in the formal role of mentor

- **Implementer**—Translates goals into results; executes visions, dreams, traditions

Service roles are not exclusive to Stage Seven. We all serve in various ways throughout all the stages. The difference between service in Stages One through Six and service in Stage Seven lies in your attachment to your role. In Stage Seven you can finally embrace service without becoming entranced with the specialness of your role. Service at this point has little to do with a sense of your own status or worth. It is simply the next step— a natural expression and extension of self into the world. Your desire, emphasis and capability are focused on collaboration, not domination.

A loving bus driver is far more beneficial to humanity than an ego-driven political activist, no matter how noble the cause.

— Elliot Sobel

In Stage Seven, you come closer and closer to being a full-time giver, because giving no longer depletes you. You're giving out of such a deep sense of heart and love that the giving itself becomes truly replenishing, regardless of the outcome. In addition to other forms of recharging, the giving paradoxically becomes a source of recharging as well, even though you are no longer giving to get.

Beware of False Leaders

Some people develop a service role for themselves before they have healed their emotional wounds. These are the mentors or the spiritual, political or business leaders who take sexual, financial or personal advantage of the people they are supposed to serve. Insufficient abyss work leads people in leadership positions into abusing their power.

One day, you are likely to meet one of these false leaders. If you have done enough of your own healing work, you will recognize him. If you are still looking for someone to fulfill your happy-ending fantasy, you may not. We describe below a few warning signs that indicate you may be dealing with a false leader. In general, you can usually spot these people by their need to monopolize power rather than their deep ability and desire to collaborate.

False Leaders Use Their Power to Pursue Special Gifts

Virtually every spiritual tradition warns against being seduced by the psychic phenomena that often accompany spiritual growth. Visions, special physical abilities (such as levitating), and astral travel are tempting distractions. However, they are the byproducts of spiritual work, not the primary goal, and they tend to reinforce a belief in a false sense of specialness.

Needing to feel special in this way is a natural consequence of some deep wound that every human being carries. Treat any signs in a leader of infatuation with psychic phenomena as a red flag.

False Leaders Use Their Power to Obtain Earthly Delights

The power that comes with service also can seduce. We've all seen leaders (spiritual or worldly) fall under the spell of the abundance that becomes available to them: expensive cars; sex with adoring, obedient followers; drug use; overeating; luxurious homes, clothing and other possessions. These excesses, usually a byproduct of egos taking on service work without the maturity gained by going through the abyss, make clear-hearted service impossible.

False Leaders Sacrifice Personal Relationships to Their Positions of Power

If a person's work in Stages Four through Six is thorough, his or her relationships won't suffer at the hands of service work. Of course, relationships do fade sometimes, and people are hurt. But when this happens to a Stage Seven person, he or she takes responsibility up front, is honest, explicit and non-defensive about the repercussions of his or her choices and is thorough in his or her amends. Someone who chronically disconnects from all his or her most primary relationships—or who avoids having a primary relationship with an equal—is not in Stage Seven. More likely, he or she is simply intoxicated by a mission.

Palestinian spokeswoman Hanan Ashrawi exemplifies the Stage Seven commitment to relationships. In an interview with Daniel Zwerdling on National Public Radio, Dr. Ashrawi talked about the challenge of balancing the needs of her family with her Middle East peace work. She told Zwerdling that, when she was offered a position at the 1991 Madrid peace talks, she asked her two daughters and her husband to help her decide whether to accept it. The family agreed to "lend" their mother and wife to the peace process, she said. Zwerdling sounded surprised. What if the family had said, "No, we don't want you to go?" he asked.

Dr. Ashrawi said she would have listened to their objections, discussed the issue with them and taken their needs and preferences into consideration as she made her decision. After all, she said, how you relate to the world is ultimately a reflection of the way you deal with your loved ones—only if your interactions with them are motivated by love can you hope to bring peace to the world.

Emotional Work: Vulnerability and Love

Blessed are the vulnerable, for they shall be broken, and being so, shall break open the heart of the Universe.

— Quaker Proverb

In Stage Seven, you continue to grow and develop your capacity to be vulnerable. You have learned to see vulnerability as the carrier of love. In this stage, you lose any last vestiges of fear (and heal the corresponding wounds) that might have kept you from being vulnerable.

Self-Responsibility Key: Preparing for Union

Underlying all your self-responsibility work in Stage Seven is the need to own the final fragments of yourself that still want to be separate, or that want to blame something or someone for anything. Full self-responsibility in Stage Seven means a full acceptance that the world you perceive is the one you have created.

Mission in Life: In Stage Seven, your mission is to reach your Higher Power through clear-hearted service to others.

Quality of Relationship with Your Spiritual Resources: Your concept of your Spiritual Resources becomes more abstract as it becomes bigger; you see your Higher Power as formless, unchangeable love. A natural outgrowth of your relationship with your Spiritual Resources is service, a weakening attachment to the world, and a growing, profoundly powerful sense that we're all siblings.

Activities: Service

Stage Seven activities are characterized by their potential to bring you closer to your Higher Power. Any service role can be a Stage Seven activity. The key is the intent: *"Am I performing this activity as a natural expression of my love for and my relationship with my Higher Power?"* If the answer is yes, and if your attachment to results is minimal or nonexistent, you have found a Stage Seven activity. However, many Stage Seven-type activities can be (and usually are) performed with something other than a Stage Seven attitude.

Examples of potential Stage Seven activities include:

- Parenting

- Creating a business that is emotionally and physically healthy for employees, vendors and customers

- Engaging in community, political or ecological activism and volunteerism

- Helping others in their healing and life journeys, either formally or informally

- Offering a product or service that brings more love, peace, playfulness, ease or comfort into other people's lives.

Stage Seven Pitfalls

The only pitfall we are aware of for people who are truly in Stage Seven is the refusal to cross the final abyss between themselves and God. People who succumb to this pitfall can get caught in doing service work as a way of avoiding a confrontation with their fear of God and the possibility of union with Him.

Stage Seven Healing Resources

The Celestine Prophecy. James Redfield. Warner Books, 1993.

The Celestine Prophecy: An Experiential Guide. James Redfield and Carol Adrienne. Warner Books, 1995.

A Course in Miracles. The Foundation for Inner Peace, 1992.

From the Heart of a Gentle Brother. Bartholomew. High Mesa Press, 1987.

From Yale to Jail: The Life Story of a Moral Dissenter. David Dellinger. Pantheon Books, 1993.

Living with Joy. Sanaya Roman. H.J. Kramer Inc., 1986.

Seat of the Soul. Gary Zukov. Simon & Schuster, 1989.

Spiritual Growth. Sanaya Roman. H.J. Kramer Inc., 1989.

Testimony of Light. Helen Greaves. Neville Spearman Publishers, 1991.

Women Who Run With the Wolves. Clarissa Pinkola Estes, Ph.D. Ballantine, 1992.

If I get the idea that God is going to save me, therefore I'm all right, that's salvation. If I get the idea that nothing's going to save me, therefore I'm all right, that's enlightenment.

– Werner Erhard

Stage Seven Healing Exercises

We're not sure what kinds of healing exercises would help people in Stage Seven. In fact, we are fairly certain we've never met anyone whose dominant stage was Seven. When you get there, please contact us. We have some questions for you.

Epilogue: Stages Eight Through Infinity

> *What the caterpillar calls the end of the world,*
> *the rest of the world calls butterfly.*
>
> — *Richard Bach*

THIS BOOK ENDS, BUT THE JOURNEY DOES NOT.

What we call The Seven Stages of Personal Healing is like the visible spectrum of light. Our limited vision permits a view of only a tiny portion, but sensitive instruments assure us there is more—much more.

We don't know of any instruments that can explore the spectra of healing beyond Stage Seven the way spectrographs can explore light. However, the flow of healing through the Seven Stages suggests what lies beyond. We feel certain of at least three truths about Stage Eight:

- It requires you to put away the map. The healing plan that brings you to Stage Seven was designed to speed up the process that you would have undertaken anyway. Here in the late twentieth century, time seems to be important. But the rest of the journey takes place outside of time. A map is not only irrelevant, but counter-productive. You may not end up where you think, today, you will go, but there is no

[40] Our thanks to the writers of *thirtysomething* for this marvelous metaphor.

doubt that you'll get somewhere at least as interesting. Look at Lewis and Clark.[40]

• It contains a final abyss: the loss of the last of all the hope you still hold that something *in this world* could make you happy, whole and peaceful. In giving up this last hope, you agree, finally, that you invented the world you see. With this act, you close the book on your illusions and release the final few strands that tie you to false hope.

• It brings the realization that nothing in this world will gain us the grandest brass ring of all—unalterable closeness with God (whatever That is)—because there is no escape from God and never could be.

If the purpose of the journey on this planet is to heal wounds, then what happens when you surrender the last of your wounds, the last of your happy-ending fantasy? Do you transcend? Ascend? Stay here, but walk through walls? Stay here as simply a happier and more useful version of yourself?

We're not sure.

What we do know is that you can count on the movement into any new stage to mark the beginning of a marvelous adventure—a fresh new journey to unexplored vistas.

Godspeed.

Appendix

Long-Term Healing Plan
for _____

My dominant stage: _____: _____   My secondary stage

Goal: _____   Goal: _____

Emotional Work: _____   Emotional Work: __

I need...	To meet my nee
Information about:	
To develop tools to:	
To network with people who:	
Professional help to:	

Date: _____

___: _____
_____
_____

ill:

Long-Term Healing Plan Form

This form is used in Chapter Twenty-Two and succeeding chapters. Photocopy this form full-size onto standard size 8½ × 11" paper. Align the upper left corner of the opposite page with the origin corner of the photocopier.

Weekly Healing Plan
for _____

Activity	How often?	When?	Potential roadblocks

For the week of _____

through _____

How will I handle roadblocks? | ✓

Weekly Healing Plan Form

This form is used in Chapter Twenty-Two and succeeding chapters. Photocopy this form full-size onto standard size 8½ × 11" paper. Align the upper left corner of the opposite page with the origin corner of the photocopier.

A Stage-by-Stage Guide to Healing Activities

Healing Activity	Stage						
	1	2	3	4	5	6	7
Journaling	☆	☆	☆	☆	☆	☆	☆
Support groups	☆	☆	☆	☆	☆	☆	☆
Reading	☆	☆	☆	☆	☆	☆	☆
Listening to speakers	☆	☆	☆	☆	☆	☆	☆
Praying or meditating	☆	☆	☆	☆	☆	☆	☆
Training in time management, problem-solving skills and clear thinking	→	☆	→	→	☆	☆	→
Workshops and classes in inner child, Focusing and company-keeping skills	→	→	☆	☆	→	→	→
Emotional release work (anger, grief)	■	■	☆	☆	→	→	→
Workshops in forgiveness	■	■	■	☆	☆	☆	☆
Spiritual retreats	→	→	→	→	→	☆	☆
Play and creativity workshops; art therapy	→	→	☆	☆	☆	☆	☆
Workshops or therapy in sex and sexuality	■	→	→	→	☆	☆	→
Lifespring or Forum-type motivation experiences	→[41]	→[41]	■	■	☆	→	→[41]
Individual counseling	→	→	☆	☆	→	→	→
Deep individual therapy	■	■	→	☆	→	→	→
Intensive group therapy	■	■	→	☆	☆	☆	→
Intensive couples therapy	→	→	→	→	→	☆	→
Intensive family therapy	→	→	→	→	→	☆	→
In- or out-patient treatment programs focused on detoxification, stabilization and early recovery	→	→	■	■	■	■	■
Residential and day treatment programs focused on healing core wounds	■	■	■	→	■	■	■
Biochemical support	→	☆	→	→	→	→	→
Bodywork	→	→	→	☆	→	→	→
Workshops and classes in interpersonal relationships	■	■	→	→	☆	☆	→
Career assessment	■	→	■	■	☆	→	→

KEY: ☆ Activity is ideal for this stage

            → Activity can help unblock you when you feel stuck in this stage

            ■ Activity is counter-indicated for this stage.

---

[41] In Stages One, Two and Seven, the value of such willpower-oriented programs as these lies in their capacity to convince you that they don't work when the problem is your unhealed wounds. In this way, they act as an irritant, which can motivate you to move into true willingness.

The Seven Stages of Healing: Some Analogies

The Seven Stages as Expressions of Evolving Willingness

Stage One: Willingness to make a commitment to healing your wounds

Stage Two: Willingness to create a new life structure to support the healing work

Stage Three: Willingness to separate from and observe your preconceptions (a.k.a. your inner critic) and to learn to have your feelings

Stage Four: Willingness to confront and heal what you're most afraid of

Stage Five: Willingness to re-discover and express yourself

Stage Six: Willingness to change the way you relate to others

Stage Seven: Willingness to change the way you contribute

The Seven Stages as Expressions of Evolving Acceptance

Stage One: Acceptance of anesthesia failure and the need to recover yourself

Stage Two: Acceptance of the rhythms of the healing life

Stage Three: Acceptance of your feelings and the responsibility for having suppressed or indulged them

Stage Four: Acceptance of the futility of your fantasies, your rightness and your pursuit of a false self and a false world

Stage Five: Acceptance of yourself

Stage Six: Acceptance of others

Stage Seven: Acceptance of having something to offer without needing it to be received; acceptance of having an impact without necessarily needing to see it; acceptance of your special role

Parallels in the Twelve-Step Recovery Community

Stage One = Abstinence

Stage Two = Sober Living

Stages Three and Four = What Earnest Larsen called *Stage II Recovery*[42]

Stages Five through Seven = Not yet mapped out in the recovery community, except as "life after recovery"

---

[42] HarperSanFrancisco, 1985.

Love, Wounds, and Self-Responsibility

	Pre-Healing *("Wounds? What wounds?")*	**Early Healing** *("I have wounds, but they're YOUR problem.")*
How I Define Love	If you love me, you behave as an extension of me and nothing else. If I love you, I control your behavior and punish you when I can't, or I turn myself into a pretzel to please you (to little avail).	If you love me, you protect me from my wounds; if you fail to do so, I'm allowed to get you back. If I love you, I protect you from your wounds; if I fail to do so, I alternate between shame and resentment.
How I React When One of My Wounds is Triggered	*"This is your problem, not mine."*	*"This is your problem, not mine. Furthermore, I can't tolerate your wounds, either, since they make me fear I will have to face my pain, so I lash out at you when you are triggered."*
What is Required for Me to Become More Self-Responsible	Major miracles	Willingness to admit my wounds are my problem. Willingness to stop blaming others

Middle Healing	Advanced Healing	
("I have wounds and they are MY problem. Except for some of them.")	*"I have wounds and I always recognize that they are my problem. Eventually."*	*"I have wounds and they are my privilege to heal."*
If you love me, you never do anything to trigger the wounds I'm not yet willing to own; if you do trigger them, you take the blame for my pain. If I love you, I try to never make you mad or trigger your wounds.	We know that triggering is inevitable and not to be feared. If we love each other, we welcome conflict. Conflict deepens our love rather than damages it, because we use it to look within and heal together.	*[Authors' note: none of us has had much experience with what love looks like at this level of self-responsibility and so do not feel qualified to comment!]*
"This is my problem, but you created it. I can't be safe around you, so I'll take care of myself by distancing."	*"This is my problem, and I need to look within for the cause."*	*"Oh—another wound. I'd like your company and input while I heal it. If you are not available, I will give it to myself."*
Willingness to heal the wounds I am avoiding Willingness to confront my need to be right	Desire for an extremely high level of healing Desire for extremely deep relationship Willingness to confront and move through even the scariest of wounds	To have healed all fear

The Twelve Steps and the Seven Stages

The Twelve Steps of Alcoholics Anonymous[43]	The Seven Stages of Personal Healing	
	Stage	*Translation*
1. We admitted that we were powerless over alcohol—that our lives had become unmanageable.	**Stage One** Willingness	Help! I've fallen and I can't get up . . .
2. Came to believe that a Power greater than ourselves could restore us to sanity.	**Stage Two** Foundation	…without some Help entirely outside my own programming…
3. Made a decision to turn our will and our lives over to the care of God as we understood Him.	**Stages Two and Three** Foundation and Feelings	…which, now that I'm in this much pain, I will finally listen to, since I'm finally willing to admit that it was my programming itself that made me fall down.
4. Made a searching and fearless moral inventory of ourselves.	**Stage Four** Healing	I uncover and acknowledge the blocks and wounds that stand between me and that source outside my programming…
5. Admitted to God, to ourselves, and to another human being the exact nature of our wrongs.		…and make them real, so I can't weasel out of it, by telling at least one other person about them in their entirety.
6. Were entirely ready to have God remove all these defects of character.		This confession solidifies my motivation to heal my wounds with Help…
7. Humbly asked Him to remove our shortcomings		…using my chosen source of Help to do so.
8. Made a list of all persons we had harmed, and became willing to make amends to them all.	**Stage Five** Rebirth	I recognize and become willing to repair the the relationship mistakes and incompleted tasks that I have created. I particularly identify those I harmed in my bullheadedness or denial, and what I did to them…
9. Made direct amends to such people wherever possible, except when to do so would injure them or others.		…whereupon I correct these mistakes and complete these incompletes in a self-responsible, compasionate and respectful way.

The Twelve Steps of Alcoholics Anonymous[43]	The Seven Stages of Personal Healing	
	Stage	*Translation*
10. Continued to take personal inventory and when we were wrong, promptly admitted it.	**Stages Five and Six** Rebirth and Clear-Hearted Relationships	I monitor myself for old patterns and promptly intervene when they appear, continually fine-tuning my plan for handling them more successfully in the future.
11. Sought through prayer and meditation to improve our conscious contact with God *as we understood Him,* praying only for knowledge of His will for us and the power to carry that out.	**Stage Six** Clear-Hearted Relationships	Having seen that this source outside my programming did indeed help, I become even more willing to seek it out in more and more situations, deepening my sense of my spirituality each time I do so.
12. Having had a spiritual awakening as a result of these steps, we tried to carry this message to alcoholics, and to practice these principles in all our affairs.	**Stage Seven** Clear-Hearted Service	I want to help others deal with the same wounds I am healing in me.

[43] The Twelve Steps are reprinted with permission of Alcoholics Anonymous World Services, Inc. Permission to reprint this material does not mean that A.A. has reviewed or approved the contents of this publication, nor that A.A. agrees with the views expressed herein. A.A. is a program of recovery from alcoholism *only*—use of the Twelve Steps in connection with programs and activities which are patterned after A.A., but which address other problems, does not imply otherwise.

How Self-Responsibility Grows Through the Seven Stages

Growth Indicator	PRE-HEALING	STAGE ONE: Willingness	STAGE TWO: Foundation	STAGE THREE: Feelings
Ability to Feel, Grieve and Heal	Virtually non-existent	Still virtually no ability, but increasing awareness of how much there is to heal	I attain an intellectual understanding of the need to learn to feel, grieve and heal	My abilities are developing; can now recognize and stay with feelings at least some of the time
Response to Pain	Avoid it or ignore it through anesthesia, blame, etc.; "What pain?"	Pain peaks, then drops; profound relief; heed it as a wake-up call, but essential hope is still to eliminate it	Pain is relieved temporarily at this stage; "pink cloud" effect; "Never again"	Begin to become willing to sweat out the pain until it passes
Boundary-Setting Skills	If present, are messy, after-the-fact, marked by guilt, fighting, shame; exist as rules and shoulds	Unchanged from Pre-Healing	Unchanged from Stage One; I'm now able to used canned boundaries	I recognize my boundaries more quickly; use resentment as indicator of missed or ignored boundary
Foundation of Self-Esteem	Based on meeting survival plan prerequisites	Gone (self-esteem shattered by admission of woundedness); replaced by feelings of failure, followed by rebirth of hope	Derived from creating new life structure and ability to create and maintain it	Found in increasing ability to feel and sweat out feelings; for the first time, self-esteem comes from resolving feelings instead of stuffing them.
Attitude toward Unfinished Business	I tolerate abundant unfinished business	My unfinished business is still abundant, but I find I can no longer tolerate it	I become willing to address debilitating unfinished business; put the rest on hold	I become willing to deal with small, daily emotional incompletes; I probably don't know it, but I'm in training for Stage Four
Mission in Life	To avoid pain and maintain addictions; to fulfill happy-ending fantasy	To break addictions, or to change my life	To become stabilized	To learn to accept all my feelings
Quality of Relationships	Dysfunctional, often volatile, lots of residue; characterized by repeating patterns	Sometimes enlivened by hope of anesthesia-free life, but still dysfunctional; hope is short-lived, followed by feeling overwhelmed by what it will take to make the hope a reality	Still frustrating; not much energy left over after stabilizing to work on relationships; time-out contracts help, as does abstinence, but it's disappointing to discover that's not enough	Still difficult; some success in working through conflicts; still many breakups; abstaining from criticism now and appreciating feelings; learning how scary it is to risk the vulnerability called for; just beginning to learn to trust again
Level of Investment in Victimhood	I'm into full-blown victimhood and victimizing others; the feeling that I'm being victimized occurs all the time	I become willing to consider the possibility that victimhood and perpetration are not the only ways to exist	I'm no longer a victim of my anesthesias; still feel like a victim of feelings, people, events; still victimizing others	Can now keep company with feelings of victimhood, but still lay responsibility for same at feet of other people, events; begin to see, feel shame about how I make victims of others
Quality of Relationship with Spiritual Resources	Higher Power consists of anesthesias, false hope and inner critic (the survival plan); relationship is marked by fear	Higher Power is the belief that there must be a better way; relationship marked at times by desperation, at other times by hope	Higher Power is sobriety and stabilization; abstinence from anesthesia and new stability allow for spiritual resources to emerge, sometimes for the first time.	Relationship with Higher Power, once heavily influenced by inner critic, now influenced more by feelings, or inner child; relationship marked by tentative trust

Note: Gray boxes indicate the self-responsibility issues that are critical to each stage.

STAGE FOUR: Healing	STAGE FIVE: Rebirth	STAGE SIX: Clear-Hearted Relationships	STAGE SEVEN: Clear-Hearted Service
Almost fully realized; can stay with feelings almost all the time; learn to stay with my deepest feelings	In full bloom; this process is now second nature; practice it daily with my own feelings and wounds	Use my ability to feel, grieve and heal to grow my relationships with others; can be there to help others feel, grieve and heal their wounds even when my own needs are not being met	Begin creating environments for others to feel, grieve and heal, even though there are no immediate gains for me in doing so; invest in others' futures
Pain peaks again; now see pain as a phenomenon of the healing process; pain is no longer avoided but embraced; use skills to negotiate the abyss	Pain is viewed as information about myself that points the way to more healing	Same as Stage Five, except for a deepened ability to hang in there in relationships when wounds are triggered	Responded to compassionately, without guilt or attachment
Good tries, poor form; tentative, sloppy, angry	Boundaries now set with increasing precision; at first, lack compassion, exhibit narcissism; move from abrasive unilateral to compassionate unilateral	Begin to be bilateral; set with compassion; marked by mutuality whenever possible	Begin to honor others' boundaries even when they don't honor their own or mine (but without codependence or tolerance for abuse)
Derived from increasing ability to heal and to confront and survive dark sides of self	Derived from expression of authenticity	Derived from feeling competent to resolve conflict with others	Expressed through how much I feel I am extending myself in love rather than reacting from fear
Become willing to deal with biggest pieces of unfinished business as core wounds are healed; then become willing to deal with backlog of emotional incompletes	Become willing to deal with backlog of logistical incompletes	Become willing to begin taking care of incompletes in relationships as they occur	Unfinished business no longer an issue; "chop wood, carry water"
To face and survive the pain of my abyss; to "gut it out"	To be my Self	To be my Self in partnership with someone else	To express my relationship with my spiritual resources
Relationships tend to suffer because the foundation (wounds) is now threatened and because I am preoccupied with the intense pain of abyss work	Boundaries are at issue; awkward birthing of a new contract for relationship; sense of excitement and empowerment; the battle for autonomy; begin to break out of old patterns; sex role differences emphasized	Full bloom of trust that we can and will work out our differences; no longer depend on them to blow over; sex role differences resolved	Find ways to express love and success with each other to the world as a team; if without partner, use relationships with friends and coworkers as vehicle for collaboration in service
I go deeper into wounds; begin a transition out of blame of self and others and into forgiveness; begin to acknowledge damage I've done to others out of my woundedness	I become bored with victimhood; make amends for damage done; manifest true forgiveness; begin to live without residue from the past	Any remaining investment in victimhood brought out in brief spurts by relationship, and is quickly replaced by self-responsibility	I become socially active out of sense of personal purpose, not because I believe anyone is truly a victim; "fight for justice without making anyone the enemy"
Hatred of God often openly admitted and dealt with for the first time; may rely on God more heavily than ever to get through the abyss	Higher Power is seen as a truly beneficent, loving presence that helps me see the gifts in all situations; relationship marked by deepening trust	Same as in Stage Five, plus shared joy with significant other	Same as in Stage Six, plus sense of service rising out of relationship with Higher Power

Glossary

ability to feel, grieve and heal
How well you recognize feelings, stay with them and work them through; the natural, innate mechanism through which people work through difficult feelings that accompany loss—pain, fear, guilt, sadness and grief. Our childhood ability to feel, grieve and heal was disrupted each time we had feelings we did not work through. If you grew up under dysfunctional or disconnected circumstances, your ability to feel, grieve and heal is stunted or missing. This makes it virtually impossible to deal with difficult emotions in any other way than suppressing them by disconnecting. One of the nine indicators of self-responsibility.

abstinence
Refraining from anesthesia use, whether the anesthesia is a behavior or a substance, previous to doing the deeper emotional work. Some people establish abstinence and never go on to deeper work.

abyss
A metaphor for feeling your deepest pain—the pain of confronting your happy-ending fantasy and the wounds that made you develop it. People who enter their abyss for the first time

report that it feels like walking into an end-lessly deep, dark cave, or stepping off a high cliff into cold, empty space. We return to the abyss whenever necessary to begin the healing of any newly discovered core wound. It gets easier. Visits are shorter and the abyss seems smaller and more familiar each time.

addiction
Anesthesia use that becomes the number-one priority in a person's life. Psychological addiction occurs when your decision-making and fantasies begin to revolve around your anesthesia. Physical addiction occurs when you need higher quantities (either larger or more frequent doses) of your anesthesia to get the same effects that lower quantities used to produce.

anesthesia
A way to hide one's feelings from oneself. Anesthesias can include: compulsive televi-sion-watching, reading, drinking, shopping, working or talking; driving too fast or eating too much or too little; obsessing about a relationship or sex; using drugs; rage—in fact, anything that allows you to ignore deeper, more painful feelings. Everyone uses anesthesias from time to time.

authenticity
The capacity, in a child or adult, to have one's own feelings, thoughts and bound-aries; the absence of a need to hide feelings, thoughts and boundaries. In an adult, the ability to choose when, with whom and

how to convey one's feelings, thoughts and boundaries in a self-responsible, non-defen-sive and respectful manner. The capacity to feel safe being vulnerable rather than through self-protections.

attitude toward unfinished business
How well you recognize and how effi-ciently you deal with emotional or logistical loose ends. Your attitude toward unfinished business reflects your level of healing; the more wounds you heal, the less unfinished business you tolerate. One of the nine indicators of self-responsibility.

Band-Aid
Anything used to hide symptoms; see anes-thesia. Like their namesake, Band-Aids don't address causes. They're great for little wounds, but a mistake when used for seri-ous wounds. Anesthesias and defense mechanisms function as Band-Aids. So do many laudable activities—like working out. Examples of Band-Aids are:

- Aspirin, when used to treat headaches instead of learning to manage stress
- Workouts at the gym to mediate against feelings instead of setting a boundary
- White-knuckled abstinence from alco-hol while consumption rate of cigarettes and caffeine goes through the roof.

boundary
A personal limit that allows me to love you (or simply work with you)—and to openly give to you and receive from you—without resenting you or compromising my

integrity or healing journey. A determination that I make about how much I can take in and how much I can give out without losing my emotional balance, my sense of self or my peace of mind.

boundary-setting skills
The ability to recognize and state your own internal limits on how much you can give or receive from others. Good boundary-setting skills come late in the healing journey, usually in Stage Five. However, it is necessary to find a way to set boundaries earlier than that to create the psychic space you need to confront and heal your wounds. One of the nine landmarks of self-responsibility.

caretaking, dysfunctional
Consciously or unconsciously, overtly or covertly, rescuing or protecting another person from feeling the effects of his or her choices. Distinguished from functional caretaking by a lack of respect for the other person's abilities.

caretaking, functional
Compensating for what another person legitimately cannot do (because of physical infirmity, illness or youth) by doing it for them or mitigating the consequences of their inability; facilitating another person's personal growth process by keeping company, offering comfort or offering asked-for advice. Distinguished from dysfunctional caretaking by a profound respect for the other person's true abilities.

codependence
A popular (and culturally condoned) anesthesia marked by an excessive focus on someone else's welfare or performance so as to avoid dealing with one's own feelings and issues.

connection
The experience of being joined.
With another person: the experience of feeling joined without losing touch with yourself.
With your insides: the experience of knowing, keeping company with and accepting your own feelings and boundaries.
With your Higher Power: the experience of being joined with a source of input or wisdom entirely outside of your programming that can be trusted to guide your choices and well-being.
Words people use to describe the way connection feels are: peaceful; serene; heartful; deeply loving; very, very full.

core belief
Any deeply held assumption that you are convinced is true. Usually, core beliefs are unconscious and limiting in nature. We tend to think of them as The Truth, even when they are born of woundedness rather than love.

core wound
The deepest, most profound and, usually, earliest wounds; the wounds that gave rise to our survival plan. Unhealed core wounds tend to run our lives. Fear of them leads to

anesthesia use. Healing them requires entering the abyss and relinquishing happy-ending fantasies. People who have healed core wounds report that their wounds no longer control them and have, in fact, created in them a unique ability to be of service in the world.

disconnection, broken connection
Emotionally withdrawing tender-hearted company-keeping from another person because your wounds have been triggered and are drowning out your love. There is only one reason for disconnecting: To protect against feeling the pain of old, unhealed wounds. Having to keep a lid on unhealed wounds is the only thing that causes us to break emotional connection from others or ourselves. Disconnection occurs in four forms:

• Abandoning—ignoring the other person or his feelings

• Attacking—criticizing or shaming a person, or physically striking him. The message is, *"Your feelings, reactions or preferences are wrong or don't count."*

• Spoiling—pronouncing feelings to be somehow "accurate" or "right" (rather than just "there"), and the people or circumstances somehow "wrong" for having triggered the feelings. In high doses, spoiling creates narcissists.

• Stealing the attention—moving the focus of a conversation away from the person who is having the feelings to the person who is supposed to be keeping company.

E.M.D.R.
Eye Movement Desensitization and Reprogramming. A therapy technique developed by Francine Shapiro, Ph.D., that uses rapid eye movements to trigger emotional memories, especially of early traumatic incidents. EMDR has been used successfully to treat post-traumatic stress disorder in Vietnam veterans, sexual abuse survivors and other trauma survivors. We have found it is an excellent tool for treating trauma with a minimum of added pain. It is especially helpful for people dealing with Stage Four (Healing) issues.

F.E.P.
Focused Expressive Psychotherapy. F.E.P. was developed by Roger Daldrup, Ph.D. Participants in F.E.P. are coached through the physical and emotional release and completion of deeply held anger. F.E.P. is especially helpful in dismantling the happy-ending fantasy and healing core wounds.

fantasy bond
A concept developed by Robert Firestone, Ph.D., to explain how infants comfort themselves when nurturing comfort is not available to them. Firestone's ideas inspired our own theories about the happy-ending fantasy. He defines fantasy bond as "An illusion of connection with the mother that is used by the infant to relieve anxiety and emotional pain…a substitute for the love and care that may be missing in the infant's environment…Later, it is extended to other individuals, mates, authority figures and other parental substitutes."

Focusing

A structured technique developed by Eugene Gendlin, Ph.D., for learning how to re-establish your capacity to feel, grieve and heal your wounds. Focusing enables people to identify their feelings, keep them company, learn from them and heal them. It is also useful for inner child work. For more information, read Gendlin's book, *Focusing*.

forgiveness

Demonstrating, through your feelings and behaviors, that you are no longer impaired in the present by the unacceptable things that you did or others did to you in the past.

foundation of self-esteem

The source of your appraisal of your self-worth. One of the nine indicators of self-responsibility.

frozen feeling

A feeling from the past, stored in an unprocessed, incomplete state, which impairs current functioning in situations in which similar feelings are triggered.

grief, grieve

Intense emotional suffering caused by loss; acute sorrow, deep sadness; mourning. Being willing to experience the grief you have inside as a result of the losses of your childhood is essential to healing. See "ability to feel, grieve and heal."

happy-ending fantasy

An imaginary relationship you create with a goal or a person to give you hope that you'll be okay someday; the delusion that a parent or other significant person or accomplishment will make you feel loved or whole. This false hope, when it permeates your adult relationships, makes you feel numb, shamed, un-cared-about, unlovable, abandoned or betrayed. Happy-ending fantasies develop out of children's need to hold on—at any cost—to the hope that it is possible to be loved the way they need to be loved, if they can only figure out how to earn it.

healing

The process of becoming emotionally and spiritually whole by gradually taking full responsibility for your own needs, feelings, thoughts and reactions. Healing is a life-long process that ultimately becomes a way of life. As *A Course In Miracles* puts it, healing removes blocks to "the awareness of love's presence." It requires you to give up anesthesias and heal core wounds. The further along you are in your healing, the less often you need to disconnect and the more skillful you are in reconnecting rapidly when you do disconnect. Healing represents the end of being a victim (or creating victims).

Higher Power

A core frame of reference through which you interpret events and make choices; an advisor; the force and logic behind your spiritual resources; a source of input entirely outside your programming that can be trusted to help you heal; an inner advisor or touchstone used to evaluate situations and make choices; the core set of values, beliefs and goals from which you derive all meaning and make all choices. None of us makes choices without consulting, on some level, a Higher Power. Everyone has a Higher Power; we can only choose which advisor to use and whether to consult it consistently and consciously, or erratically and unconsciously. *Quality of Relationship with Your Spiritual Resources*, of which your Higher Power is the core, is one of the nine indicators of self-responsibility.

hope, false

The belief that *If I can hide me and/or change you, I'll get love (or at least safety)*. In childhood, false hope is a life-saving maneuver; in adulthood, it sabotages your dreams and wishes by preventing you from seeing yourself, others and circumstances as they really are. False hope forms the foundation for the survival plan.

hope, genuine

The conviction that you can, with the help of your spiritual resources, heal your original wounds and recover from the survival plan you invented and embraced (and that saved your life) as a child; an understanding that you can learn to love and nourish yourself, and thereby learn to love others without giving up yourself; the awareness that you need never again be a victim.

hopelessness, false

A defeated, negative belief that there is no way to ever feel better despite evidence and input to the contrary. Similar to learned helplessness.

hopelessness, genuine

The recognition that nothing you can do will ever elicit love from others in the way or to the extent that you needed (and didn't receive) when you were a child; the awareness that nothing you could have done as a child would have succeeded in getting you more love than you did. Fighting genuine hopelessness makes you try harder to get others to love you. Surrendering to it allows you to grieve deeply and move into self-love, which draws to you people who love you.

inner child

A metaphor used to describe two parts of you: The *wounded inner child*, who carries your unhealed wounds and your need for anesthesias and self-protections, and the *precious child*, who contains your genuineness; part of the true self who lies behind your wounds and self-protections.

inner critic

A metaphor used to describe the part of us that holds the rules of our survival plan; the part that watches and judges. In wounded people, the inner critic can be vicious and unrelenting, with something nasty to say about almost everyone. The critic's voice can turn against the self, against others or both. When people begin to heal core wounds, their inner critic can become an ally. For them, the critic's observations are important pieces of information about people, events, objects and situations that help them make decisions.

investment in victimhood
Your willingness to view the cause of your pain as existing outside your own behavior, feelings, perceptions and projections. Your level of investment in being a victim declines as you heal core wounds. One of the nine indicators of self-responsibility.

keeping company
The art of being a tender-hearted witness who listens attentively and compassionately to your own or someone else's feelings without saying how to feel or what to do.

mission in life
Your prime motive; the driving force in your life; your special task or calling. As you heal core wounds, your mission in life tends to move from self-protection outward to emotional vulnerability. One of the nine indicators of self-responsibility.

personal competence
How well you manage your time and energy so you can express your authentic self; how effective you are in creating your home, career, financial picture, method of self-expression, etc., in a way that reflects who you truly are. Personal competence tends to increase over the healing journey. As you heal, your sense of what makes you competent also changes, from external fac-

tors (for example, how well you perform in a given capacity) to more internal factors (for example, who you are as a soul).

prerequisites to happiness
The requirements your happy-ending fantasy says you must fulfill in order to feel happy, worthy or safe. These requirements are based on false hope and therefore never lead to the outcome you desire, no matter how well you meet them.

programming
The set of rules and beliefs you carry around that block you from feeling connected, loving and peaceful. Healing requires you to be open to ideas that come from outside your own programming. We think of programming as unhealed wounds and self-protections.

projection
An ego defense or self-protection in which you see in others what you don't like or can't accept in yourself, thus protecting yourself from the pain of acknowledging these disowned parts.

purgatory
A state of dead disconnectedness. People in purgatory don't know that's where they are. In fact, they usually think they have the corner on reality and the rest of the world is living in a naive fantasy. People who choose purgatory are convinced that there is no other place to be, even though it may be cold, lonely, frightening or just boring.

quality of relationships

How you deal with other people, especially in the face of conflict. One of the nine indicators of self-responsibility. The quality of your relationships is deeply affected by five other indicators of self-responsibility: *Response to Pain, Boundary-Setting Skills, Ability to Feel, Grieve and Heal, Mission in Life* and *Investment in Victimhood*.

quality of relationship with your spiritual resources

Your perception of and the flavor of your dealings with your Higher Power. On the healing journey, people tend to move from fearing what they perceive as a vengeful Higher Power to trusting what they perceive as a loving Higher Power. One of the nine indicators of self-responsibility. See *Higher Power*.

residue

Unfinished emotional business between two people that leads to resentment and conflict; usually caused by lack of resolution of past conflict.

response to pain

How you perceive and react to emotional or physical pain; your view of the purpose of pain determines your response to it. Pre-healing, people tend to try to avoid pain at all costs. Embarking on the healing journey means looking at pain in a more and more positive light—finally even embracing it. One of the nine indicators of self-responsibility.

rightness

A frozen belief that a particular perception or interpretation is the truth or reality; being closed to evidence that does not support such a belief; the thinking equivalent (or, sometimes, the result) of a frozen feeling.

rightness addiction

An unswerving conviction, sometimes approaching delusional intensity, that your fundamental beliefs about yourself, others and the world are correct and unchangeable; the ego's desperate attempt to prove your limitations to you; an insistence on maintaining your perceptions, interpretations and beliefs by downplaying evidence that does not support them, while denying that it is your perceptions that cause your pain, unhappiness, ineffectiveness or disconnection from others. Being right is what the ego does best.

Rubber Band Effect

The consequences of trying to avoid a wound by skipping over painful stages or digging in your heels so you can stay in a current, relatively comfortable stage. The purpose of the Rubber Band Effect is to bring you back into alignment with the healing journey principles and keep you from avoiding your unhealed wounds for long. If you try to move ahead too quickly, it pulls you back to the wounds you tried to ignore. If you stay in one stage after your work there is completed, it pulls you forward to confront the wounds of the next stage. The symptoms of the Rubber Band

Effect include feeling stuck, confused and dissatisfied.

self protection

A survival mechanism to keep you from feeling your own emotional pain. Shame, fear and control are at the heart of all self-protections. In adulthood, these behaviors at best delay—and at worst, deepen—the need for healing. Also known as *defenses* and *defense mechanisms*.

self-responsibility

Understanding of, and acceptance of, the fact that your interpretations, not outer circumstances, determine your ability to respond to people and situations, your feelings, your awareness of choices available to you, and, ultimately, your behavior. The opposite of a self-responsible attitude is victimhood.

shame

A feeling of deep unworthiness and unlovability. Develops from a child's need to feel responsible for being "the problem," so he can believe he has the power to solve it. The child's alternative to this delusion is stark hopelessness; shame is preferable.

sobriety

Abstinence plus support (generally, of a recovery program). Usually, *sobriety* refers to refraining from using substances such as alcohol, drugs, or food to numb the emotions. We often use it to refer to any healing journey founded upon a commitment to experience emotions without the numbing effect of any substance or process, such as promiscuous sex, gambling, rightness addiction and so on.

survival plan

A defensive structure or pattern of thoughts, beliefs, behaviors and habits you create to shield yourself from the pain of emotional disconnection. You create your survival plan when you have insufficient support to feel the pain of disconnection and heal your wounds. See *happy-ending fantasy, rules* and *anesthesias*.

time out

A method of cooling off a hot emotional situation by planned, conscious distancing. Parents can decree a time out for a misbehaving child. Adults can give themselves a time out during an argument when they sense they may do something damaging, by either physically leaving the scene or by "going away" for a few moments internally.

transference

An essential aspect of therapy in which you (the client) begin to respond to your therapist as though her or she were your parent or some other important figure from your childhood.

trigger

(as a verb) To re-open an unhealed wound through events, words, sounds, behavior (or any other stimulus) that somehow reminds you (either consciously or unconsciously) of the original wounding event. When you are triggered, you behave as if you are again

experiencing the wounding event, and you tend to act to protect yourself from the pain. *When my supervisor shakes her finger in my face, it triggers an unhealed wound I have around critical women, and I am flooded with rage.*

(as a noun) The stimulus that causes the unhealed wound to re-open. *Ambivalent men are a real trigger for me—they remind me of my dad in a way that makes me pursue them even when I know they are not particularly interested in being with me.*

turn it over, turning it over
An expression used in twelve-step circles that means giving up to your Higher Power your efforts to change or control some aspect of your life or your feelings. *Turn it over* is good advice when you are free of unfinished emotional business. Turning over an emotional issue when you still have emotional work to do on it is the same as stuffing feelings, and will, sooner or later, trigger the Rubber Band Effect.

twelve steps
A structured program for recovery from addictions first developed in Alcoholics Anonymous and now used in over two hundred different self-help recovery approaches.

unfinished business
A loose end, emotional or logistical; an incomplete. Unfinished business results when we leave a situation without a sense of peace about the adequacy of our actions in that situation. *Alcoholics Anonymous,* the "big book" of A.A., calls unfinished business "the wreckage of our past." Attitude toward unfinished business is one of the nine indicators of self-responsibility.

visualization
A healing tool in which you use your imagination to picture a desired goal or outcome.

victim
Someone who believes that his happiness, integrity or capacity to love is in the hands of another person or situation. See "investment in victimhood," and "self-responsibility."

wake-up call
A signal that your survival plan is failing you; external pressure to change. Wake-up calls appear in a variety of forms and degrees of intensity, from catastrophes such as auto accidents or being fired to a simple loss of inner peace. They indicate that a repetitive pattern in your life is not working, that your anesthesia is failing and the effects of your anesthesia use are becoming increasingly destructive.

willingness
An attitude of being genuinely open to input from a source entirely outside of your programming that promotes healing your wounds.

window of willingness
A response to a wake-up call in which you temporarily become willing and able to discontinue your anesthesia use. A "window-sitter" appears eager to do something—anything—to make the pain go away. However, a window-sitter's true, unconscious aim is to reduce pain levels by getting rid of the wake-up call itself. So as soon as the pain goes away, the willingness to discontinue anesthesia use and heal wounds goes away, too.

wound
A feeling or set of feelings that have frozen in place, instead of being allowed to flow through you and out. Strong feelings (fear, anger, grief) freeze when you are not allowed to release them. Unhealed wounds block your ability to love because they cause you to react to present events as though you were re-experiencing the past. This limits your range of creative and effective responses to today's events.

Index

80-20 rule   154,155

ability to feel, grieve and heal   337
    and disconnection   14
    and response to pain   133
    as an indicator of self-responsibility   129
    in children   8
    in Stage Three   324
    loss of, as a price of survival plan   76
abyss
    and Body Work   345
    and Prayer and meditation   343
    and Self-Help Groups   344
    and therapy   343
    as kitchen remodeling   340
    avoidance of   349
    benefits of making it through   356
    common questions about   338
    fear of   338
    importance of foundation skills in completing   342
    insufficient incentive for completing   355
    insufficient work in   385
    nature of ~ work   337
    premature   248
    tools for   336
Academy for Guided Imagery   329
affirmations   96

amnesia
    influence on the length of your journey 241
anesthesia
    exercise as an 69
    failure of 82
    function of 67
    positive thinking as 95
    stress management as 94
    worsening side effects of 82
anger 15
    and blame 52
    and boundary-setting skills 141
    and inner critic 60
    and premature forgiveness 348
    and relapse 277
    release 358
    venting 361
authenticity 76, 369
authority figures 192

Band-Aid 81, 82, 289
boundary 138
    difference between self-protection and 144
    examples of 138
boundary-setting skills
    as an indicator of self-responsibility 138
    in Stage Five 368
    in Stage Six 382

challenging your notions of normal 293
children
    as interpreters 45
criticism 82

dabbling 246
damage
    influence on the length of your journey 240
disconnection
    by abandonment 10
    by attack 10
    by spoiling 11
    by stealing the attention 12
    chronic 23
    pain of 9, 36
downward spiral 90

E.M.D.R. 359

"Enough" Principle 279
    evaluating healing activities 303
exercises
    activity evaluation 321
    anesthesias 71
    broken connections 16
    cause-and-effect inventory 298
    connection indicators 167
    contract for willingness 299
    discharge letters 361
    disconnections 332, 365
    feelings indicators 135
    happy-ending fantasy 54
    Higher Power 319
    inner critic 332
    inner selves dialogues 363
    internal guidance 332
    life and relationships as 388
    life mission statement 320
    goals 377
    incompletes 377
    mission statement revision 376
    personal power indicators 151
    price of your survival plan 78
    rightness inventory and release 363
    rightness release 378
    self-inventory 378
    self-victimization patterns 377
    support network 320
    survival plan failure 85
    survival plan review 363
    trauma inventory 362
    wake-up calls 85, 99, 107
    wounds 28
Eye Movement Desensitization and Reprogramming
    359

falling in love 246
False Hope/Hopelessness Continuum 53
false leaders 390
fantasy bond 42
Focusing 329
forgive
    unwillingness to 346, 372
forgiveness 15
    as a prerequisite to healing 346
    defined 346
    premature 348

foundation of self-esteem
    as an indicator of self-responsibility   145
    in Stage Five   369
foundation skills
    biochemistry   305
    crisis containment   310
    daily life   308
    exercise   304
    family   313
    food   304
    friends   312
    Higher Power work   305
    home   309
    inner work   306
    learning   307
    mentors   312
    money   308
    physical activities   303
    play   307
    sleep   304
    social   311
    spiritual activities   305
    support groups   313
    time   309
friends   354

God sidestep varieties   248
Grief Recovery Institute   329

happy-ending fantasy   43
    and authenticity   124
    and false hopelessness   52
    difference between ~ and true goal   49
    forms   49
    symptoms   51
healing journey length
    and amnesia   241
    and damage   240
    and willingness   241
healing plan
    and pain levels   252
    and Rubber Band Effect   251
    and the speed of the journey   253
    benefits of   250
    long-term   258
    revising   274
    troubleshooting   281
    weekly   266

healing principles   24, 242, 279
    and the Rubber Band Effect   244
Higher Power   163, 164, 305, 319
holy instants   384

I've Arrived! Full Halt   248
influences on the length of your journey   240
inner
    child   165, 324, 325, 363
        and pace of healing   172
        and Stage Three   184
        spoiled   327
    critic   51, 324, 325, 332, 363
        and Rubber Band Effect   251
        as fault-finder   60
        as interpreter   57
        as keeper of rules   56
        as maintainer of hope   57
        as provider of "love"   59
        source of   56
insight
    believing that ~ heals   327
    premature   315
Interactive Guided Imagery   329, 358
inventories
    cause-and-effect   298
    disconnection experiences   365
    incompletes   377
    rightness   363
    self   378
    self-victimization patterns   377
    trauma   362

letters   342
    "Dear John"   361
    discharge   361
    from inner critic, inner child   281
    giving back your traumas   362
level of investment in victimhood
    as an indicator of self-responsibility   148
    in Stage Four   341
    in Stage One   292
life
    and the Rubber Band Effect   249
    energy   74
    mission   320
long-term healing plan   258
looping   328

mission in life
    as an indicator of self-responsibility 157
    in Stage Five 369
    in Stage Seven 393
mission statement revision 376
motivational techniques 96

pain
    and healing plan 252
    and misery, difference between 134, 205, 328
    diversions from 296
    inevitability of 120
    of disconnection 9, 36
    of healing 120, 239
    response to 292, 341
parenting 324, 328
parents 13
    personal competence 145, 146
pitfalls
    Avoiding Your Abyss 349
    Believing that Insight Heals 327
    Cross Addictions 355
    Dependent Therapist 372
    Depth Therapy 314
    Fear of Feeling Too Good 373
    Frightened Friends 354
    Ignoring the Risks of Stage Five Work for
        Relationships 372
    Insufficient Incentive 355
    Mistaking Abstinence for Healing 314
    Mistaking New Levels of Happiness for Healing
        314
    Premature Forgiveness 348
    Premature Insight 315
    Putting Down Roots 327
    Relapse 326
    Rightness Addiction 349
    Spirituality as Drug 326
    Spoiled Inner Child 327
    Therapist Issues 350
    Two-Five Jump 315, 326, 373
    Unwillingness to Forgive 346, 372
    Your Own Insufficient Abyss Work 385
    Your Therapist's Insufficient Abyss Work 386
prayer and meditation 165, 227, 305
    and abyss work 343

premature
    abyss 248
    forgiveness 314, 348
    insight 314, 315
proclaiming 295, 299
purgatory 97

quality of relationship with your spiritual resources
    as an indicator of self-responsibility 163
    in Stage Five 369
    in Stage Seven 393
    in Stage Two 302
quality of relationships
    as an indicator of self-responsibility 159
    in Stage Six 382
    pre- and post-Stage Six 197

relapse-recycle phenomenon 276
repetition compulsion 25
response to pain
    as an indicator of self-responsibility 131
    in Stage Four 341
    in Stage One 292
revolving door between Stages Five and Four 191,
    342
rightness 349
    addiction to 248, 349
    release of 378
Rubber Band Effect 243
    and dabbling 246
    and falling in love 246
    and the God sidestep 247
    and the *I've arrived!* full halt, or setting up camp
        248
    and life 249
    and the premature abyss 248
    and recycle/relapse 275
    symptoms of 251
    and the two-five jump 244

self-help groups 293
self-responsibility 75
    benefits of 119
serenity prayer factors 240
Setting Up Camp 248
shadow self 335
sociopathy 37

spiritual resources
 and Higher Power 163
 and hope 39
 inner critic as 61
 and purgatory 98
support groups 344
support network 320
surrender 102

therapist
 dependent 372
 insufficient abyss work 386
 red flag behavior 353
 therapist issues 350
 transference 350
 unhealed or unwilling 352
therapy 325
 art 357
 depth 294, 297, 314, 327, 343
 family sculpture 357
 Focused Expressive Psychotherapy 358
 gestalt 357
 group 344, 352, 370, 371
 in Stage Five 371
 in Stage Four 343, 357
 in Stage One 294
 in Stage Six 384
 in Stage Three 325, 327
 in Stage Two 311, 314
 like kitchen remodeling 340
 psychodrama 357
 sand tray 357
 transference in 350
transference 350
trauma 21
triggering 26
two-five jump 244, 373

unfinished business, attitude toward
 as an indication of self-responsibility 153
 in Stage Five 369
victim 346
victimhood 346
 level of investment in 292, 341

Wake-Up Call Intensity Continuum 84
wallowing 328
weekly healing plan 266

willingness
 appraising 294
 as a factor in the length of your healing journey
  241
 boosting 78, 294, 296
 defined 101
 in recycling 277
 putting ~ into action 179
 to be self-responsible 110, 118
 to do your healing work in an orderly way 241
 to feel your feelings 129
 to re-organize your life 241
 window of
  attributes of 92
  defined 91
  typical activities 94
Willingness Works resources 318, 331, 360, 375, 387

About the Authors

DAVID GRUDERMEYER, Ph.D., and REBECCA
GRUDERMEYER, Psy.D., are the co-proprietors of
Willingness Works, which they founded in 1988 in
Del Mar, California. Through Willingness Works,
they give presentations, conduct workshops and
consult on the Seven Stages of Personal Healing,
spiritual and emotional growth and relationships.

The Grudermeyers have more than three
decades combined experience in personal growth fields. David is a Licensed Psychologist and
Marriage and Family Therapist and received degrees from Alfred University and the California
School of Professional Psychology. Rebecca is an Occupational Therapist and a Licensed
Psychologist and Marriage and Family Therapist. She received degrees from University of
Puget Sound, Antioch University and the Oregon Graduate School of Professional Psychology at
Pacific University, and holds a certificate in Alcohol Studies from Seattle University. They have been
married since 1986 and live and practice in Del Mar, California.

LERISSA PATRICK holds a B.S. in journalism from the University of
Colorado and has more than twenty years writing experience, including
newspaper articles, classroom instruction guides, advertising copy and
children's fiction. As an instructional designer, she helps speakers and
seminar leaders design dynamic, engaging classes and presentations on a
variety of topics. She lives in San Diego, California.

We hope you found *Sensible Self-Help* helpful and enjoyable. We would like to know as much about your experience with this book as possible. Your comments can teach us how to improve it for future readers.

1. What I like most about this book is:

2. What I like least about this book is:

3. My specific suggestions for improving the book are:

4. Other comments:

Optional:

Your name: _____ Date: _____

Occupation: _____

May we reprint your comments, either in promotional material for *Sensible Self-Help* or in future publishing ventures? ☐ Yes ☐ No

If Yes, may we use your name? ☐ Yes ☐ No

If Yes, please give your address and a daytime phone so that we may contact you:

Address: _____ Phone: (_____) _____

Thank you! — *David Grudermeyer, Ph.D., Rebecca Grudermeyer, Psy.D., and Lerissa Patrick*

Willingness Works Press ❦ 1155 Camino Del Mar #516 ❦ Del Mar, CA 92014
800/915-3606 ❦ Fax 619/942-1572

In addition to *Sensible Self-Help: The First Road Map for the Healing Journey*, the following tapes, workbooks and materials pertaining to the Seven Stages of Personal Healing are available from Willingness Works:

Tapes, Workbooks and Workshops
(T = Tape, W = Workbook)
- ☐ *Acceptance Makes You Powerful* (T)
- ☐ *Answering Your Wake-Up Calls* (T)
- ☐ *Boundaries: Your Key to Empowerment* (T)
- ☐ *Breaking Free of Power Struggles* (T)
- ☐ *Fantasy Bond: The Core Wound in Search of Healing* (T & W)
- ☐ *The Fantasy Bond Revisited: The Secret Source of Relationship Sabotage* (T)
- ☐ *Feelings: An Owner's Guide* (T & W)
- ☐ *Finding Your Inner Purpose* (T)
- ☐ *Forgiveness: An End to Wounds* (T)
- ☐ *From Victimization to Empowerment* (T)
- ☐ *From Inner Critic to Inner Helper* (T & W)
- ☐ **Getting Done With Your Anger** (T, W & workshop)
- ☐ *Getting It Done: Ending Procrastination* (T)
- ☐ *Healing the Abandonment Wound* (T)
- ☐ *How Do I Know When I'm Triggered?* (T)
- ☐ *How to Benefit from Everything that Happens* (T)
- ☐ *How to Journal* (T)
- ☐ *How to Stay Responsible Around Irresponsible People* (T)
- ☐ *How to Stop Repeating the Same Patterns Over and Over Again* (T)

- ☐ *If I'm Right, Why Am I Unhappy?* (T)
- ☐ *Integrating Your Many Parts* (T)
- ☐ *Know Your Narcissists* (T)
- ☐ *The Power of Self-Responsibility* (T)
- ☐ *The Power of Willingness* (T)
- ☐ *Reaching Your Goals by Stretching Your Comfort Zone* (T)
- ☐ *Self-Responsibility: Healing's Secret Ingredient* (T)
- ☐ *Sensible Self-Help: The Tape* (T)
- ☐ **Sensible Self-Help: The Workshop** (workshop)
- ☐ *Sorry It Happened, But What's the Plan?* (T)
- ☐ *Stop Sucking My Energy!* (T)
- ☐ *A Therapist's Guide to the Seven Stages of Personal Healing* (T)
- ☐ *Using Relationships as a Spiritual Path* (T)
- ☐ *What a Healthy Relationship Looks Like* (T)
- ☐ *What Do I Do When I'm Triggered?* (T)
- ☐ *Why Do You Bug Me So Much?: Owning Your Projections* (T)

Additional Materials
- ☐ Updated *Healing Resources Guide*
- ☐ Extra copies of Dominant and Secondary Stage Assessment forms
- ☐ Packet of blank Healing Plan and Activity Evaluation forms

For a catalog and information about ordering tapes and workbooks, or for information about Willingness Works workshops, call 800/915-3606. Or fax us at 619/942-1572. Or write to:

Willingness Works Press ✽ 1155 Camino Del Mar #516 ✽ Del Mar, CA 92014

Wishing you the best success on your healing journey!